Ancient Ways for Current Days

Women, Goddess & Communities of Peace

Jennifer Cameron

First published by Ultimate World Publishing 2021
Copyright © 2021 Jennifer Cameron

ISBN

Paperback: 978-1-922597-41-0
Ebook: 978-1-922597-42-7

Jennifer Cameron has asserted her rights under the Copyright, Designs and Patents Act 1988 to be identified as the author of this work. The information in this book is based on the author's experiences and opinions. The publisher specifically disclaims responsibility for any adverse consequences which may result from use of the information contained herein. Permission to use information has been sought by the author. Any breaches will be rectified in further editions of the book.

All rights reserved. No part of this publication may be reproduced, stored in or introduced into a retrieval system, or transmitted in any form, or by any means (electronic, mechanical, photocopying, recording or otherwise) without the prior written permission of the author. Any person who does any unauthorised act in relation to this publication may be liable to criminal prosecution and civil claims for damages. Enquiries should be made through the publisher.

Cover design: Ultimate World Publishing
Layout and typesetting: Ultimate World Publishing
Editor: Marinda Wilkinson
Illustrative drawings: Kaye Moseley

Ultimate World Publishing
Diamond Creek,
Victoria Australia 3089
www.writeabook.com.au

This book is dedicated to all our foremothers, on whose shoulders we stand. We remember and celebrate you.

The writer acknowledges the traditional owners of country throughout Australia and their continuing connection to land, waters, culture and community. I pay my respects to elders past, present and emerging. I recognise that First Nations' lands were never ceded and honour the care and custodianship of the First Nations people of Australia for the Earth Mother over thousands of years. In particular, I acknowledge the Wurundjeri people of the Kulin nation on whose land this book was written.

Cover photo: Hollow pottery whistle figurine from the Remojadas culture, Veracruz, Mexico, 400–750 CE. Dimensions: 30 x 14 x 24.5 cm (11.8 x 5.5 x 9.6 in). A society as patriarchal as any in Mesoamerica, the Remojadas did include worship of an Earth Goddess who wears a snake girdle. Designed as a very melodic whistle for ritual purposes, when played she would indeed have 'spoken'. This woman stands in her personal authority and seems to demand answers. National Museum of the American Indian, Smithsonian Institution (22/2310). Photo by NMAI Photo Services.

Testimonials

'This is a refreshing and easy to read exploration of ancient Goddess-loving peoples and cultures demonstrating all the wisdom they have, which can contribute to the development of a renewed Earth-loving, matrifocal world culture in the future. Full of wonderful information and ideas. It's a great book!'

**Kathy Jones,
author, founder of the Goddess Conference and recipient of the Demeter Award for Leadership in Women's Spirituality**

'Jennifer Cameron's sweeping tour of female-centred and egalitarian cultures, from the Palaeolithic era to today, is a passionate plea to take better care of the earth – and of ourselves. Challenging the idea that patriarchy is natural and inevitable, and taking inspiration from our ancient ancestors as well as from today's First Nations peoples, it invites readers to (re-) imagine a more cooperative, consensual way of life in which women are equal with men, violence is rare, the accumulation of wealth for its own sake makes no sense, and the earth is respected and cared for rather than ruthlessly plundered.'

**Robyn Arianrhod,
science writer and associate in the School of Mathematics, Monash University**

'*Ancient Ways* is a deep dive into the matrilineal and matrifocal past of human history. Sweeping in its vision – from the ancient past to the present moment – Jenny Cameron draws from many disciplines to present an overarching alternative history: that for the majority of human existence our values have been life, cooperation, and peaceful coexistence with others. *Ancient Ways* is inspiring in its breadth and impassioned central premise: that societies that centrally value women and children are possible, have always existed and still exist, and offer a solution to the imperilled state of our planet.'

**Jane Meredith,
author of *Journey to the Dark Goddess*
and *Aspecting the Goddess***

Contents

Introduction	1
Chapter 1: Palaeolithic Mothers	7
Chapter 2: Neolithic Flowering	35
Chapter 3: And Matrifocal Culture Is?	57
Chapter 4: Matrifocal Megalith Builders	87
Chapter 5: The Maltese Phenomenon	115
Chapter 6: Continuity from the Deep Past	135
Chapter 7: The Onslaught of Patriarchy	147
Chapter 8: The Battleground of the Female Body	161
Chapter 9: What's Civilised?	177
Chapter 10: The Survivors – Hidden Matriarchies	215
Chapter 11: The Oldest Continuous Living and Thriving Culture	239
Chapter 12: Modern Matrifocal Re-emergence	267
Chapter 13: Creations of Nature – Our Kin	275
Chapter 14: Regaining the Motherworld	285
Bibliography	309
Index	323
About the Author	353
Acknowledgements	355

Introduction

In 1978, I travelled across Europe and the Near East in a campervan for a year. I was with my then partner and we had journeyed from Australia in search of any evidence or trace of matriarchal societies in the distant past. We found it in spades. We used a pioneering book by Elizabeth Gould Davis, *The First Sex*, which listed many options to explore. Following these leads, we drove to places of ancient European culture, and to those where Western women were rarely seen, across roads with great holes and poor signage.

We were looking for any remnants to indicate mother-centred cultures (matriarchies), rather than the cultures of father rule that we were living in, in other words, patriarchy. Looking back over 230,000 years, we found what we sought. We came to realise the apparently inevitable patriarchy that dominates today was at most only 4,000 years old, just a small blip on the radar of human existence on the planet. We were exhilarated, but saddened that our 'herstory' had been so removed from us.

Perhaps only 10 years ago I started to become aware that there were in fact societies currently operating as matriarchies, or the term I prefer, matrifocal social systems. Some had operated continuously since ancient times. They were overtaken by colonialism only in the last 100 years and forced reluctantly into the patriarchal social form. I found maybe four or five of this sort.

Then I came upon Heide Goettner-Abendroth's work, in particular *Matriarchal Societies*, which only became available in English in 2012. In this thoroughly academic work, she meticulously lays out the whole story across the globe. She looks at the past and discusses many living 'matriarchal' (the term she prefers) societies, in 17 regions of the world. She shares many, many, stories and details of these people. Some of these cultures have been included in this book.

Matrifocal societies are still alive, based on their ancient ways even today – but in addition, women driven to the end of their endurance by male violence, have newly adopted the model for current times. In 1990, women established villages run by women for women in Kenya, and in 2016 a similar village was established by women in Syria. They are setting new ground rules, based on the needs of women and children.

In a time of unprecedented neglect of Mother Earth, often called Gaia, we are confronted by a system at its extremes. To continue as we are courts disaster, possibly extinction – for us and huge numbers of species. We are neglecting our role as custodians and have gone down a destructive path. Does the matriarchal/matrifocal model offer a viable alternative? I believe it does, and hope this book contributes to awareness that there are other options we can use now, to forge an egalitarian society for all genders.

Jennifer Cameron

Technical notes

This is not an academic work seeking to prove the case. I assume the case is proven already by the academic research completed by the professionals in the field. So I draw upon these primary

Introduction

and secondary sources to support the ideas brought together in the book. We live in a world of difference and there are those who would readily dispute my interpretation here.

Interpretation of findings are debated to the finest detail in archaeological circles and practitioners are often loathe to proffer an overview, until they can find yet another piece of evidence. The views I reject are usually those I perceive as informed by the blinkers of patriarchy and the unquestioned assumption of male superiority or dominance as the norm throughout time.

I have not written for an academic audience. I want to share this news with regular people and I hope that a broad audience will find it easy to read and thought-provoking. I write for people seeking another way to live from the one that has got us to the place we are in. I hope it will provide ideas for the way forward.

We can make a change. We can be strengthened by our ancient past, shared by both women and men. The task is not to recreate, but remember. What worked before? Now is the time of imbalance of male energy over female. What can we recover? ... and reuse!

A note on time references

In discussions of the ancient past we come across various ways of describing time – BC, BCE, AD, CE, BP. All these are acronyms.

Since the time of Christian domination, we have used **BC – Before Christ**, and **AD – Anno Domini**, Latin for **Year of our Lord**, referring to Jesus. Some think of AD as After Death, because it commences upon the supposed date of the death of Christ. This is the year zero (Year 0) of our calendar.

Ancient Ways for Current Days

In our more cosmopolitan world it hardly works for people of other faiths to adopt such alien terminology. Not least out of respect for different faiths other terms have been adopted.

Common Era (CE) has thus also been adopted to refer to anything after Year 0.

Before Common Era (BCE) stands for anything before Year 0.

Simple.

Before Present (BP) years is a time scale used mainly in archaeology, geology and other scientific disciplines to specify when events occurred in the past. Because the 'present' time changes, standard practice is to use 1 January 1950 as the commencement date (epoch) of the age scale, reflecting the origin of practical radiocarbon dating in the 1950s.

Personally, I find BP confusing because I think of now as the present, not January 1950. For this reason I have not used it in this book. When talking about huge spans of time, 70 or so years hardly seems to matter, and to work out how many years ago objects were made, you can add the current year to the BCE date. For example if something dates to 3,000 BCE, you add 3,000 plus the current year, say 2020, to get 5,020 years old – it gives you the idea.

Sometimes I say something is a certain number of years old, to convey the gravity of the age, but I do not use BP because I am not being strictly accurate if I do.

I use BCE and CE throughout this book.

Introduction

Time periods in pre-history

I have used the commonly employed and accepted periods of time that are applied to Western developments in pre-history, many of which you have probably heard of. Different cultures have different ways of describing history and pre-history in their countries.

In the West, a terminology is used based on technological material used in the time, e.g. stone, pottery, copper (the Chalcolithic), bronze, iron. Timing can be problematic, because these behaviours developed earlier in some places compared to others. The periods are usually based on timing of events in the Near East, roughly also known as the Levant. To be consistent with this the periods used in this book are as follows:

Palaeolithic
2,000,000 years ago – 8,300 BCE
Epipalaeolithic (Near East) or Mesolithic (Europe): 10,000– 8,300 BCE

Neolithic
8,300 BCE – 4,500 BCE

Chalcolithic
4,500 BCE – 3,300 BCE

Bronze Age
3,300 BCE – 1,200 BCE

Iron Age
1,200 BCE – 586 BCE

After 586 BCE is considered the historical period, rather than pre-history, because human activities started to be recorded in written forms that have been deciphered. This gives us a written history. There were earlier scripts, some disputed, some accepted as written language (e.g. the Minoan script from Crete – Linear A) but which we cannot read … yet!

Key definitions

Matrifocal – That which focuses on the mother, in particular mothering and the values that arise from the mother/child relationship.

When a culture focuses on what works for women and children, the result enhances life for everyone. It automatically excludes war and violence, especially against women and children. It provides an equal voice to women and men, each with their diverse roles. Such societies are usually also matrilineal.

Matrilineal – Kinship traced through the mother's line.

CHAPTER 1

Palaeolithic Mothers

*Our ancestors knew how to walk closely to the Earth,
and how to align themselves with her rhythms.
Their DNA lives on in us, which means that somewhere in us,
we know how to do this too.*
Elizabeth Childs Kelly, writer, researcher, educator. *Human Parts,* **Nov 2019**

Western civilisation as we know it has been centred on a religion of one male God. This has not worked out well for women. Allah, God/Jesus and Yahweh have dominated. When we look back, this has been in place for over 2,000 years. Yet that is just a tiny segment of the time that humans have been on the planet.

What happened before that? Before these one-god religions dominated, there was a period of worship of both female and male deities that lasted for about 4,000 years, more or less, depending on where you were. That's a long time! BUT before that, it was the Mother alone who was worshipped in a great variety of forms – worldwide! There were no images of gods at all. As we see below, potentially the first created image is of a woman (from Berekhat Ram), which is 233,000 years old.

We can imagine this spread of time, if we allow 5 centimetres on a timeline for male gods and twice as much for a period that included both female and male deities before that. We would have a timeline of 15 centimetres. If, before that, we add to our line the Berekhat Ram figurine, we would need to extend our timeline 5 to 6 METRES back, during which a Goddess was the only deity.

Patriarchal religions are a blip on the timeline. An aberration. For at most 4,000 years under patriarchy this ancient, female deity has been reviled, denied, but never completely obliterated. Why has this ancient depiction and spiritual expression been treated thus? This is a big part of what this book explores, but first let's clarify what has been concealed of our human past.

In 1981, by the shores of a lake in the summit crater of a sleeping volcano, at Berekhat Ram near the Golan Heights in Israel, a corpulent female figurine was found by archaeologists, and she is 233,000 years old. Only 35 millimetres (1.4 in) tall, made of scoria, she is now displayed in the Jerusalem Museum of Archaeology.

This object from such ancient times has at least three incised lines that mark head and arms. There are those who dispute that it was intentionally made, and if so that it represents a woman. The same can be said of another figure, of the same period, found in Morocco at Tan. Rather than being made by modern humans (Homo sapiens) these, it is argued, would have been made by Neanderthals or perhaps even earlier by Homo erectus, hunter-gatherers and tool users. What if we accept these are not statues, but merely serendipitous shapes formed by natural geological

Palaeolithic Mothers

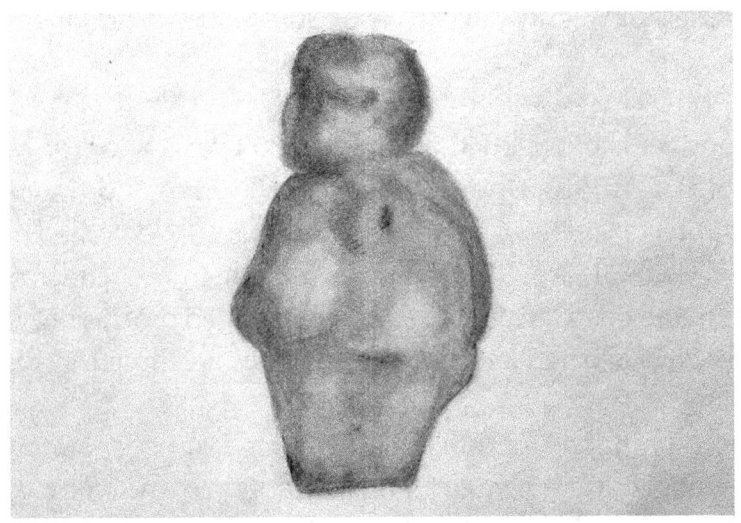

1. Berekhat Ram figurine – Front view
A 233,000-year-old figure of a corpulent woman, potentially the first created image. Found by the crater lake at Berekhat Ram, Israel. 35 mm (1.4 in) tall, of scoria. Jerusalem Museum of Archaeology. Drawing: Kaye Moseley ©.

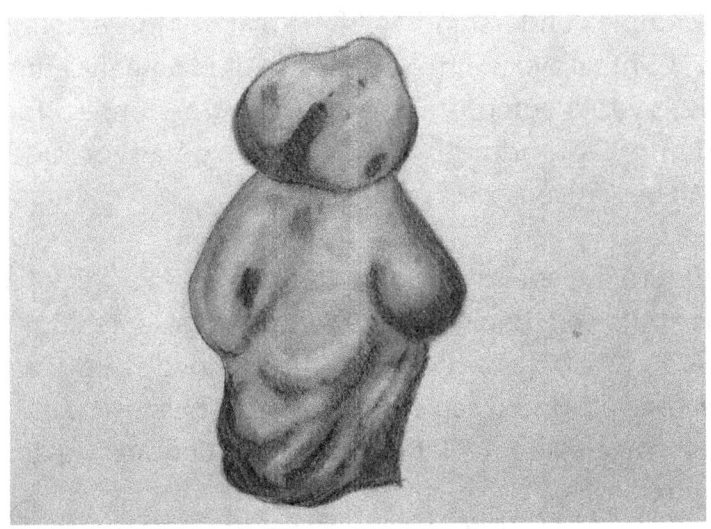

2. Berekhat Ram figurine – Side view
Drawing: Kaye Moseley ©.

processes. How long ago can we be sure Goddess figurines were produced?

The answer is between 35,000 and 40,000 years ago. The Venus of Hohle Fels is an Upper Palaeolithic figurine and the oldest undisputed example of figurative prehistoric art. Unearthed from a cave in Germany in 2008, she is hewn from mammoth tusk ivory. In place of the head, the figurine has a perforated protrusion, which would have allowed its owner to wear it as an amulet.

I should perhaps mention that all female figurines found from the Palaeolithic are named in the convention of the word 'Venus' followed by the name of the place it was found. Venus was the Roman Goddess of beauty and appeared in myth thousands of years after the Palaeolithic 'Venuses'. Archaeologists named them thus on the assumption that they represented an ancient concept of beauty. Our interpretation of them has today gone far beyond this stereotyping of the viewer's eye, to a much more complex understanding of the place of these figurines in human spiritual evolution. A better accepted nomenclature than 'Venus' is yet to emerge, although the terms 'female figurine', 'Woman of', 'Grandmother of', 'Nude woman' or 'Goddess' have all been used.

To return to the 'Venus' of Hohle Fels, the date for this, at 35,000 BCE, is at the very beginning of the Upper Palaeolithic (40,000–8,300 BCE), which is associated with the assumed earliest presence of our species, Homo sapiens in Europe. These were the same people who created the famous cave paintings (e.g. at Lascaux; Altamira).

About 70 centimetres from the figurine a flute made from a vulture bone was found. Additional artefacts excavated from

Palaeolithic Mothers

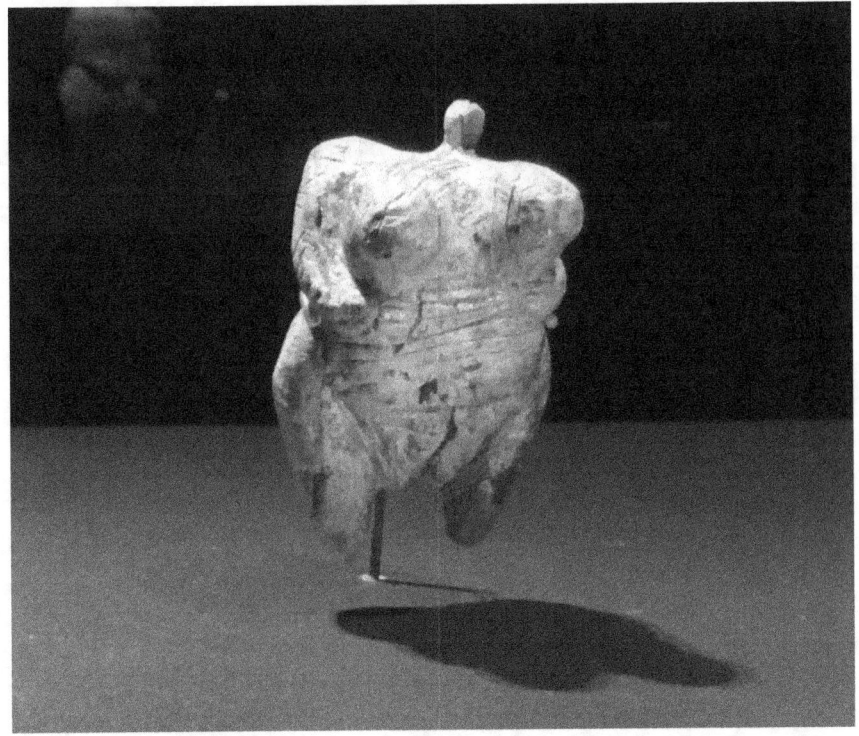

3. Goddess of Hohle Fels
35,000 BCE, Early Upper Palaeolithic period. Oldest undisputed female figurine. Found in a cave in Germany in 2008. Mammoth tusk ivory. Could have been worn as an amulet. Photo: Kaalii Cargill.

the same cave layer included flint-knapping debris, worked bone and carved ivory. Also found were remains of tarpans (extinct wild horse), cave bears, woolly mammoths, reindeer and Alpine ibexes.

What does the Hohle Fels Goddess show us? She is a figure of abundance, fertility, health and survival. She embodies a desire by the artist to be connected to these qualities. It may also be that she was associated with ritual practice, perhaps including the magic of music, in the dark of a cave, in the body of Mother Earth. She is now released to speak to us again.

*4. Goddess of Kostenky
30,000 BCE from Russia. Made of mammoth bone. Could
have been worn around the neck. Pregnant woman with
well-developed buttocks and pendulous breasts. A fringe or
girdle at waist (rear view). Drawing: Kaye Moseley ©.*

The Hohle Fels Goddess was the oldest, but not the first to be found, of what became thousands of discoveries of such figurines produced across Europe, North Africa and Siberia, carved out of bone, antler or stone. The Venus of Kostenky (from Russia) is the next oldest known figurine. Dated to 30,000 BCE she is also made of mammoth bone. This statue has a hole between the ankles, so if she was worn around the neck, the wearer could look down and see her looking up. It shows the characteristic pregnancy, well developed buttocks and pendulous breasts of many such statues. In the rear view, she can be seen to be wearing a fringe or girdle around the waist.

Next is the most famous Goddess figurine of all – the Venus of Willendorf, uncovered by a workman during an archeological

Palaeolithic Mothers

5. Venus of Willendorf, Austria
Artistically developed limestone statue of a naked woman, 11.1 cm (4.4 in) in height, coloured with red ochre. Dated between 30,000 and 25,000 BCE. The stomach and breasts are large, and the pubic area is emphasised. Photo: Kaalii Cargill.

excavation in 1908, in Austria. Artistically developed, she was found prior to the other two discussed above. Carved from limestone, she is 11.1 centimetres (4.4 in) in height, coloured with red ochre (iron oxide) and dated between 30,000 and 25,000 BCE. Like the earlier two, the stomach and breasts are large, and the pubic area is emphasised as the portal of birth.

The pubic area is a triangle shape, which became the symbol for the Goddess for millennia to come and even today is recognised in the Tantric tradition as the primary symbol of life. The red ochre pigment covering the Venus of Willendorf is thought to symbolise menstrual blood. Red ochre represents a life-giving agent, that was to be used for thousands of years, on sacred artefacts, sacred paintings and in burials, particularly of women.

The Venus of Willendorf looks down on her own abundance (McCoid and McDermott 1996). She is probably not an individual but a symbol of all that women provide. The figurine's hair is braided in seven concentric circles; seven, in later times, became regarded as a magic number used to bring good luck.

Context of the Goddess imagery

Politically, it can be speculated that women, due to their life-giving and nurturing capabilities, might have had an esteemed role in the society. Matriarchal or matrifocal societies were always associated with 'the worship of a supreme female earth deity' (Bachofen 1973).

The number of these figurines found is staggering. These pages could be filled with examples. Why was it so? Why were these abundant women produced? It was no simple matter to create the images – it is estimated that the Hohle Fels figure, using the stone implements of the time, would have taken tens and perhaps even hundreds of hours to carve. This needed strong motivation and determination.

The journey of Goddess imagery begins in a time where ongoing life was a wonder. The fact that women produced children was a wonder. People observed that with the changing seasons plants became dormant. From their perspective, they appeared to die (like leafless trees) but came alive again as the seasons moved on. The cycle of birth, life, death and rebirth was very evident.

It has been estimated that between 40,000 and 16,000 years ago the entire population of Europe was only 4,000–6,000 individuals. The average lifespan of people at the time is estimated to be 25 years – for us that seems unreasonably short. But looking past averages, in actuality if you could live past childhood, you could live to 75 years.

The highest death rate was among children. They were particularly vulnerable (65% of deaths) to a variety of infections and diseases, especially gastrointestinal and respiratory (Volk and Atkinson 2013) that we can now prevent using vaccines or cure with antibiotics. Only half the infants born lived long enough to become adults of those times (Wallois in Ates 2002). Their vulnerability to sickness and death made the offspring of Palaeolithic peoples very precious.

This concern for species continuation was paramount, and in this context, there is no evidence of fighting or violence. There was an abundance of food – research shows in addition to vegetables, the people mostly ate reindeer (95–99% of their game), a high nutrient source. Securing food does not appear to have been a problem. Settled village sites have been found later in the period indicating housing was not a problem either. Species survival was.

Art and spirituality turned in the direction of ensuring fertility and life. A study by anthropologist Marshall Sahlins (1968) demonstrated that Palaeolithic people needed to work only 15 to 20 hours a week to feed, clothe and shelter themselves. This leaves ample 'downtime'. Sahlins argues that hunter-gatherer and Western societies take separate roads to affluence, the former by desiring little, the latter by producing much. He asks, ' … what do human beings do when they need work only 15 hours a week? Well, for one thing, they devote time, energy, and community resources to creating great works of spiritual art.'

In those ancient times humankind lived in intimate contact with the Earth, and it was crucial to understand the seasons, moon cycles, and growth and decline of the light of the sun across the year. They were hunter-gatherers and, as in all traditional societies of this type (outside of arctic regions), 65 per cent of the diet was made up of plants, including fruit, nuts, grains, legumes and berries. Animal products made up the remaining 35 per cent (Crittenden and Schnorr 2017). Men hunted larger game and women gathered all manner of plant life and small game like snakes and lizards. Women provide the staple diet and men added meat to that. The term used should perhaps be 'gatherer-hunters'.

It was evident that life came from things which were female and, therefore, the female was not just respected, but revered. Unlike men, women could bleed and not die. Miraculous! Mothers nurtured their offspring from before birth and into adulthood and with this came the bond of love. Love, the Mother and the Earth were linked.

An endearing story comes to light with the Goddess of Dolni Vestonice, found in 1924, in two pieces, at an archaeological excavation in the Czech Republic. Not of bone or stone, she is ceramic pottery, 11.5 centimetres (4.5 in) in height, and dated between 26,000 BCE and 24,000 BCE – the first ceramic sculpture known in the world. The fingerprint of a child, estimated at between 7–15 years of age, has been identified, fired into the surface (Kralik et al. 2007). The curious child handled the figurine before it was fired – so it is reasonable to assume that the youngster was not kept away from this sacred object.

Found in 1922 in a cave in France at the foot of the Pyrenees, the Venus of Lespugue is a nude female figure carved from mammoth tusk ivory, approximately 150 mm (6 in) in height. She was unfortunately damaged during the excavation. She wears a skirt of twisted fibre frayed at the ends, hanging from below

Palaeolithic Mothers

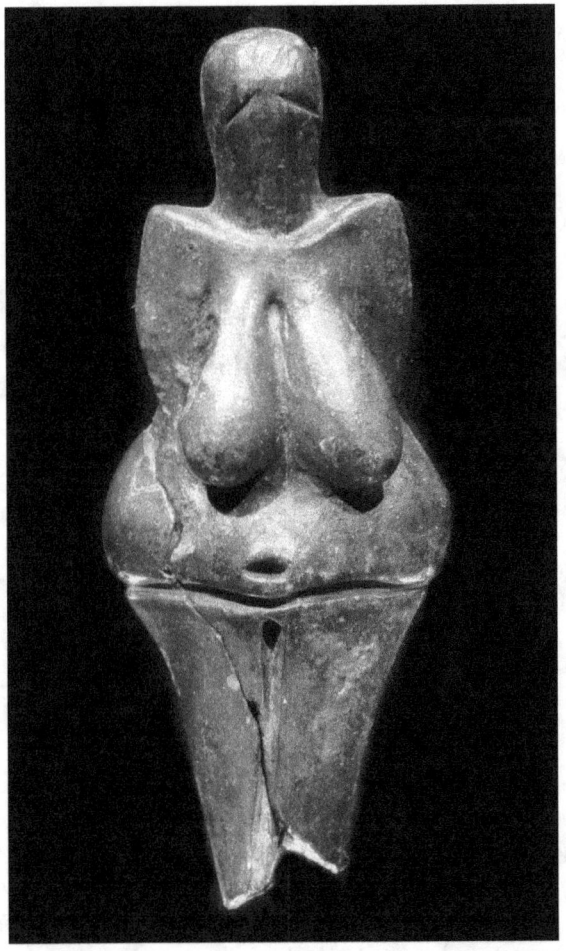

*6. Goddess of Dolni Vestonice, Czech Republic
Ceramic, 11.5 cm (4.5 in) high, dated between 26,000 BCE and
24,000 BCE – the first ceramic sculpture known. The fingerprint of
a child is fired into the surface. Photo: Petr Novák, Wikipedia.*

the hips. She is dated to between 26,000 and 24,000 BCE and, of all the figurines of the period, appears to display the most prominent hips, stomach, vulva and buttocks. Additionally she has extremely large, pendulous breasts. With these proportions, it is highly unlikely that this was a copy of an actual woman. How do we explain this?

Ancient Ways for Current Days

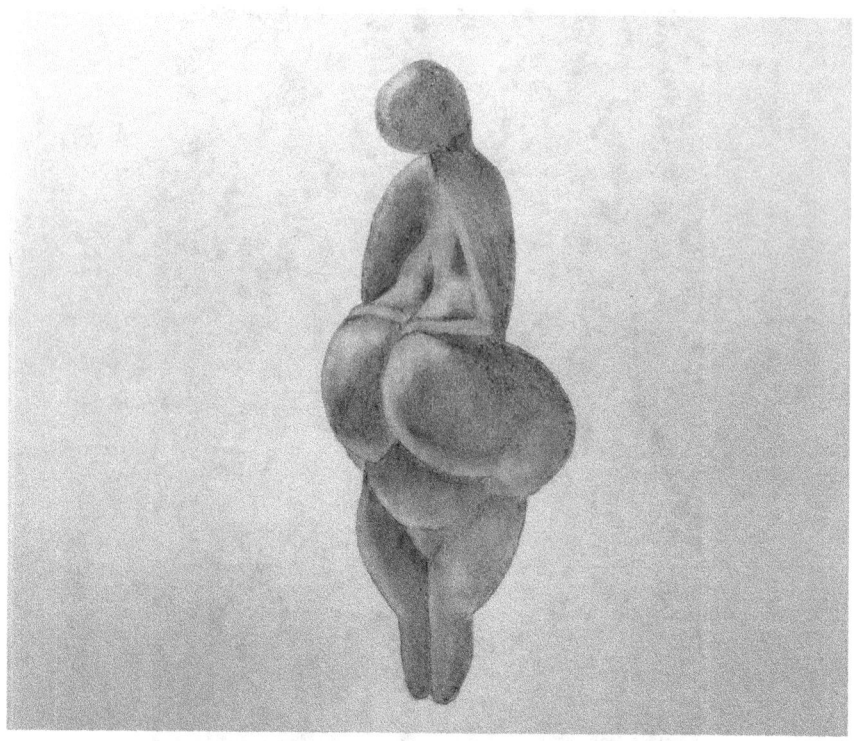

7. Goddess of Lespugue, France
Nude female figure carved from mammoth tusk ivory, approximately 150 mm (6 in) in height. Wears a skirt of twisted fibre frayed at the ends, hanging from below the hips. Dated between 26,000 and 24,000 BCE. Of all the figurines of the period, appears to display the most prominent hips, stomach, vulva and buttocks and extremely large, pendulous breasts. May show egg symbology. Drawing: Kaye Moseley ©.

Her whole body is a repetition of egg shapes, emphasising her role as the source of life (Gimbutas 1974). Since the art of the Upper Palaeolithic, the egg has been present as a fundamental element in the world of symbols, mostly connected to the bird and the woman. In these early times everything was believed to come out of an egg – this idea produced bird-headed Goddess-woman statuettes. The Venus of Lespugue is said to be one of the earliest examples.

Palaeolithic Mothers

8. Goddess of Laussel, France
Found 1911, limestone relief sculpture dated to about 23,000 BCE. A nude ample woman with traces of red ochre, 43 cm (17 in) in height, holding an animal horn with 13 markings, possibly menstrual cycles in a year. Drawing: Kaye Moseley ©.

Also created in France was the Venus of Laussel, which differs from other images in that she was carved into the limestone of the entrance to a rock shelter, as a relief sculpture. Discovered by a psychiatrist interested in archaeology in 1911, the block of stone had fallen from the rock-face and was transported to the Museum of Aquitaine in Bordeaux. A nude woman, once painted over in red ochre, her physical features resemble those of the other figurines already described. Measuring 43 centimetres (17 in) in height, she is the most beautifully executed relief sculpture of several found at the Laussel rock shelter; these are the earliest reliefs of a human (about 23,000 BCE). Laussel is located only about 20 kilometres (12.4 mi) from the caves of Lascaux and their famous Palaeolithic artwork.

When found, the Venus of Laussel was smothered in the sacred red ochre. She is one of five female reliefs, plus one of a man who may be dancing, and these occupied a ceremonial area of a rock shelter. The Venus of Laussel has hands and fingers but no feet, arising straight out of the rock, and the sculptor used the contour of the stone to enhance the pregnant belly. In her right hand, the woman holds up a bison horn which contains 13 notches – these may symbolise the number of menstrual cycles in one year. Her left hand, as if to help us make the link, directs the gaze across the pregnant belly to her vulva area.

At the shelter there are vulva marks and vulva stones, plus one vulva shape carved onto what may be a penis stone. One somewhat indistinct statue has what appears to be a large penis. This interest in the sexual organs of both sexes, but particularly women, together with the fulsome Goddess reliefs focusing on pregnancy and on breasts for nourishment of the promised new life, all marked the place as a sacred venue for women's mysteries.

Into the Earth

The Earth was seen as the Great Mother. Caves and cracks in the Earth were entrances to the Mother's body. A spring was her vital fluids poured as a gift out of her body, to aid all creatures. In Europe, the caves sometimes crept underground for kilometres into the

Palaeolithic Mothers

mountains, for example in France at Niaux for 2.5 kilometres (1.5 mi); at Rouffignac for 10 kilometres (6.2 mi). Dark and sometimes difficult to get to, these were not homes but spiritual (or as we shall soon see, 'shamanic') environments. No objects of daily use are found in these deep caves, though they were at the entrances. The caves were kept extremely clean as befits a sacred place. Here the people would gather for certain days or events.

People were very comfortable to enter the caves, as if coming into the home of the Mother, even taking their children into the depths, as footprints captured in clay display. The art of the Palaeolithic caves is renowned for the clarity, colour and beauty of their simple and realistic images, mainly of animals; paintings of hands; and abstract patterns. The oldest are 40,000 years old, they are of animals, and are found in France, Spain, Indonesia and Australia.

Various means of dating have been used in the past, but the most specific available now are carbon-dating and uranium isotope decay measurement. Both of these use a small amount from the area of the painted material, so have to be used precisely.

Carbon dating needs pigment which has to have been mixed with something organic (like animal fat or a vegetable) as these have carbon in them to measure. Carbon dating loses reliability after about 35,000 years.

Uranium isotope measurement relies on water dissolving minerals over stone – the way a stalagmite is formed – on or under the artwork. Uranium decays into thorium over time. By measuring the amount of thorium in a sample (if there is any), using a mass spectrometer, researchers can determine how much time has passed since the layer was formed. This methodology is reliable to over 500,000 years in the past.

Shamans and spirituality

All known religious traditions have an ecstatic component to allow followers to enter into an altered state of consciousness. These can include one or more of the following: trance, meditation, prayer, chanting, drumming, rhythmic dancing/movement, deprivation (e.g. fasting), pain, eyeball pressure or consuming plant-based material. Discovery and ingestion of plants that altered perceptions could have been a very early human or even proto-human experience.

Today those who use plants to induce altered consciousness for spiritual purposes are referred to as shamans. They take these mind-altering sacred drugs to 'perceive and interact with what they believe to be a spirit world and channel these transcendental energies into this world' (Whitely 2008). The shaman is seen to act as an intermediary between the human and spirit world.

In the Palaeolithic era, upon returning from this state, the shamans strove to record what they saw or felt, perhaps verbally, but very probably by painting and carving on stone. Supporting this contention, in experiments today with psychedelic substances, the shapes that subjects record are very similar to those of the ancient past (Lewis-Williams and Pearce 2009). They are recurring geometric patterns – grids, parallel lines, dots, zigzags, nested curves, meanders and spirals.

In modern times a shaman is as likely to be a woman as a man and the same seems to be true in the distant past. One cave drawing from the Lascaux cave complex shows a stiff stick-like man lying on a 45-degree angle with an erect penis, before a wounded bison. Present-day shamans report that the out of body experience is

Palaeolithic Mothers

9. Lascaux ithyphallic shaman figure
Cave drawing in black oxide from Lascaux cave. A stiff stick-like man, possibly a bird-headed shaman, lying on a 45-degree angle with an erect penis, before a wounded buffalo. 15,000 BCE. Drawing: Kaye Moseley ©.

felt as a lift upwards out of the body, on an angle, and producing an actual erection of the penis for the male. The one in this image seems to wear a bird mask and is accompanied by a bird totem on a pole. It would appear that the shaman has represented both his experience and trance vision in this image.

In a rock art painting in Arnhem Land, Australia, the First Nations Australian artist shows a woman, her mouth open as if in wonder, who 'appears to be floating in space' (Chaloupka 1993) on this 45-degree angle, before a large image of a mythic female being (Fig 177, Chaloupka 1993; Fig 5, Ch.15, Foster 2013) who gestures in her direction. It is entirely possible that, like the figure in the Lascaux painting, this also reflects a shamanic trance experience, although I have been unable to discuss or confirm this with the traditional owners.

Ancient Ways for Current Days

In other caves, elsewhere in Europe, there is a handful of images of a male wearing animal skins, including the still furred skull – perhaps representing what it might be like to experience being that animal while in trance.

Archaeologist and anthropologist Marija Gimbutas notes that less than three per cent of statues from Europe in prehistory were of men. These include some male figures known from cave engravings and paintings, the shaman image from Lascaux just discussed being one of them. Most are fantastic composite beings arising 'from the imaginative pairing of man and horned animal. A number of them are grotesque and enigmatic figures and rather carelessly engraved'. They are naked and often hairy, and appear to be moving, maybe dancing. One in particular seems to be driving a herd of animals before him. Gimbutas hazards a guess that these images could be a 'Master of Animals' figure.

Returning our discussion to the trance events in the caves, according to author Judy Foster in her book *Invisible Women of Prehistory*, the role of nurturing and preparing the plant material for the trance ritual was a task undertaken only by the female shamans, due to women's traditional horticultural and agricultural knowledge as the tribal food gatherers. In some cultures, for example the Yeoh of China, only women could be shamans due to their ability to facilitate rebirth.

In southern Sweden the grave of a woman who has been interpreted as a shaman, given her distinctive burial, has been found. She was buried upright, seated cross-legged on a bed of antlers. A belt fashioned from more than 100 animal teeth hung from her waist and a large slate pendant from her neck. A short cape of six different types of feathers covered her shoulders. In life she would have stood a bit under 1.5 metres (5 ft) tall, been dark-haired and pale eyed and was about 30 to 40 years of age when she died. She lived about 5,000 BCE and as such was probably from one of the last hunter-gatherer groups of Europe (Romey 2019).

Research by historian and professor Mircea Eliade (reported in Goettner-Abendroth 2012) established that the shaman is a person of higher than normal intelligence and ability to concentrate, beyond what is possible for most people. His research also shows shamans have a higher than normal capacity for memory, and play a role as keepers of oral traditions and in healing.

It is likely that Palaeolithic humans saw spirit inhabiting everything, even rocks, rivers, mountains and stars – items to which the westernised anthropologist would never have thought to assign life. The Palaeolithic people saw animation or life all around them. Many peoples who are living traditional and ancient lifestyles today believe that a spirit from one of these elements of nature, or from areas where ancestors were buried, sparked new life in the womb of a woman, leading to the birth of a child (even when they know the physical role of the male in conception) (Goettner-Abendroth 2012). In the Palaeolithic, with no accurate understanding of how reproduction worked, women would have been seen as parthenogenic – self-fertilising, creating life from within themselves, alone (Carr-Harris 2011).

Some caves have ample space for art, while other areas have images piled on top of each other. This tells us that the place itself was important for the ritual drawing. Recent research indicates that Palaeolithic cave art was located in areas which produce strong vocal resonance (Kreisberg 2014) – meaning speech, song and chanting would have had powerful effects, possibly even for healing. According to the innovative American Palaeolithic archaeologist,

Alexander Marshack, the caves were often visited by pregnant women, fertility rites were held there, and certain parts of the caves 'were most probably' where women came to deliver babies. Those special parts of caves used for fertility rites were regarded as the uterus of the Mother Goddess. In other parts of the cave, groups came to worship.

'Gaia' and the Environment in the modern era

Worldwide today there is a modern movement of people seeking to revive the idea, and related practice, of the Goddess as a focus for spiritual experience. The female side of existing deities may be recognised again (e.g. Sophia, as knowledge, in the Christian tradition). Perhaps more commonly, as with this ancient Palaeolithic belief, many people involved in the Goddess movement today consider the Earth to be a living Goddess. For some this may be figurative, for others literal. This literal belief finds resonance with the scientific theory proposed in the Gaia hypothesis (by the scientist James Lovelock). Indeed, the Goddess name 'Gaia' is now sometimes used as a synonym for the Earth.

The Gaia hypothesis proposes that planet Earth is a super-organism, which for most of the past 3.8 billion years has been responding, through the natural systems of the Earth, to perpetuate the conditions for life on the planet. Living organisms interact with inorganic matter in a way that regulates the environment across the planet, to keep it habitable.

With the loss of our ancient spiritual connection to the land, in Western cultures at least, came the replacement of the female nurturing principle subsumed by the religions 'of the Book' (Judaism, Islam, Christianity). These religions predominantly inform morality today, and one outcome has been that modern humans, influenced by these faiths have lost the sense of oneness with nature, and of responsibility to care for the land, the Earth. The first book of the Old Testament quickly states:

> Then God said, 'Let us make humankind in our image, according to our likeness; and let them have dominion over the fish of the sea, and over the birds of the air, and over the cattle, and over all the wild animals of the earth, and over every creeping thing that creeps upon the earth'. Genesis 1: 26–28

In the context of this passage, Christianity took 'dominion' to equal 'power over', the right to dominate, subdue and even exploit nature. Man was seen as the most valuable part of creation and all else had value only insofar as it benefited mankind. In the worst expressions of patriarchy, it was taken that it had to be men who benefited, without regard to the effect on women and children.

The archaeologist Brian Boyd makes an argument that in looking back from our position in time and social attitudes, we focus too much on the role and centrality of the human in the environment. Instead, we should look at the relationship as an engagement amongst different forms of life – 'the mutualism of the human-plant-animal relationship'. This view sees all life forms interrelating.

The modern perspective has been to think of humans as dominating – the active agent in hunting or in domestication of species, plant or animal. However, there are stories of native people asking a tree if they can cut it down and explaining why; or thanking an animal for giving up its life for the hunter's needs. In this worldview, the issue is not about having power over another, but living in collaboration and respect with other living beings. A view we could do well to adopt more broadly today.

Ancient Ways for Current Days

The UN Environment Program (see Chapter 13) informs us, for example, that in the culture of the Maori people of New Zealand, humans are deeply connected with nature. The two are interdependent, even kin. By guarding and protecting the environment the Maori respect the elders and secure the future. In his books, author and professor Enrique Salmon explores this 'kin-centric' ecology – the kin or relatives include all the natural elements of an ecosystem. He discusses in particular the Raramuri people of Mexico with the view that, without human recognition of their role in the complexities of life in a place, the life suffers and loses its sustainability. In the face of species extinction on a grand scale today, it would appear that this ancient belief is proven true.

Traditional matrifocal/matriarchal cultures do respect their environment. Instead of domination, they emphasise custodianship, caretaking or stewardship in our relationship to Mother Earth. This means taking responsibility for our actions that could have a negative impact on the natural world and righting the balance as quickly as possible. This is the ethos Gaia, the Earth, cries out for now. She has been suffering through 4,000 years of neglect and exploitation under patriarchy. Reinvigorating matrifocal principles will provide us with a path to right this again. Only change at a fundamental level will help us now.

The artists of these ancient caves, such as Lascaux, Trois Freres, Chauvet, Pech Merle (all in France) and Altamira and El Castillo (in Spain), saw their work as a form of communication not only with the Goddess in particular, but also with the viewers of the art. Cave art provided a strong link between humans and the natural world. These were seen as intertwined. Linked to the Goddess figurines, we see that the fertility of the land and its creatures and the fertility of the people, were as important as

Palaeolithic Mothers

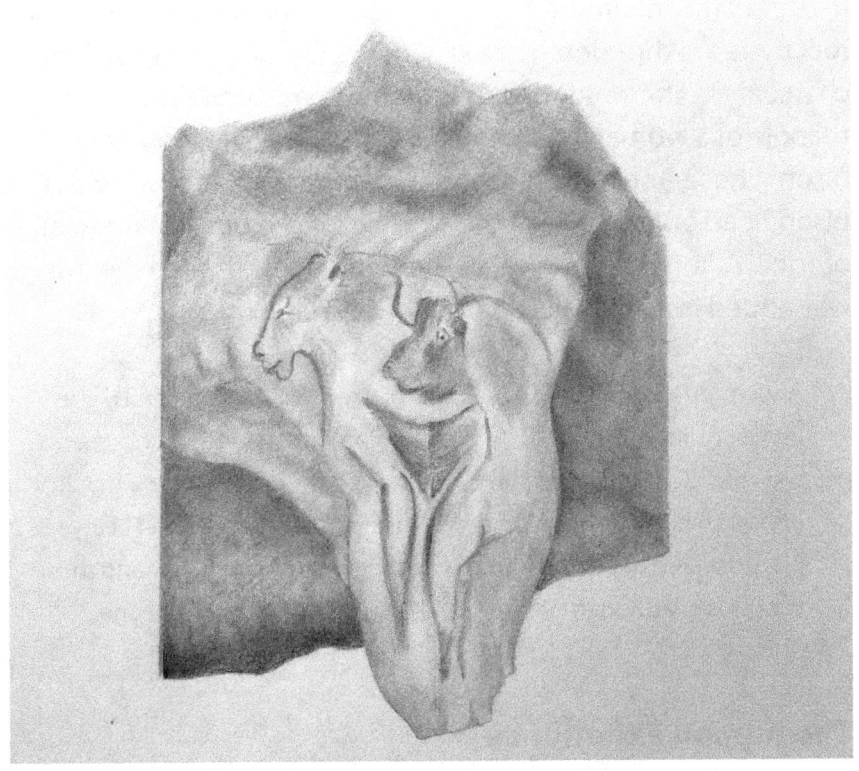

10. Goddess of Chauvet
Drawn in black charcoal, three combined images painted at different times on a pendulous rock hanging from the roof of a deep limestone cave at Chauvet, France. The first painted was the female pubic triangle. A vivid portrayal of the interconnectedness of fertility across land, animals and humans. 32,000 to 30,000 BCE. Drawing: Kaye Moseley ©.

each other. Humans and animals were perceived to be of one and the same energy.

A vivid portrayal of this interconnectedness of fertility across the land, animals and humans comes from the last and deepest of the cave chambers in the Chauvet Cave, in a feature called the Venus of Chauvet (or Venus Pendant). From the ceiling of the chamber, a vertical cone of limestone hangs down ending in a point 1.1

metres (3 ft 6 in) off the floor. On this pendulous part of the rock roof there are three integrated images which were created in black charcoal at different times. The oldest image portrays the pubic triangle of a woman and her legs. Added later are, on the right, a bison whose front leg is the left leg of the female form, with the bison head on the belly of the woman placed on a rounded area of rock. A lioness who shares the right leg of the female image was added last. Soetens describes the image thus:

> A woman's vulva, legs and illusion of pregnant belly given by the contour of the rock … .The pubic triangle is shaded in and then the vulva slit cut though the paint and yellow rock surface so that it appears white. The bison body, with her leg becoming his and his eye placed where her belly button would be, was painted after and the lionesses head added later still … .This Goddess and bison are one … .

The human experience

Who were the people who came with their multicoloured paints and charcoal, by the light of a small oil lamp, deep underground? The sacred experience of the caves was for everyone, not just the shamans of the time, with different cave areas for different purposes.

Handprints and silhouettes were among the images found in the caves, for example at Pech Merle, France (between 25,000 and 13,000 BCE). They are also found in Australian First Nations' cave artwork. For silhouettes, the red colour used was held as a liquid in the mouth and carefully blown around the hand which was used as a stencil for the image. All ages and genders are represented in the paintings of hands. However the analysis of the archaeologist Dean Snow and his colleagues at Pennsylvania

Palaeolithic Mothers

State University, determined that 75 per cent of the cave art hands were female.

Rachel Corbett, in visiting the El Castillo caves for the BBC, recalls her urge to place her hand up to reach out, mirroring such an imprint. The archaeologist with her, Marcos Garcia Diez of Madrid University, commented that he thought this was why they were there – to connect with descendants and ancestors through placing your hand against the image of theirs. The wall was more than a canvas; it was a threshold, 'a being' (Diez in Corbett 2014).

You will recall the tale of the child who left a finger imprint on the pottery of the Goddess of Dolni Vestonice statue. Pech Merle has its own child imprint to share with us. Further into the cave at Pech Merle, footprints of children, preserved in what was once damp clay, have been found a kilometre (more than half a mile) underground. Chauvet Cave has imprints of a child and a wolf or dog walking side by side.

An earlier proposition was that the cave art was made in the belief that it would ensure hunting success. However, it is held by many now that most of the art was made by shamans (both female and male) who went into trances to try to connect with the spirit world, as was discussed earlier. 'If you go into one of these caves alone, you start to suffer from sensory deprivation very, very quickly, in 5 to 10 minutes,' David Whitley, a world expert on Palaeolithic caves has said. He added, 'It can spin you into an altered state of consciousness'. A shaman would have experienced an altered awareness, interpreted as connection to the world of spirit.

The dating of the Cave of Altamira artwork in Spain, shows it was created over a period of at least 10,000 and up to 20,000 years, starting about 36,000 years ago. Dating in the Chauvet Cave in France indicates that the artwork was created from 37,000 years ago through a period of about 9,000 years (with a 2,000-year break in the middle), after which the entrance was closed by a landslide.

The limestone El Castillo caves in Spain have the oldest known cave paintings, dated to at least 40,800 years old. Like the other caves mentioned, El Castillo was used over a long period of time. Diez has said of El Castillo, 'This cave is like a church and that's why ancient people returned, returned, returned here for thousands of years.' (Diez in Corbett 2014). This Palaeolithic worldview survived dramatically over a vast period of time and could only have done so because it served the spiritual needs of the people.

The works in the caves may indicate a quite complex knowledge system, with ideas put forward by the French researcher Chantal Jègues-Wolkiewiez, among others, that the arrangement of animals on the walls can be seen to replicate star patterns in the night sky.

From an Upper Palaeolithic site at Mal'ta in southeast Siberia, comes a rectangular piece of polished ivory tusk, 13.8 cm x 8.1 cm (5.4 in x 3.2 in), with a small central perforated hole (26,000 BCE). On one side are carved three wriggling snakes and the other side is incised with many dot markings in a concentric line going around from the perforation. On the edges are other groups of dots forming spirals. This has been described by a number of authors (e.g. Renfrew et al. 1991) as a calendar-astronomical device. Archaeologist Alexander Marshack identified that this plate had 365 holes marked in it, which happens to be the exact number of days in a year.

In the Abri-sous-Roche Blanchard rock shelter in Dordogne, France, interesting markings were found on a section from a reindeer antler. Through microscopic analysis, Marshack pointed out that this shows in perfect pictures the astronomical movements/phases of the moon within a period of two months – following the moon phases is a more reliable way of charting time than the sun – and moon phases are used by women to chart their menstrual cycle. Another feature of the same rock shelter complex is the frequently found vulva sculptures and stones.

On the basis of extensive research of markings in 146 painted caves, paleoanthropologist Genevieve von Petzinger proposes that there are 32 symbols or pictograms of a graphic code found in caves all over Europe. If this is the case, then here is another form of communication, based on the same concept that eventually resulted in written language in historical times.

There was a vibrant intelligence and complex spiritual interpretation at work in the Palaeolithic period and it was linked to women. Burials of women are similarly presented as those of men and indeed of children. When buried all bodies were usually placed directly on the earth, often in a foetal position, with crumbled red ochre over the bodies or in small lumps in the graves. The bodies could be wearing adornments such as a cap, necklace, armband, bracelet or anklet, made from stone, teeth and shells – including cowrie shells. Often shells, and particularly the cowrie shell shape, noticeably resemble the female vulva, the focus for birth, so clearly marked on the Goddess statues.

We may go so far as to conjecture that those buried in such graves are in the position they were/will be in when in the womb – perhaps, the living looked forward to rebirth. This is certainly true in later matrifocal communities when the importance of the woman was underscored by her being the source of both birth and rebirth. Women became the more sacred because everyone relied on them to be the means through which one would be born again.

Through an extraordinarily long period of time humans developed a living belief system that centred on life – on the Earth as the Mother of all life. This informed and motivated their quests into the spiritual dimension and spurred their inquisitiveness about the stars and moon, and ways to communicate in both this life and in a spiritual dimension. Perhaps they developed skills in this arena that we have lost or might scoff at today.

Women were viewed as a wonder in what they could achieve through reproduction, and they were inevitably linked to the Earth Mother image – they were the model for her. Humanity was an integrated part of the natural world. Then, after the next period, the Neolithic, the culture seemed to have slipped away ... or had it? Through archaeological exploration we are now uncovering the truth: that in the remaining pockets of matrifocal cultures available today we can identify important social principles. These principles may nurture a new way of being in the world as we face the greatest human disaster, centred on the climate challenges we have created. We will explore more about this fascinating story in the chapters that follow.

CHAPTER 2

Neolithic Flowering

Let us be the ancestors our descendants will thank.
Winona Laduke, Native American environmentalist and activist (1959–present)

I want to talk about the Neolithic period because it continues the theme of the ancient role of women and men as collaborative equals, rather than that of two sexes engaged in a 'power-over' interplay that became the norm under patriarchy. I want to trace the story of matrifocal culture into this important developmental time for the human species, the period called the 'Neolithic'.

With the warming that ended the Palaeolithic Ice Age, more opportunities opened up for human beings in terms of where they could thrive and the ways that they could care for themselves. Taking up these opportunities took a transition from one lifestyle to another. We move from the 'Stone Age' where tools and implements were chipped from stone to the Neolithic ('New Stone Age'), where tools were still of stone but were ground or polished.

Pottery, spinning and weaving were also developed and there is evidence of sophisticated woodworking. People began to choose to live in permanent settlements and eventually domesticated crops and then animals. As the climate and the world became more liveable, one of the major events of the period was a rapid increase in population.

Overall, this period is sometimes called the 'Neolithic Revolution'. But it was not a violent one. From the time when anatomically modern humans appeared, through to about 3,000 BCE, warfare, aggression and conflict are noticeable by their absence in human history.

Generally, this period is dated from about 10,000 BCE. It was a gradual transition, with a variety of manifestations, and common to them all in terms of culture and belief, remained identification with the Earth and her creatures, including reverence for the deceased. In that context, what an explosion of religious expression it was!

Who were they?

Who were the people of the Neolithic period? They were building on their learning and practices over the preceding aeons. The basic group to which people would probably have felt connected was the clan to which they knew they were related. They knew they were related because they shared the same mother and her sister/s and their children also made up the clan. The role of men in procreation was not yet known, something that could only be worked out once animals were domesticated. As illustrated by matrifocal cultures still in existence today, if the mother had a sexual partner, he may have shared living in her house or returned to his mother's hearth in the morning. All living fairly close together, many discussions about plans and issues would have occurred. Through a consensus system, decisions most people could agree with (or live with) were reached.

In many traditional societies, that of First Nations Australians included, there is a clear gender division of tasks, and this division is called upon when important decisions are to be made. Some business is decided only by the women, some only by the men, and some require each gender group to consider an issue before they come together to negotiate. We have no indication that there was a hierarchy during these ancient times to suggest that one individual or select group made decisions and imposed the outcomes on others. Indeed, the evidence shows the opposite.

A place of worship

While some things continued, the Neolithic was a period of transition, particularly at first. An example of this is the spiritual site of Göbekli Tepe, in south-eastern Turkey, dated to around 9,500 BCE to 7,300 BCE. This site was developed by nomadic hunter-gatherer tribes, and may be the oldest known human-made place of worship. Perhaps the site has been sacred ever since – the highest point of the mound is known as the Hill of Ritual, which has a wishing tree and local women still frequent the site (Sever 2011).

There was no permanent housing in the area, but large numbers of animal bones have been found. These were left over from feeding the various clans who gathered there to share festival events. Hundreds of people were probably required in order to create and erect the pillars, which are the focal point of attention here.

Ancient Ways for Current Days

11. Göbekli Tepe excavation
A temple sanctuary with at least seven stone circles containing limestone pillars (up to 6 m /20 ft high, weight up to 9.07 tonnes /10 tons), carved with stylised people, animals, insects and birds. Typically there were two central pillars, as seen here. The 'T' shaped pillars are carved in one piece. Turkey, approximately 9,500 to 7,300 BCE. Photo: Kaalii Cargill.

This is a very early example of megalithic building that emerged to full expression elsewhere (e.g. Israel, Malta, Britain) around 4,000 BCE. It is also an example of the sophisticated decision-making that had to occur to create such an innovation.

This site tells us that the desire for religious expression was a huge driving force such that permanent sacred sites, where spirit could be expressed, were more important than creating permanent settlements. It has now been found that, on the other side of Europe in the Orkney Islands, in their early Neolithic period, they too built megalithic sacred structures – in their case burial mounds

Neolithic Flowering

– before they built settlements (Kerns in Nash and Townsend 2016). It is also the case that many people remained hunter-gatherer from choice, even when lives as sedentary crop-growers had been adopted by others (Romey 2019).

At Göbekli Tepe, carving was the dominant art form, while earlier in Europe it was cave painting. In this temple sanctuary there are at least seven stone circles (and possibly 20), covering 10 hectares (25 acres), which contain limestone pillars carved with animals, insects and birds. In the earliest phase, each pillar was up to 6 metres (20 ft) high and weighed up to 9.07 tonnes (10 tons).

One of these carved pillars is like a totem pole that shows three figures, one above the other. While the top one is damaged the next clearly births the one below which, in turn, has a head emerging between its legs. We can only assume three women are depicted. Here is the story of a motherline – the newborn has three ancestors shown before it.

In the level dated to about 7,350 BCE, rectangular buildings, without doors or windows were built, with shorter and fewer pillars, but still including the two central ones. In one of these the only clearly female figure at Göbekli Tepe was found engraved on a flat plaque/stone benchtop, placed between the two central pillars (Sever 2011). The woman is naked and probably in the process of giving birth. The waters seem to have just broken. The important reproductive role of women has been honoured here. The pillars have carved reliefs of felines (possibly lionesses or leopards). The association of a birthing woman and felines is one that we will later see strongly developed at Çatalhöyük, also in Turkey.

Ancient Ways for Current Days

12. Göbekli Tepe birthing stone
A carving on a stone slab showing a woman in the traditional birthing position, waters having just broken they flow from her vaginal area. The slab was placed between two pillars carved with felines, in a rectangular room. Urfa, Turkey, approximately 7,350 BCE. Drawing: Kaye Moseley ©.

The introduction of the female form is unusual because, like the cave art tradition of earlier times, few humanoid figures are shown at Göbekli Tepe. Of these it could be said that the sex is indeterminate, but it could be more accurate to say that they are androgynous. Later we will see evidence that huge stones were representative of female and male ancestors in matriarchal/matrifocal cultures, which may have been the case for the Göbekli Tepe stones.

What is clear is that the animal and other images give no indication of organised violence. There are no depictions of hunting raids or wounded animals. The creators of the pillar carvings generally ignore game on which the society depended for food, such as deer, in favour of formidable creatures such as lions, snakes, spiders and scorpions. Perhaps they were clan totems. Like the earlier cave art in Europe, what we see here is respect and veneration of the natural world and a desire to align with it. The later cultural shift to praise of violence (as seen in Sumer and Egypt) had not yet occurred.

The awakening of this new era provided great diversity. Every group had its innovations, which is evident in the ways they honoured ancestors, celebrated the Goddess spirituality, and expressed themselves through art. They traded and/or exchanged gifts with each other and shared their knowledge. The Earth was seen as the Great Mother. Caves and cracks in the Earth were entrances to the mother's body. A spring was her vital fluids poured as a gift out of her body, to aid all creatures.

Honouring ancestors

At 'Ain Ghazl in Jordan, a cache of 15 busts and 15 statues has been uncovered. They were created over a period of at least 200 years sometime between 7,200 and 6,500 BCE. They are constructed of lime plaster over reeds with bitumen to outline the irises. The statues represent women, men and children; women are recognisable by features resembling breasts and slightly enlarged bellies, but neither female nor male sexual

Ancient Ways for Current Days

13. Double figure ancestor statue.
Constructed of lime plaster over reeds with bitumen irises. The figures are part of a cache of 15 busts and 15 statues. 'Ain Ghazl, Jordan, created between 7,200 and 6,500 BCE. Photo: J. Cameron.

characteristics are emphasised, and none of the statues have genitals. The only part of each statue fashioned with any detail, was the faces.

These representations are taken to be re-creations of ancestors and are located in time and place close to the clay covered human skulls first found near Jericho, Palestine. To date approximately 60 plastered skulls have been found from Jordan to Turkey and across the Middle East, dated to between 8,000 and 6,000 BCE.

Neolithic Flowering

In a couple of instances, the artists went further and created stands for the heads. At Tell Ramad, Israel, archaeologists state the two finest skulls are of women, aged between 18 and 20 years. To accompany such skulls artists created seated female clay figurines about 23 centimetres (9 in) high without heads, coated in plaster and painted in red. These served as stands for heads of both women and men. In northern Syria two striking headless female figurines were found which may have served a similar purpose. They are fine, strong figures; possibly pregnant, with large breasts and thighs. Each has a long, slim neck which ends in a flat platform.

The usual interpretation for these mortuary practices is that the skulls and statues offered a means of preserving, communing with and worshiping ancestors. Some experts maintain that there is a religious aspect to the practice, reflecting a belief that life continues after death, possibly assisted by preserving the individual characteristics of the deceased. In both practices women, men and children are treated the same, indicating gender and age is of little importance.

In the next great flowering, at Çatalhöyük in Turkey, we see a similar identification with animals and the clear message that the Goddess has not been forgotten, she remains integral to the human spiritual world.

The first urban centre – Çatalhöyük

Çatalhöyük was a very large Neolithic, and then Chalcolithic, settlement in southern Anatolia, which existed from approximately 7,400 BCE to 6,000 BCE, illustrating a very stable lifestyle spanning at least 1,000 years. It is the largest and best-preserved Neolithic site found to date, if not quite a city, then certainly the first urban centre in the world. About 8,000 people lived there. Mostly hunter-gatherers, they kept some animals and stored excess grain.

This fascinating site, when found, was a mound rising gently from the flat Konya plain, beside an old riverbed. It was first identified and excavated by the archeologist James Mellaart (digs were conducted from 1958 to 1965), who enthusiastically interpreted the findings as evidence of a matriarchy. There was a 27-year period where excavation was forbidden by the Turkish government, until a new dig, supervised by the archaeologist Ian Hodder, was permitted (1993 to 2018).

Contrary to Mellaart's energetic and rapid excavation work, Hodder adopted a thorough and laborious approach utilising every modern technique available. He has been unwilling to continue the earlier Mellaart interpretation in his findings; nevertheless, he contributed new insights, especially into clan life and procreation behaviours. Çatalhöyük was a discovery which stunned the archaeological world, creating controversy, intrigue and delight to the present day.

In 6,500 BCE the Konya plain was a scene of lush vegetation and teeming wildlife. On the southern and western limits of the plain lay the heavily wooded slopes of the Taurus mountains. From here a number of streams flowed from the great mountain lakes to the plain, including a major river which split into three forks as it crossed the wide flat land to a lake about 10 kilometres (6 miles) away.

On the central branch of this river, the town of Çatalhöyük was established. Indeed, the new arrivals may have followed the river on foot, or paddled canoes from the mountains, for the seed they

Neolithic Flowering

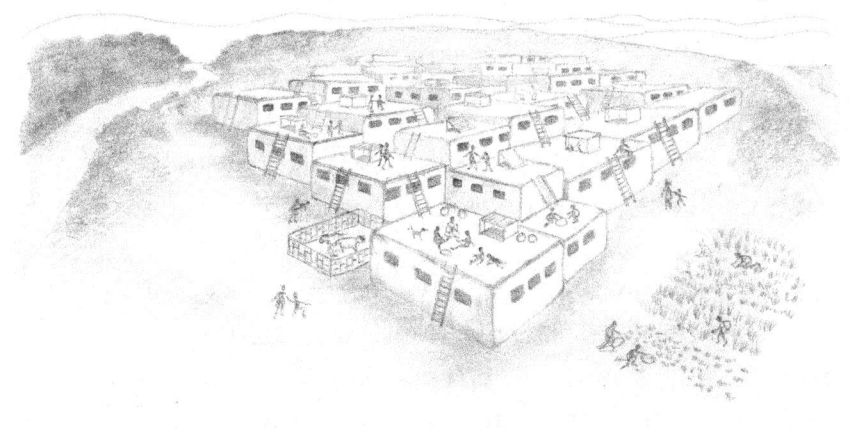

14. Çatalhöyük, Turkey
Artist's reconstruction of the city showing ladders, high windows,
flat roofs with doorway/chimney. Drawing: Kaye Moseley ©.

brought with them is native to hill-country, not to the plains. Across the grasslands roamed herds of huge aurochs, a kind of cattle now extinct. This new home was abundant in game and vegetation for food. The settlers grew at least 14 different crops and knew about field rotation and fertilisation. They made interesting meals, including sweet desserts; baked loaves of bread; ate porridges; made yoghurt, wine and beer; dried and salted meat; and stored grain for the cold of winter when snow covered the land.

The urban centre these people built was unique, made up of regular rows of mudbrick houses, each one higher than the last, rising in steps up the mound. There is no grand central building and no fortified wall. Not a road or alleyway was to be seen – blank white walls stared out at the outside world, with animal pens built against them here and there, and the occasional wooden ladder to climb up to a roof. The rooftops were the roadway, and work areas – further ladders took you up to higher buildings. People would have passed by their neighbours, chatting and sharing exchanges. A small, three-walled verandah sheltered a hole in the roof of each house. To visit, or enter your home, you went down this hole, via another ladder. Çatalhöyük covered 13 hectares (32 acres), when most settlements of the times were only a half to one and a half hectares. Given there was an active trading culture dealing in raw and finished goods that attracted travelling traders, the city would have been legendary.

Even more fascinating are the interiors of these dwellings, which were kept very clean and neat. There were fixed benches for tables, beds, seats and workspaces. There were niches in the walls which were used as shelves for storage or for stone lamps; a quern was set in the floor for grinding flour. Beneath the entry hole in the roof was the hearth and an oval oven with its back against the wall that had a flat top to keep things warm. Unfortunately, this did lead to smoky homes and inhaled smoke fibres built up in the lungs (Hodder 2016). The room was a rectangle and had open windows under the eaves for light and ventilation, which is why the houses rose one behind the other. In one wall was a round, doorless hole leading into a narrow storeroom built beside the house.

The whole interior of each building was finished with smooth, white mud or gypsum. Reed or rush as mats were on the floor, or as matting on the bed platforms. These platforms were also spread with cushions, bright kilim rugs and blankets. Sometimes, a panel of the wall was painted in a pattern, or in plain red – the sacred and protective colour of life. Sometimes, there was a scene painted on the wall giving a glimpse into events in the people's lives – one shows a volcano nearby erupting.

The art of the painter was a highly developed one. Since no paint or painting tools were found in burial sites of men, only in those of women, it would appear that women were the artists. Archaeologists have deduced from the many plastered layers of paintings, that

Neolithic Flowering

15. Reconstruction of a dwelling at Çatalhöyük
Ladder to entrance to the rooftop street. Smoke also exits here from the oven immediately below. The Goddess on the top of the far wall is in the birthing position and we can assume the bullock heads below her are the result of this. To the right is a sleeping platform waiting for bedding and there is one out of view in the foreground. Skeletons of deceased ancestors were found under such platforms. The whole interior is plastered in white clay. Neolithic period, approximately 7,400 to 6,000 BCE. Museum of Anatolian Civilisations, Ankara, Turkey. Photo: Elelicht. Licensed under Creative Commons, Wikimedia.

they were regarded as powerful in some way. Perhaps created for a certain ritual or ritual period, they only remained on display for a short length of time before being plastered over.

We can infer who slept on the beds, because after death their bones were buried underneath them. In each home in the centre of the east wall was the woman of the house. A red painted post in the wall at either end of the platform marked this place. The man of the house slept on the platform farthest from the door; the youngest children initially slept with their mother then moved to other platforms (Mellaart 1975). Up to eight people at a time could share a home.

From earliest times, red was a sacred colour representative of the menstrual blood of women and of the life provided by the womb. It is so frequently used it is understood that it was more than decorative. It was the colour used to bestow blessings, safety, abundance. In some burials, the bones are stained with red ochre, and they are bones of women. This linked women to the Great Goddess who provided all life, as well as to ancestors and rebirth. Additionally, some women's burials contain polished obsidian mirrors, their rarity making them mysterious and probably part of a priestess' ritual tools.

A ritual centre

The town provides many examples of statues of the Goddess. Particularly renowned is the fired clay Goddess with felines circa 5,800 BCE. She is seated and we are at first taken by her nakedness and sheer bulk. It is a corpulence that exudes both abundance and serenity. The air of calm is shared by the leopards, panthers or lionesses, one on either side, which raise their heads in pleasure as she fondles their ears, their tails curl over her shoulders. She is mistress of the animals. Her breasts are firm and full, ready to suckle the newborn child, who is so easily emerging, between her legs. Yet this monumentally majestic figure is only 18 centimetres (7 in) in height! She was found placed in a bin used to store grain, possibly to protect this precious resource, or to protect a house which was about to be rebuilt.

Çatalhöyük was a world where the sacred, the spiritual, were indivisible from ordinary life. Author Liz Carr-Harris refers to it as

Neolithic Flowering

16. Seated Mother Goddess of Çatalhöyük
Baked clay. Approximately 6,000 BCE, Anatolia, Turkey. Corpulent and fertile, she is giving birth while seated between two felines – either panther, lioness or leopard – indicative of her influence with animals. Drawing: Kaye Moseley ©.

a 'temple community' with a full religious expression – and every home was a temple. However, some buildings were exclusively temples, or shrines – huge figures, twice life-sized, were moulded onto some of the walls, often without clear sex, although they are usually pregnant, which tells us they are female. Sometimes they are zoomorphic (have animal features), though definitely human.

Fortunately, we have the sculptures, and they are almost all of women, often holding their breasts and corpulent. There are some statues of males, usually boys, which were found in the later stages of the settlement and constituted about 20 per cent of all statuettes made.

In the region, small statues of a double or twin Goddess have been found. Such an image, quite stylised and large, is on one of the temple walls at Çatalhöyük. Legs on these relief images are usually wide apart, indicative of the birthing posture. Emerging below will be the head of a bull shaped in plaster, actual horns fully intact.

Bull-skull and horns are called a bucranium. This was a highly favoured, symbolic motif in shrines at Çatalhöyük – in one raised bench, at right angles to the wall, there were seven bucrania, one behind the other, sunk into the bench with the horns protruding out either side. At first the horns of wild animals were used, but later domesticated ones were incorporated. This reveals that the clever people of Çatalhöyük had managed to tame a very formidable creature into herds that they controlled.

The bull motif continues into other later cultures linked to the Goddess (notably Minoan Crete), and one interpretation (Cameron 1981) is that the skull closely reflects the shape of the womb, with the horns as the fallopian tubes. They were even used, much later, in Greek and Roman building decoration.

Sometimes in the shrines of Çatalhöyük there are also sculptural breasts protruding from the wall. Excavation revealed that they have been moulded over the skull of an animal – the sacred is both death and life, and the Mother is the intrinsic part of the entire cycle.

This 'temple community' illustrates that, like the megaliths at Göbekli Tepe, the urban town of Çatalhöyük had religious significance before the domestication of animals occurred. People were driven first by the complex belief systems they held – their cultural life. Hodder has said that they were driven by the desire to relate – they wanted to be as close as possible to each other and very much wanted to live near the ancestral houses where significant people were buried.

In one shrine there is a series of murals that confront and confound modern thinking. On all four walls are different depictions of animals, surrounded almost exclusively by men. The men have pointed beards and wear leopard loincloths. There are some figures that appear to be musicians – percussionists, pipers or harpists, making it a festival or ritual scene. The men are interacting with the animals – chasing an animal, pulling the tongue, pulling the tail, swinging from the horns, jumping on or over the animal's back, one appears to be poking his butt towards the animal. The men don't have weapons. The aim was not to injure the creatures, but to represent the relationship of the man to the animal.

The animals shown are the bull, horse, stag deer, bear and wild boar, all of which are large and potentially dangerous to human beings. The things the men are doing appear to be acts which a person could never in reality do with these animals. The animals are shown as large, the humans very small. This discrepancy in size emphasises the bravery of approaching the animal. Perhaps the images were used to bolster the courage of the young men through a ritual, before participating in festival games. These festivals may have been an opportunity for males to show bravery and experience public excitement – a bit like a rodeo today. As there were no sacrificial sites at Çatalhöyük, one imagines that this may well have ended in the animal being killed and eaten in an atmosphere of celebration.

Otherwise, the paintings on the walls portray stylised birds, vultures, flowers, stars, butterflies, bees, plants and landscapes. There are also geometric patterns that may have covered the whole wall or as a half panel. Goddess images are shown, similar to the statues that have been found of her. Mellaart claims that the power of the Goddess is shown by her link, in the house/shrine paintings and wall sculptures, to powerful animals and to the vegetation needed for the provision of food and therefore, life.

An egalitarian culture

Çatalhöyük has strong evidence of being an egalitarian society. Hodder calls it 'an aggressively egalitarian society held together by a complex network of ritual, social and economic ties'. There are no houses more richly adorned than others, for example where royalty or a religious hierarchy might live. There is no war equipment (such as shields), only hunting tools (arrows, lance or javelin). Nevertheless, there were arguments between residents, which may have been settled by fighting – there are a few skulls with head wounds, and some arm fractures sustained from blocking a blow – perhaps from a person, perhaps from something falling. If fighting was a method of dispute resolution, it may have been sanctioned by the clan priestesses as a way to resolve differences before they could disrupt the peace any further.

Hodder's findings reveal little social distinction based on gender, with women and men receiving equivalent nutrition and equal social status, as also typically found in Palaeolithic cultures. For Hodder, this means it was not a matriarchy. He is falling for the notion that a matriarchy is the same as a patriarchy, but with women on top. What we see clearly is that these people shared a matrifocal culture, in which equal and complimentary gender roles are the norm.

Women organised religion and social matters; household order; agricultural activity; and pottery, weaving and painting production.

Neolithic Flowering

Men concerned themselves primarily with herding, hunting, mining and trading. They were also occupied with craftwork associated with their trading, including carving and tool-making. Both females and males were physically fit and many trained as dancers.

The challenge for us, looking back from within patriarchy, is to understand how all this development occurred without a leader or executive group. As we will see in later matrifocal cultures, the links of collaboration are by relationship, which would have been based on the mother-line. In charge of the domestic domain, women were the household priestesses and some would have led group rituals as well. It may be amazing to us, but analysis of teeth at Çatalhöyük indicate that children were not raised by their biological parents. They were fostered out early in life to another family to raise. Thus was created a network of relationships and support through both birth and child rearing.

Not all houses have burials. Some houses were preferred places of burial, showing that all these people felt connected to that house or those buried in it, although not necessarily of the one biological family. The sense of history and of ancestral connection was important.

Hodder proposes, from the urban layout, that the people were divided into two groups who lived on opposite sides of the town, separated by a gully. Furthermore, because no nearby towns were found from which marriage partners could be drawn, he proposes that this spatial separation must have marked two intermarrying kinship groups. This is entirely compatible with the analysis of marriage patterns in matrifocal communities, explored in Goettner-Abendroth's work.

Ancient Ways for Current Days

First Nations Australians have a kinship system whereby the people are divided into two halves (called 'moieties'), and then four quarters (sometimes more), that classify a person into a kin group or 'skin group', depending on who your parents were. Every group has equal status. The kin group includes both blood relations and specified others. A person's 'skin' determines among other things, who would be an eligible sexual partner. It places the individual firmly into a network of relationships – both obligations and support. 'Skin groups were further subdivided according to generation, occupation, gender and educational status' (Poulter and Nicholson 2018). The culture of Australian First Nation people show many aspects of a matrifocal culture, so they provide a model that may illustrate the sort of arrangements we are seeing at Çatalhöyük.

Also compatible with a matrifocal system is the notion that at Çatalhöyük there may have been interlinked customs of obligation to assist one another. There is not a lot of storage space in the houses – groups did not hoard for themselves, but took their allocation as distributed, in all likelihood by the elder women, from the grain storages. This distribution system occurs in some matrifocal cultures even today.

In matrifocal societies, systems of gift-giving and exchange maintain connectedness and obligation. The same gifts could rotate to others several times – the connection is in the handling and passing on of such objects to others in the friendship/relationship/obligation chain.

In this system of exchange, at Çatalhöyük, after bodies had been interred for some time, in some cases they were dug up and the skull removed, often then plastered to restore features (as in Jericho, above) and then displayed in a shrine-room. Sometimes other bones were also removed. These retrieved bones were then kept in another house – presumably where there was a social or biological connection. Similarly, sometimes bucrania were dug up from earlier habitation layers and reused in the current house, which is evidence of their importance in family or clan histories.

The challenge of urban living

This was however an early experiment in city dwelling, and Larsen et al. (2019) comment that Çatalhöyük human biology reveals 'increasing cost to members of the settlement'. There was no sanitation in the city, so that refuse areas had to be used as excrement dumps, both within and outside the city. While the ash also dumped there provided some sanitation, this refuse system exposed the people to a higher level of pathogens than ever before – there was more disease and more infectious disease from living closely together; higher incidence of dental and oral infection; and increased chance of a localised skin infection from cuts and abrasions.

Humans were also unaware of the health costs of a heavily cereal (carbohydrate) based diet, compared to the very varied diet of hunter-gatherers. Neolithic farmers became significantly shorter than their Palaeolithic ancestors. The steady supply of food, and the convenience and security of settled life did fuel fertility. However, the creation of this food also created greater stresses, due to the extra workload demanded by farming, which was undertaken by both adults and juveniles.

Gradually, crops took over all areas close to the city, so the herders had to travel some distance to reach the grasslands their animals required (sheep/some goats, and late in the period, cattle). Trees for building were no longer close to the city either. Perhaps the site was becoming overburdened by the needs of the people and their lifestyle. Added to this the area was becoming gradually drier. The city expansion and increasing population density led to some behaviours involving interpersonal violence. In the late period of the settlement, people started to move away, a new settlement started beside the original, until the site overall was eventually abandoned.

Introduction to a matrifocal culture

Our visit to Çatalhöyük has shown us many of the features of a matrifocal culture – ancestral connection, role obligations, social relationships, gender equality, exchange practices, a sharing economy, common spiritual beliefs and practical support; together these ensured social cohesion. Priestesses provided guidance and promoted consensual resolution of issues. The deity was a Goddess, who fulfilled many roles. She was the embodiment of warmth and protection; the patroness of the arts; she was at one with the wild animals; mistress of life, death and rebirth. She was the source of fertility for humankind, for their fields, and indeed for all natural places such as the forests. With women as the heads of households and inter-family relationships, the city experienced a period of peace and prosperity totaling nearly one thousand years: a feat that later cultures, our own included, have found hard to match.

Later we will discover what happened to at least some of the descendants of Çatalhöyük and the contributions they made to new endeavours. We have seen how there were very ancient matrifocal indicators in Europe, the Mediterranean and Turkey. Before continuing this ancient journey, it is time to find out what exactly the elements of matrifocal cultures were – and are.

CHAPTER 3

And Matrifocal Culture Is?

> The feminine principle attempts to relate.
> Instead of breaking things off into parts, it says,
> 'Where are we alike? How can we connect?
> Where is the love? Can you listen to me?... see me?
> Do you care ... ?'
> **Marion Woodman, Canadian mythopoetic author,
> Jungian analyst and feminist (1928–2018)**

What would it mean to live in a place where respecting women was not optional? How would that change the way masculinity was expressed? We can explore it because it has been done for thousands of years in the past, as this book shows. We can explore the ideas because some cultures do this – today, now. We will explore this, in this chapter.

I am not proposing that we go back to life as it was in the deep past. Nor am I saying we all should live in tribal clans as some matrifocal groups do today. I hope that on this journey we can gain a genuine feel for what this concept of a matrifocal society is, and if it is possible to bring it, or key aspects of it, into the world we need to create now. As a minimum, it is important to know that we can be different – and better.

A simple starting point for the term 'matrifocal' is that these societies are matrilineal – biological descent is traced through the mother's line. They are also matrilocal, because in a sexual partnership, the woman stays with her biological family and the man moves to her household/compound. More likely, he visits her there and then returns to his mother's family to fulfil his required duties by day (and these are discussed later).

How do these arrangements help anything? They help because the woman's needs are put first – she has inheritance and she has safety. A woman who stays in her community is safer than if she was to travel to a new home, possibly without access to her own support system, out of reach of friends or advisors who have her best interests at heart. In contrast, in her matrilineal home she has the women of her family to advise and support her, her uncles and brothers around for protection, and she can flourish in her own community.

In the past, women were treasured for their ability to give life – without this, social groups would die out. In our society, this power is not considered very valuable. We have lost connection to the appreciation of this wondrous capacity. Heide Goettner-Abendroth, the world expert on matriarchies has said, 'Matriarchal societies are anchored in maternity. An abandoned child or woman is unheard of within them'.

Goettner-Abendroth also explains that 'matriarchy' (her preferred term for these cultures) means 'mothers are at the centre of society'.

And Matrifocal Culture Is?

I am very fortunate to have benefited from her comprehensive research, originally in German and translated to English in 2012, and I refer to her frequently in this book. Through her extensive study of matriarchies she used her own research in the field, recorded studies of anthropologists, and work by many other researchers into particular societies across the world, both past and present. She thus distilled the key attributes of matriarchal/matrifocal societies. The goal of this chapter is to summarise these principles for you, and so it almost entirely reflects her work. I therefore do not cite her throughout this chapter, unless it is a direct quote. Rather, I have cited others when an idea is not from her work or they support her.

Archaeologists have in the past been primarily male. They assumed and asserted that if rule by women (matriarchy) had ever existed it would look the same as rule by men (patriarchy), just that the person on top was a woman, not a man. This simplistic reading overlooked the fact that women are completely different in their interests, concerns and ways of going about things, from men.

What you look for, to find a matriarchy, is very different from what is displayed within patriarchal societies. Not being able to find anything to fit their expectations, the male archaeologists, rather than change their narrow expectations and definitions, declared that there never had been matriarchies. Patriarchal systems provide rich burials of men, weapons of war, glorification of war and killing, a class system, racism, slavery and women in an oppressed situation. When a culture is found to be peaceful, gender-egalitarian and without a class system, this will not be declared a matriarchy (e.g. Hodder on Çatalhöyük; the first interpretation of Knossos [later revised] by Evans) because there is no queen at the top. The lack of a dominant ruler, female or male, is exactly the point in a matrifocal or matriarchal society and a fine indicator that this is what you have found.

17. Powerful Goddess, North Africa
Clay statue with vulture-shaped head, she is in a pose with upraised arms, common to a type of figurine from Predynastic or Kemetic Egypt, about 4,200–3,400 BCE. Drawing: Kaye Moseley ©.

It took the extremely brilliant Lithuanian-American archaeologist and anthropologist, Marija Gimbutas (1921–1994) to stand up to this limiting paradigm and, through her extensive research, propose that there had been a Goddess-centred and woman-centred ancient social system in Europe. Gimbutas was ridiculed and suffered a professional backlash at the time for this position, but her theories have since been widely accepted and supported by later research. Her discoveries are also foundational to what is presented in this book.

And Matrifocal Culture Is?

Key values – a sharing economy

In an interview in late 2019, Goettner-Abendroth said of the values represented in matriarchies:

> They are egalitarian, considerate and nurturing, in the sense that taking care of others and their wellbeing is self-evident. In the Khasi culture in India, the clan mother – the chief of the village – is chosen according to her ability to help her people.
>
> Everyone is respected, regardless of their age or sex. They take care of the elderly until their death. There are no hierarchies among people. Decisions are made by consensus, unanimously. They conduct a sharing economy and condemn the concept of accumulation.

Can you imagine that? Living in a world that condemns the concept of accumulation, the foundation stone of the capitalist system under which we live. Instead, within matrifocal societies, the members of it engage in what is known as a sharing economy (that often incorporates a gift economy). Traditionally, matrifocal societies are agricultural and the fields and homes are a common resource for the people of the clans. The clan mother is the central authority and is custodian (not 'owner') of the clan property. All produce, and income from a clan member's labour is handed over to the 'matriarch' of the clan.

Can you imagine that? Freely handing everything over to one woman? Why risk it? Because you know the clan mother will take care of you and those you care about; she will distribute what is available fairly. Her role is to look after all the children of the clan at every age and stage of life. It is an honour and responsibility, and it is not about using the clan goods for personal gain. It is about measuring surplus out equitably to meet the needs of the clan, storing against difficult times, and investing in the clan so that everyone can thrive.

It is not Communism, which is giving everything to the state. Or perhaps having it taken by the state. No, this is within the arms of the family, the mother and the values of mothering. If there are troubles, everyone shares in it; if there is abundance, everyone benefits, not just a ruling elite. Clan mothers frequently also fill the role of the main priestess. Either way they have no enforcement officers – police, military, officials. The power that they have is to give advice and counsel, not command through force. Their advice is voluntarily accepted.

Key values – shared decision-making

The clan mother/priestess is not alone; she is assisted in her work in several ways, not least by her brothers, one of whom is selected to be the delegated representative to the Councils outside the clan. If there is no brother then it may be an uncle, or a male child may be adopted in anticipation of this.

The male in this role can convey the decisions of the clan but can make no decisions on his own. He has to return to the home base to consult. This role in the outside world meant that when patriarchal invaders, like the British, asked for the chief, the delegated brother stepped forward. This made the true power structure invisible to westerners, who could not conceive of what was really going on.

And Matrifocal Culture Is?

Male parenthood

The role of the uncles and brothers is a pivotal one. They are the mother's helpers and protectors. The children are regarded as related only to their mother and carry her clan name. The children and grandchildren live with their mother in the clan house. The biological 'father' is not seen as related to her children. His own nearest relative is his sister and her children. He fulfils the role of parent, the social father, with these children – his nieces and nephews as we would understand it. If he should express a wish to be also more involved than is usual with his biological children, the clan will facilitate a way for that to happen. The biological father would take affectionate care of his wife's children – in stark contrast to patriarchal fatherhood that encourages domination by the father of the family, and in its worst form, subjugation of the wife and children.

The matrifocal approach to male parenthood seems incredible to us, who are so embedded in the idea and experience of the nuclear family. Many of us have happy memories and experiences within that format, but the nuclear family is separated from others; it is the place where domestic violence occurs, where isolation of the woman involved can lead to anxiety and depression. It is a flawed model, but it is the one that works for patriarchy, where the males need control over female sexuality to be sure they can trace their biological descendants. Thus men can confidently designate property inheritance to their biological offspring, and until fairly recent times, usually to the boys.

Under a matrifocal system the separation of the individuals in a sexual partnership means that, should a couple choose to part, there is nothing much involved. The children are not a focus of argument. They are safe in the clan home. There is no property to split up nor opportunity for acrimonious division of goods. If the male in the partnership were to become upset and agitated, the woman would be protected by the men who surround her – brothers and uncles.

Enjoyment, sex and safety

For matrifocal people monogamy is seen as a form of repression against women. Matrifocal people do not have several partners at once, but they do regularly change partners. Both the woman and the man who are separating are free to develop a new sexual partnership elsewhere. If one partner becomes infatuated with another person, then it is time to part.

This attitude is supported by a society that regards sexuality as fun, a game, an enjoyment. Compare this to the Western traditional attitude that looks upon free sexuality as somehow shameful, and where women who have partners rather than a husband are viewed as promiscuous, (a man who does this is not). The matrifocal approach is completely opposite. In the matrifocal culture sexuality is valued highly and satisfied sexuality is regarded as leading to health, peace and culture.

In this situation prostitution and rape are unknown. Now you are going to say that I am idealising. But no, it is true. The idea of domination simply doesn't exist. Further, a man would not dare to touch a woman against her will. Women, their sexuality and power to give birth, are too much respected. The clan system protects each woman.

This is not to say that the people produced through a matrifocal system are better than other human beings. It is just that the way that their society is structured facilitates peace. Much of our behaviour is learned. Many of the social messages given in Western society are negative, violent, disrespectful. Yet, in our times, there are men as well as women who are insisting on, and demonstrating, a different way of being and relating, a different expectation of masculinity and of equitable power relationships between women and men. A change has already begun.

A motherline

Under patriarchy it is traditionally the eldest son who inherits – the eldest prince becomes the king. Again, the matrifocal system turns this around completely. It is the youngest daughter who inherits from the clan mother. She takes up the honours, rights and duties of the clan's head. As the youngest she is still young, fit and able when this occurs. She can ensure that the outgoing woman is properly cared for, should she have stepped aside, rather than died. She can seek advice without doubt arising about her abilities, given her youth. If she is underage, the uncle or brother who represents the clan will act in her stead, ensuring that the responsibilities of her role are undertaken. In some matrifocal clans the matriarch may be elected, based on capability, from the women of the line.

The designated role of this brother or uncle of the matriarch is the management of the clan land or of the estate. He is well-respected and is a member of the neighbourhood council, representing the clan in outside matters. In internal matters, on a day-to-day basis, the clan mother (the matriarch) is in charge and supervises the household expenditure, workspaces, directs women's work in the kitchen and gardens, attends to the education of girls and ensures domestic ancestor rituals are observed. She is revered by women and men alike.

Balance between sexes

So, despite women's authority, and centrality, a balance was maintained between female and male areas of activity. The tasks are not stereotyped, and can be set out somewhat differently in different tribes. As Goettner-Abendroth says, 'It is the job that is gendered, not the individual who is sexualised'.

In a matrifocal system, both ceremonially and politically, women and men receive equal dignity – they are in balance. Women and men respect each other's dignity, value and spheres of responsibility.

Marriages do occur in matrifocal cultures and one of the common formats for this is the sisters-brothers group marriage. Here a group of sisters marry a group of men who are brothers from another clan. It is usually the same clans that regularly do this, so it is really cross-cousin marriage.

In some forms it is brothers-polyandry, where one woman has several men who are brothers, as her husbands. This produces fewer children and so is often preferred, as it is an effective mechanism for population control. This could be overly demanding for the one woman, but those involved adhere to specific rules of encounter that effectively exclude conflict and jealousy.

Also, within these arrangements all participants are free to engage in romantic sexual liaisons. It is not unusual that men prefer older women as partners, because they are more respected and experienced. The women choose younger men. Romances are insignificant and do not affect the system of group marriage.

The women stay in the home of their mother and the man visits from his clan. The cross-cousin (including brothers-polyandry) marriage form is predominant in Tibet and occurs from there to China in the east and Afghanistan in the west. In this region, this is the marriage practice of at least 30 million people.

Consensus and the power of two

The balance between the sexes is constantly re-established and maintained via the political medium of creating consensus. Matrifocal cultures are egalitarian consensus societies. Core politics is developed and carried out in the clan house – the domain of the women. The women's vote carries significant weight, because without women's agreement, men can do nothing. Clan-house politics represents 'the sacred will of the people' (Goettner-Abendroth 2012).

The importance of the concept of balance of two is discussed by Gimbutas, who refers to the 'Power of Two'; Goettner-Abendroth who refers to the 'Twinship Principle'; and H.R. Bell who shares the First Nations Australian Law that there are always two (see Chapter 11). In *The Language of the Goddess*, Gimbutas proposes that the importance of two first expressed potency or abundance intensified. She traces the power of two, beginning with the double egg shapes of the Goddess of Lespugue from 21,000 BCE. She notes the short parallel lines, in groups of two, on pregnant animals in Palaeolithic cave art; the double Goddesses of Neolithic Turkey and the Aegean; the double symbols (for example, of seeds and plants) on pots throughout Neolithic Europe; and a complex ritual arrangement in north-eastern Rumania (4,000 to 3,600 BCE).

In this ritual arrangement, inside a large lidded vase, at the four compass points, an upright Goddess figurine was placed. Gimbutas points out that 'the concept of dualism had advanced from simple replication to a more complex recognition of opposition – life and death, summer and winter – which accepts the cyclicity of nature … .' This can as well be seen as balance, complementarity. The Twinship Principle as described by Goettner-Abendroth recognises 'the matriarchal principle of balanced collaboration between two equivalent powers'. Often this is associated with the designated areas of concern for women and men – the Iroquoi of America saw women as the Keepers of the Field, men were Keepers of the Forest. In all matrifocal cultures the values of consensus recognises the power of two, the reconciliation of two views, which is always more productive than disagreement.

In matrifocal cultures men are clan delegates to the forums of the outside world and can only convey what the women have agreed to and must return and give an account of their actions. Women can intervene in the men's clan or tribal councils to present their side of the issue or to ensure consensus. Thus women must also have a good understanding of the wider political sphere to have input into it, through the clan councils. Women elect chiefs and can, therefore, also unseat them. In this way they determine the make-up of all larger political bodies. As detailed above, the clan has two chiefs – the 'matriarch' and a male clan representative.

Confederations of equals

Matrifocal alliance-building is based on organising confederations of equals. Every village is self-sustaining, autonomous (village republics – this is mentioned in the discussion of the culture of the Indus Valley, Chapter 9) and egalitarian. The alliance-building represents the ideal of a society based on relationships. In Briffault's very early anthropological study of this (1927), he found that the authority of the mother holds the female clans together and guides the sons,

And Matrifocal Culture Is?

in their outside marriages, to form ties with other clans to weave the matriarchal society together. The alliances are formed through direct or symbolic matrilineal lines of kinship. The inter-clan marriage systems would operate as part of this. The two clans may trace their lineage back to a common female ancestor. All these aspects were confirmed as the case in Goettner-Abendroth's work.

A wonderful example of this confederation concept was the creation of the Iroquois Confederation, among five nations of Native American peoples, in 1142 CE. This included the 'Great Law of Peace' – the legal framework for the Confederation or League of Five Nations. These tribes saw themselves thereafter as related to each other and each nation had all of the clan names. Thus, the matriliny was preserved as a matriarchal kinship society, which was what held the confederacy together (Goettner-Abendroth).

The Confederation made it possible for the Iroquois people to remain sovereign over their vast territories until the end of the eighteenth century. When the white people of the original 13 American colonies decided to unify as the United States, it was the Iroquois framework that was used as a basis for the political system, unfortunately though, under a patriarchal model.

The Iroquois Confederation renewed and reformulated the ancient matriarchal principle of balanced collaboration between two equivalent powers. This is the twinship of female and male. Female power was associated with the Earth and was local; male power with the sky and was federal. Intrinsic to the concept is that there is the female part in the overall male and a male part in the overall female. Clans are female, and include males; nations are male, and include females. To reach a conclusion all matters must circulate in an ongoing process between these two interlinked powers. This reflects the traditions of matrifocal culture.

In line with the matrifocal principles outlined earlier, all matters were first considered by the women, who would then pass relevant items on to the men. If the men's council did not resolve the matter in a way that the women preferred, the women could take up the matter again, reformulate it and return it to the men's council. As Goettner-Abendroth describes:

> However, this does not mean the Women's Clan Council had too much power, because it included consensus, not just of the women of the council, but the consensus of the people – all the clan houses, including the men, women and children who belonged to them.

Also under the Confederation, women were the exclusive guardians of war and peace. They decided these matters on the grounds that women and children had the absolute right to peace and security. The women retained the weapons and only gave them to the men when the women had agreed to war. Traditionally this happened only rarely with feuds resolved through sports, games or one-on-one contests of well-matched opponents.

The necessities of life were in women's hands: the land, housing, food. As the farmers, the women had control of the major food supplies – if women did not supply the food required for an activity (e.g. war) it did not happen. Women turned food into nourishment and were seen as providers.

Matrifocal economy

In matrifocal culture women own the markets where agricultural and domestic products, including textiles and pottery, created by women, are sold and bought. As such, the women manage the economy. Long-distance trade is generally the province of men,

And Matrifocal Culture Is?

again reflecting the separate spheres of local for women, the wider world for men. At the local markets, it is not the selling price that matters most, but rather the good neighbourly relationships created and maintained by the conversations between the women at the marketplace.

This brings us to consider the concept of the 'gift economy'. The Mother Earth herself provided the guiding principle for the matrifocal economy and so, as with the Earth, sharing and giving away out of an abundance are actions aligned with its supreme values. The gift is thus the lynchpin of the economy, patterned after the continuous gift-giving of Earth and sky. Commonly, material wealth is not accumulated, taxes are not levied.

Giving begins with the mother-child relationship according to Vaughan – the mother giving life, nourishment, language and all sorts of social skills to offspring, from birth. The ultimate goal is to build strong relationships. This notion is at the base of the development, in matrifocal cultures, of circles of gift-giving and of the gift economy. Goettner-Abendroth explores ways in which the matrifocal principles are expressed in various existing cultures and one example is the culture of the Tobriand Islanders.

The Tobriand Islanders are Melanesian people, living on lush, coral islands in the Pacific, equidistant from New Guinea and Australia to the west and the Polynesian Islands to the east. They practise the matrifocal custom where the most important relationship is between a woman and her brother. However, in this culture, there is a key difference from other matrifocal cultures we have explored. Here the 'walking marriage' is not practised, with the woman remaining in her matrilineal home and the man visiting overnight. Upon marriage, it is the man who stays with his matrilineal family and, although a woman goes to live in the village of her husband, her welfare is still taken care of by her brother, described below.

The men do the work in the matrilineal clan gardens until harvest time, but the end produce is taken to the women – their sisters. It is with great pride that a man delivers his harvest to the elaborately carved yam storehouses of his sister. The brother gives the harvest to his sister through the husband, emphasising the importance of the act of giving – in this case between brothers-in-law.

The yam is the staple food and it belongs to the sister, providing not only for her and her children (who belong to the matrilineal clan), but also for her husband. Thus, the husband is dependent on his wife for food, which encourages him to be on good terms with her. A woman can easily divorce her husband and return to her matriline in their village, with her children.

The husband in turn takes the produce from the garden that he has been tending, to his own sister in another village. The circulation of the yam harvest brings a man great prestige. The better the brothers provide for the sisters, the greater the clan prestige.

The gift of giving

All prestige stems from the ability to give in the Tobriand Islander culture. Giving forms good relationships – typical of the 'gift-economy'. The women in turn have sharing circles where they give 'Doba', which is a spiritual gift given at funeral ceremonies. This is the exchange of two gifts, one of the clothing women wear – skirts of coloured grasses – the other of bundles of dried, hand-worked banana leaves. The creation of these items is complex and so some must be obtained in exchange with other women.

And Matrifocal Culture Is?

Traditionally yams, and in more recent times under colonisation the money earned by the husband, can come into the exchange. These gifts are high value.

Both the yam gift and the Doba exchange occur at different public festivals. Through them, relationships between siblings and in-laws are reinforced and displayed in public.

Finally, in terms of the Tobriand gift-economy, the concept is extended more broadly, to the widely dispersed Trobriand Islanders. This is the 'Kula Ring' which was identified in detail, and made famous to the wider world, by the twentieth century ethnologist, Malinowski. Kula is an extensive friendship system, based on gift-giving. It involves men of the clan visiting other islands by canoe, travelling 2,000 miles in a vast circle over the ocean, to visit people who are of no kin to them at all. The items of gift-exchange are two different kinds of shell jewellery. Like the Doba gift for women, the Kula is considered a spiritual act for men. At the same visit items of trade are exchanged, but the most important business is the gift-giving.

The gifts are not held for long. The men sail back out and give them again in a strictly pre-determined order – for example, long necklaces of red mussel shells are distributed clockwise and white mussel shell bracelets, counter-clockwise. The Kula is carried out with clear rituals and ceremonies. The ritual gifts are usually reciprocated with appropriate return gifts, but this cannot be demanded or it loses the freely giving character.

The Kula Ring promotes a wide network of friendly relationships among a large number of Melanesian people. It promotes peace – a key matrifocal value.

Women, Goddess and rebirth

In matrifocal cultures, girls and women embody the various manifestations of the Great Goddess in different stages of their lives and may be worshipped as such. The stages are recognised as the Maiden, Mother and Crone and there are usually different Goddesses to represent each of these phases (e.g. Kumari, Lakshmi-Parvati, Kali in Hinduism; in European paganism examples would be Kore, Demeter, Hecate). Nevertheless, these are in reality different phases of the one, three-fold matrifocal Goddess.

At the centre of religion and spirituality is veneration of the ancestress (mother of the people) and her bond to the Goddess, along with the associated belief in rebirth. Within this belief system the idea of rebirth is not an abstract concept, but a firm understanding of reality. Children are not seen as sired by men, but are accepted back into life from the world of ancestors.

Each woman is a daughter of Mother Earth and participates in her capacity to bring forth life. This is recognised at the time of first menstruation. The initiation ceremony for girls is, for all matrifocal peoples, the most important festival and there is nothing similar for boys.

The event is a celebration. In the ceremony the girl's transition to womanhood is blessed, and she becomes a full member of her society. At this time, women pass on the knowledge of their life-giving abilities, the control of this gift and the enjoyment of sexuality. This is usually undertaken by the mother of the girl and/or her female relatives. She is also instructed in the economic, social and religious knowledge of her society.

And Matrifocal Culture Is?

Gender roles

There are some matriarchal societies that practise adopting alternative gender roles – girls can become 'sons' and boys 'daughters'. The practice includes acceptance of same-sex love. Choosing to change gender roles mainly reflects the work a person is interested in, since spheres of work are gender defined (as occurred in Minoan Crete – see Chapter 9). For example, usually women are the horticulturalists and agriculturalists and produce the food from raw materials; the men's work is hunting, fishing and external trade. Gender reversal can also be useful when there is a shortage of brothers to fill this important social role. These practices reinforce the matrifocal cultures' basic premise of female-male polarity/interdependence, which may be practised and expressed differently in different matrifocal cultures.

Both ceremonially and politically, women and men are in equal balance and experience equal dignity. Men do not feel oppressed or want to revolt against the role of the matriarch in their cultural group. Women and men respect each other's dignity and value. For both genders, the matrifocal culture provides their ethnic and cultural identity.

While the capacity to give life is honoured in a woman, motherhood as such is not raised to any cultic level within matrifocal cultures. Sisters share the general mothering role, thus lightening the load and restrictions of individual motherhood and protecting the children. It was only under patriarchy that motherhood per se became iconic (starting with Mother Mary), which reduced women to that one child-bearing function, even if against a woman's will, interests and abilities.

Shamanistic spiritual leadership

In matrifocal societies the priesthood originally was female, and remained so either exclusively, or shared equally with men. Between priestesses there is no hierarchy and the same is true among priests. These principles have been held across the ages and today women in matrifocal societies still act as the religious facilitators within the families and clans, even where patriarchal religion has been superimposed. Where men have established their own temples and forbidden them to women, the royal clan's family priestess, nevertheless, remains the highest sacred authority (e.g. Polynesia).

The priesthood of women was shamanistic. The female shaman attempted to transition to the 'otherworld' and there entice the souls of the ancestors back to this world for another rebirth. They may have sought advice, wisdom and healing there (as in megalithic Malta). Their tools were dance, music, ecstasy, potent herbs and trance journeys and could include the spirits speaking through the shaman. Goettner-Abendroth states that shamanism was, for a very long time, a purely female phenomenon. In Northeast China, for example, there is evidence that the eldest daughter did not marry but became the family shaman; in Northwest China, it was the youngest daughter.

First ancestress, Goddess and seasonal ritual

In matrifocal religions the creation of the world is the work of one or more primordial Goddesses. The primordial ancestress – the woman from whom the matrifocal group see themselves descended – is often deified as a Mother Goddess. The main senior woman (or 'matriarch') is a reflection of this original Goddess, representing her in ceremonies. In the home, the ancestors are venerated by the mother at the fire, thus the hearth at that time becomes a sacred place.

We see in this the wide importance of rituals in matrifocal cultures. Central in these rituals are the annual cyclic agrarian festivals, around the productive power of the earth. Spring festivals celebrate the appearance of new growth, this comes to harvest in summer followed by barren land in winter, which is a period of diminished food supplies, returning again to the new life of spring. The Earth is considered the everlasting provider, the all-encompassing mother, the Great Goddess.

Religious practice originates in the first ancestor; and in the feminising of Earth as the Mother. Thus the seasonal festivals based on the fertility or dormancy of the earth are the central basis of ritual, with life-stage ceremonies interspersed (e.g. birth, menstruation, marriage, death). These are public festivals, not secrets of cults, demonstrating the ancient traditions of equality. Usually they are celebrations, even for death. Honouring the dead with feasting, dancing and erotic encounters might occur, all to entice the spirits of the dead to return for rebirth.

The natural annual process of plant life provided clear information that life was cyclical and that what died was reborn. Rebirth is assumed in matrifocal religion and women are the means through which individuals achieved that rebirth. Women were thus precious on many levels to everyone.

Parity and balance

We have discussed the female-male polarity or balance in matrifocal cultures. It is important to understand though, that this does not make the culture dualistic or oppositional as is the case in patriarchal thought. Raised as most of us have been in a world that defines so much by opposites, it may be surprising to you that the matrifocal religion does not recognise concepts of 'good' or 'evil'. There is, instead, parity between different, but complementary energies; they represent two sides of the world, both cosmos and earth, and determine the cycle of life. This is a cyclical worldview, rather than linear. Further, each part must cooperate with the other, rather than being opposed, for anything to be successful.

The partner of the Great Goddess is a sacred king, seen for example in Celtic and Hindu mythology. In Europe, he was said to rule for a year and then he would be sacrificed to ensure the fertility of the crops or in the hope that the Goddess would grant a better life for the people. This was regarded as the highest form of sacred sacrifice.

For us, this is a rather shocking idea, but in the ancient times and tribes in which it was practised it was seen as part of the exchange between humans and the Earth – the Goddess who had given so much was given one life in return. In matrifocal culture the sacrifice of the sacred king was based on the principles of free will (assured by many rituals) and the firm belief in rebirth. It was believed that the king would almost immediately be born again, like stepping through a door. In later times, the sacrifice of a male animal, or other symbology, replaced the death of the king. The animals sacrificed, too, were considered to be reborn and the principle of free-will respected (as far as possible).

And Matrifocal Culture Is?

The sacred landscape

Shrines and sacred grounds do not appear arbitrarily. There is usually a symbolic order across the landscape. Author, lecturer and researcher, Paul Devereux states that:

> Ancient and traditional people used the whole landscape as a mnemonic, an aid to memory, a place where they could lodge their myths and their religious, social and moral concepts.

The 'songlines' of Australian First Nations people are a rich example of this. As they walk across landscapes they know, they sing the stories associated with features in the landscape. This embeds knowledge of the route in the mind and honours the Creators who made the world.

In matrifocal societies earth and water features are seen as the body of the Goddess, as shown in the landscape at the Callanish Stones, Lewis Island, Scotland, for example (see Chapter 4). The direction of the rising sun, the east, represents life. The west, where the sun goes down, represents death.

There are many reminders in Nepal of a matrifocal past, some related to this. In the Kathmandu Valley for example, the valley is framed by four ancient stone shrines placed at the valley edges in each of the compass directions. At each shrine there is a 'pitha' or vulva-shaped stone, and this is the object of worship, representing Mother Earth.

The living environment of matrifocal societies can vary from planting cultures of digging stick and hoe, to agricultural societies combined with building megaliths (e.g. Malta), and highly developed urban societies (e.g. cities of the Indus valley in India/

Ancient Ways for Current Days

Pakistan; the Minoans in Crete, or matrifocal cultures in modern times that include clan members living in cities).

Matrifocal peoples were master builders and it is likely everyone in a community was involved. However, among the Hopi pueblo people of Colorado, America, who built in mudbrick, it was the women and children who did the building. It was reported by the first Spanish missionaries (arrived 1596 CE) that when a priest asked local men to build a wall, it brought gales of laughter from the women and children, to think that men would know anything about construction (Goettner-Abendroth 2012). No doubt in other matrifocal cultures the men did engage in this work.

As pointed out in earlier chapters, megalithic constructions are found all over the world, wherever matrifocal, agriculture-based societies have settled. Some societies still make them, for example, the Khasi in North-East India, the Parayan in South-West India and others throughout Indonesia (Steimer-Herbort 2018).

People of matrifocal cultures built megalithic constructions that took both sacred and secular forms, as Western culture defines them. It should though, be pointed out that the matrifocal people themselves observe no distinction between sacred and secular; the entire world is sacred, and every action is infused with that understanding.

Sacred works include stone rows, circles, rectangles, and pyramids used for various religious purposes. A specific sacred type was the monumental grave, described in some detail in Chapter 4. In some cultures, stone figures were created such as the 'Moai' on Easter Island, or the carved menhirs of South Sulawesi, Indonesia. In North Africa, the Berber and Tuareg peoples have simple stone shrines, grottoes and archaic stone tombs where they honour the ancestors. The secular megalith examples are ditches, dams, roads and water pipelines, including aqueducts. Nine-storey stone homes have been built in Tibet since ancient times.

The stones in all of these works usually fit very tightly together without the use of mortar. Very fine examples are found in South America, including by the matrifocal Arawak peoples whose descendants still honour the stones today. They can also be artfully decorated in sacred contexts.

How the idea spread

You will have noticed how widely geographically dispersed are the examples I have provided. This book has emphasised the European context, but Goettner-Abendroth has also identified the highlands of the upper reaches of the great East Asian rivers as one of several birthplaces of matrifocal cultures (and megalithic construction). As long ago as Neolithic times there were movements of people from there, north to Tibet and into China, then from there further north into Japan.

They also moved south from Central and South China through Vietnam/Cambodia and from there into Indonesia, with their ever-improving boats and sea-faring skills. Some left the coast of East Asia, settled Melanesia and reached New Guinea, Australia and Fiji. The original Polynesians came from the Yellow River delta (China) and, developing long-distance sea-faring capacity, little by little they settled in Taiwan, the Philippines, Micronesia, Hawai'i and Polynesia. From Polynesia they eventually moved south to New Zealand, and further east from Polynesia to Easter Island and the coast of South America. Seafarers from Hawai'i even made it to Central America. Agriculture in the Americas began at these places; one example of which was crops of sweet potato.

The oral history of these people is that the female clan elders, or 'Grandmothers' led their people's migrations. At any point when consensus in a group could not be reached, one solution was that one part of the clan moved away to establish themselves elsewhere. This could also be a solution when population growth exceeded available productive agricultural land.

Matrifocal societies are first of all relationship societies. Differing from most patriarchal empires or states, matrifocal expansion was never by warfare, but by trade, marriage politics, and alliances based on good relationships. Where matrifocal realms developed each clan retained its autonomy and self-sufficiency with respect to the royal clan and no taxes were involved.

Response to patriarchy

Goettner-Abendroth could find no example where a matrifocal society, in and of itself, developed into a patriarchy. They change from the outside, from powerful pressures from patriarchal societies, over long periods of time. This pressure was and is strongly resisted both passively and actively by the matrifocal society, usually in a combination of actions by both women and men.

Generally, matrifocal cultures had a highly-developed ability to tolerate and integrate outside influences and new elements. This meant that even patriarchal religions could be (superficially at least) accepted. But if so, the ancient matrifocal beliefs lived on in ceremony and in adaptations in their expression of the patriarchal religions surrounding them.

And Matrifocal Culture Is?

When first confronted with patriarchal aggression typically, rather than become aggressive themselves, if they could, the matrifocal clans would remove themselves from that contact and set up their homes elsewhere. Unfortunately, this often led them to marginal places such as into the mountains, down to the shorelines or into landscapes such as deserts, that were less hospitable for their farming practices.

Sometimes the only option, or the chosen option, was to stay and defend. On several continents, these circumstances led to women defending themselves away from any men at all, and the Amazon social system developed. In them the women became professional warriors and protected their way of life militarily.

With their role in the wider world, the ways for men to defend their culture ranged from political involvement, intellectual discourse, to armed resistance. In the case of armed resistance there were societies where the women took up arms and fought alongside their men, particularly in Africa and in South America, and especially where invaders threatened to destroy the matrifocal culture.

In times of crisis the matrifocal women leaders, known in Africa as queens, could choose to become warlords against foreign invaders. The need to defend was driven by the scarcity of arable land. In these environments agriculture lost its prominence and clan members became herders (examples still exist in Tibet, South America and East and North Africa). Among these were the Tuareg of the Hoggar Mountains in West Africa. The women would stay in their encampments of tents with the goats, while the men took to the deserts with the herd – the property of the women – in an annual cycle in search of fodder for the animals. The men dreamed of return to the women and when they did were treated to full attention, to feasting (compared to what they had lived on), to traditional music, storytelling and poetry evenings relaxing with the women.

In some clans in Africa men would undertake long trading journeys with camels, perhaps carrying salt, or animal products prepared by the women, to support the tribe. The women spoke the tribal language and created the literature, the men had to learn several languages for their role in trade. The foodstuffs and other goods acquired by the men were (and are) given to the women to decide on its distribution. If food scarcity became too desperate, one crisis solution was for matrifocal men to leave to ensure that the women survived, and hoping it would be possible to return when things improved.

In Africa, clans displayed the matrifocal dual leadership we have seen earlier in this chapter, with a queen mother in a primary partnership with a man (who she usually selected from her relatives) as king, who deferred to her and acted as the clan representative to the outer world. The queen had a court of justice over women and the king held one over men. Veneration of female and male ancestors was, and is, the main ritual duty of the queen and of the king.

Many of these queens led their people against European invaders such as the English, French, Italians and Portuguese. Notable among these was the queen mother Yaa Asantewa of the Ashanti people (Ncube 2015, Goettner-Abendroth 2012). Even when the British thought they had defeated them, the Ashanti people would continue to place their own kings on the throne-stool. The Golden Stool of the Ashanti is made of gold, stands 45.7 centimetres high, 61 centimetres long and 30.5 centimetres wide (18 in x 24 in x 12 in), and was deemed so sacred that it never touched the ground.

And Matrifocal Culture Is?

The ruler never actually sat on it, but was lowered and raised over it at the ritual when he took on the role of king.

In 1896 the English abducted the king, his close relatives and advisors and the British governor stated he would sit on the Golden Stool. This was when the invaders were confronted with the dual nature of matrifocal society. In spite of her advanced age, in 1900 CE the queen, Yaa Asantewa led her people in a last desperate war against the hated Europeans. She had successes, surrounding the English in their fort and holding them captive for three months. Women went into battle with men, the menopausal women among them fighting and spurring the others on to greater efforts. It took over 1,000 English soldiers to eventually subdue Yaa Asantewa, who spat in the face of the officer who arrested her.

The Ashanti are part of the Akan people who continue aspects of their matrifocal culture to this day and praise Yaa Asantewa, their queen mother, for the survival of their culture. There are five million Akan in West Africa. They are excellent traders contributing to the overall economy, for example, their trade supports cocoa production in Ghana.

Land scarcity led to displaced populations and these people then became invaders elsewhere. The turmoil created an imperative to have charismatic leaders and professional fighters. This, in some instances, led to the development of male secret societies (e.g. Africa, North and South America) or warrior castes and traditions, as an attempt to extend men's power. In an effort to mimic the girls' initiation rites, the men would develop practices where boys were 'reborn' into manhood through their association with other men (e.g. parts of Africa, India, Australia and Central America) rather than with women. Sometimes this involves experiences of pain, bleeding and scarring.

Ancient Ways for Current Days

Throughout this chapter, we have examined in detail the key aspects of matrifocal cultures as identified through the work of Heidi Goettner-Abendroth. In summary, we have identified that matrifocal cultures are matrilineal and matrilocal, where the needs of women and children are put first. These societies are therefore considerate, nurturing and there are no hierarchies. A balance between the sexes, rather than the dominance of one over the other, creates a relationship of working together, with equal dignity and respect. Women are strongly supported by their brothers. Alliances in the wider world are also based on good relationships, creating confederates of equals. All of this facilitates peace – a key matrifocal value.

Important is the gift-giving economy, and a sharing economy to ensure the wellbeing of all ages and stages of life. Sexuality is valued as health-giving, culture-producing and peace-promoting. Choice of sexual partners and gender is respected. All this is embedded in an earth-based, nature-loving tradition, respecting the female principle through a Goddess, and including ancestor veneration, and importantly rebirth as a basic principle.

In her research on traditional dance, Laura Shannon identified the patterns of such wisdom, in Europe, encoded in Balkan circle dance traditions, perhaps as signposts for today. She suggests these values are 'exactly the values we need to rekindle in order to ensure a sustainable future for our planet'. How would we do that? A question that is explored in the final chapters of this book.

CHAPTER 4

Matrifocal Megalith Builders

Megalithic constructions are encountered all over the world, whenever matriarchal, agriculture-base societies have settled.
Heidi Goettner-Abendroth, philosopher, feminist, researcher, world expert on matriarchies. (1941–present)

The megalithic world where stones could speak, and spark, and resonate, was a culmination of an integrated vision, an understanding that humans are one part of the physical, natural world. Strategically placed by human hands, huge megalithic stones could revere a Goddess shape in the landscape, or for those with the knowledge to see, direct attention to major celestial events, like solstices. In death, the tombs that the stones formed would cocoon a person's bones back within the womb of Mother Earth, a pathway to the divine and to eventual rebirth. The construction of the megaliths was imbued with meaning for the people of those times, expressing a sophisticated spiritual tradition.

The new knowledge of the Neolithic lifestyle gradually spread with people who moved steadily westward across Europe, eventually reaching the end of the journey in the British Isles. Thus, the Neolithic in Western Europe occurred some 3,000 years after the period started in the Middle East. The new people arriving in Western Europe mixed little with those already there, who continued the ancient hunter-gatherer ways; the two cultures existed in parallel over a period of about one thousand years (Malmstrom et al. 2015).

Enter the megalith

In North Western France, the abundance of crops enabled Neolithic people to develop a new building phenomenon – the megalith – a concept, it is now contended (Schulz Paulson in Handwerk 2019), that started there as early as 4,000 BCE and was spread by people travelling by sea along the continent's coastline, in several migratory waves.

The first manifestation of the culture of the megaliths was burial mounds. The oldest known is in Brittany (France) and is reckoned to have been constructed about 4,800 BCE. Very well-developed examples have been dated to 3,500 BCE in Ireland. The megaliths indicate to us a culture of at least 2,500 years' duration, and as such they are not to be ignored.

You may wonder how these megalithic constructions relate to a tale of matrifocal culture. The answer is that, starting from a matrifocal base, it is a period of possible power transition to more male leadership, though with great strength of matrifocally-based philosophical beliefs developing and transferring over time. We can examine the information we have discovered, the archaeological remains, the continuities from earlier cultures, and the various interpretations available, to garner an understanding of this richly rewarding phenomenon – to let the stones speak to us.

The word 'megalithic' comes from two Greek words – *megas* meaning 'great', and *litho* meaning 'stone'. It is a method of building rather than a period of time. These enormous stones are found alone, and forming circles, avenues, graves and temples. They have been found in Malta, Sicily, Spain, Portugal, France, England, Ireland, Wales, Scotland, Russia and all around the Baltic Sea. They have been found in Israel, Mongolia, China, Korea, Vietnam, South Asia, Melanesia, Polynesia, Easter Island, North and South America; some are found in Indonesia and India and in both countries, they are still constructed. There are over 35,000 megaliths in Europe alone. We will discover in later chapters, that tracing the path of the appearance of megaliths traces the arrival of a matrifocal group of people in new places (Goettner-Abendroth).

To understand megalithic architecture, we must first recognise that all these striking stone buildings are huge sculptures into which the Neolithic people put all their important ideas and beliefs.

Burial chambers and Mother Earth

In the great stone burial chambers, we can discover what ancient Europeans thought about life and death. The basic design of the chambers is a circle with a passage leading out. The chambers were created by fitting huge slabs of stone together to form the circle and the passage. The ceiling was also made of stone slabs. Sometimes side chambers were added to the design.

Ancient Ways for Current Days

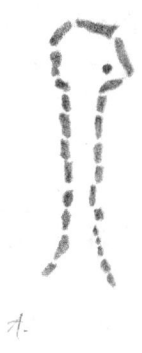

18. Interior design of Long Barrow: A – Bryn Celli Ddu Passage Grave, Isle of Anglesey, Wales
This internal plan demonstrates the basic passage (8.4 m/ 28 ft long) and round chamber plan, interpreted in terms of birthing/rebirthing as the vagina passage and womb. The sun shines down the passage at summer solstice. This particular passage grave has an upright stone behind the back of the main chamber, incised with three snake shapes moving from the ground to the top of the stone. Snakes are a symbol worldwide of the Earth Mother Goddess. The carved stone may have been part of the stone circle that preceded the grave. Earliest dating here is 3,000 BCE. Drawing: Kaye Moseley ©.

19. Interior design of Long Barrow: B – West Kennet
This larger barrow was designed for a whole community over a long period. It shows the same long passage (13 m/42 ft) and final chamber construction but additional spaces have been added to the design, two on either side of the passage, opposite each other. The second set of two had a blocking stone to achieve the sense of a long passage to the final chamber where the death rituals occurred, before bones were interred in one of the four rooms along the passage. Burials were of both sexes and all ages. Part of the Avebury group of megalithic constructions, it was built around 3,650 BCE and used for at least 1,000 years. Drawing: Kaye Moseley ©.

Incredibly, in a time before people knew how to work with the metals, the slabs were quarried and shaped using only flint tools and antler picks (which have been found in the quarries). In some places, the people discovered that salt together with bitumen (both available from the sea) could be used to chemically crack a block away from a rock face. Another technique was to lay twigs soaked in fat on the desired line and set it alight, then pour cold water over that, so that the change in temperature made the stone easier to crack.

Whole village populations would assist in hauling the stones after they were quarried. The wheel had not yet been invented, so to transport these massive weights, logs were placed underneath a block, and with fibre ropes around the stone, they were then hauled by people. In some places (e.g. Malta) round stone balls were possibly used instead of logs. These tools and techniques indicate what a supreme effort the creation of megaliths was, and how determined the Neolithic people were to construct them.

Once all of the slabs had been fitted into the burial chamber design, the people covered the whole construction with layers of earth to form a small hill or mound. In time, grass grew over the mound and only the entrance was visible.

Burial chambers were tombs for the dead. When people died they were placed in the tombs, usually knees to chin (the foetal position), and covered in symbolic blood (red ochre). We have seen in earlier chapters the deep significance of the colour red as symbolic of menstrual blood, the blood of childbirth and of life. The bodies would be left to decay completely, and then the bones would be stacked to one side when space was needed for a new corpse.

It appears that the people had a special reason for burying their dead in this manner. The clue is in the shape of the tomb and the way in which the corpses were laid out. The tomb represented a womb. The people were placed like unborn babies, in the womb of the earth. Perhaps there was a belief in rebirth evidenced in this position. In the Palaeolithic, we saw that caves provided this sense of entry into the earth, the mother of all. Now the people constructed the same concept near at hand – near to their permanent homes and crops.

From the outside of the burial chamber, the large mound that contained it could be interpreted as a sculpture of a pregnant belly.

Ancient Ways for Current Days

Inside is the long, usually low passage, replicating the vaginal canal, that connects the inner womb with the outside world (Gimbutas 1989). Now we see the beliefs begin to emerge – the earth was a great mother who gave life and took it back again. The Great Goddess was all the aspects of the natural world – the concept of 'Mother Nature' goes back to these times.

Over time entire communities were buried in megalithic tombs. Women, children and men are all represented. According to Denmark's National Museum, one burial chamber in western Zealand had over 100 skeletons in it. Recent genetic studies reveal there were close kinship relations between those buried in megaliths, traced through the male line. This indicates a change from the traditions of the earlier Neolithic where the norm was for women in a settlement to be related and the men came from outside (Rodenborg 1991).

In some places (e.g. Orkney in Scotland; in Sweden and in Spain) equal numbers of male and female interments were found, in England there were more men than women buried in megalithic tombs. This tells us social patterns were in a process of change. While male skeletons were not predominant in all megaliths, they were more likely to be buried in the megalithic tomb. Nevertheless, the random placement of bones suggests the Neolithic communities were not hierarchies. In this regard women and men were treated equally, which is a trait of matrifocal communities.

It was not a time where personal wealth was the priority. There are no kings, queens, or chieftains buried in splendour and riches as we find in later, patriarchal periods. No households were put to death to accompany a specific dead man. There were no weapons, shields, nor any pictures or carvings of them, and no evidence of war. The absence of these features indicates an egalitarian approach which is a further marker of a matrifocal social system.

Matrifocal Megalith Builders

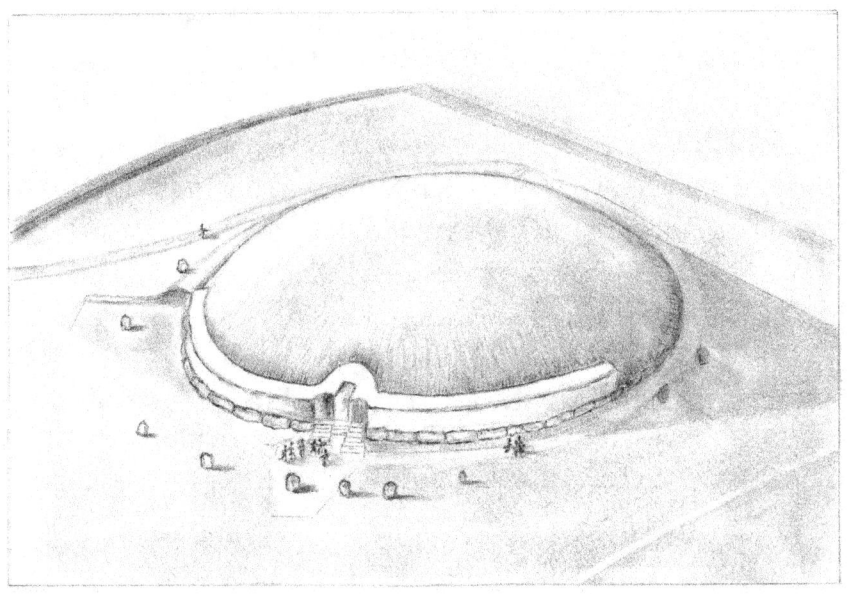

19. Newgrange exterior
A passage tomb and probable temple, now reconstructed, with white quartz gravel around the entrance. A large mound of alternating earth and stones covers a long passage created with megalithic stones. This reaches a central room from which a chamber, probably to accommodate bones of the dead, is added to each of the three sides. In each chamber is a horizontal stone. Complex carving on stones of spirals and other geometric forms, especially on the horizontal entrance stone. Near the Boyne River, Ireland. 3,300 BCE. Drawing: Kaye Moseley ©.

In Ireland there is a splendid burial chamber, called Newgrange (or Bru-na-Boinne,) dated to 3,300 BCE, which shows that the Neolithic Irish had surveying skills, a knowledge of astronomy and mathematics, and understood both the construction and the acoustic properties of stone.

The mound, or pregnant belly of Newgrange is enormous – 12 metres (39 ft) high and 85 metres (279 ft) across. Inside it has a passage 19 metres (62 ft) long, which opens into a great chamber. The roof of this 'womb' chamber is a dome made from corbelled stones – the stones are shaped like wedges that overlapped each other inwards and are tightly packed to further secure it.

Archaeologists have also uncovered a whole network of grooved stones within Newgrange which formed a drainage system. As a result, over thousands of years, the chamber has remained dry from any rain which could have seeped into it.

Astronomy and crystals of the Earth at the tombs

A special feature of Newgrange, is an opening set high above the entrance. It looks like a big letterbox opening, and has a block of white quartz set in it. Each year on December 21, the stone that blocked this opening, or roof-box, was moved aside – no doubt to do so was a great honour and responsibility. Then, at dawn, the rays of the rising sun shone through the opening into the tomb. In our times this occurs a few minutes after dawn, but astronomers have calculated this delay is due to a movement of the Earth's rotation since Newgrange was built. This supports the idea that the tombs doubled as temples or shrines for rituals other than for death. The position of Newgrange and its unusual roof-box was planned to align with this phenomenon.

This was a planned special event for the shortest day of the year – winter solstice. The light phenomenon still does this, and over a period of 17 minutes the light slowly passes through the 'birth canal' or entrance passage and comes to rest on the two spirals engraved in a specially decorated stone at the back of the tomb/womb.

With winter solstice, the light begins to increase and the dark of winter to retreat. The east, where the sun rises is often associated, in matrifocal cultures, with new life. The return (or increase) of light is something that is essential for life and growth, symbolised here by the light entering the womb to start life again.

Why was white quartz used for the roof-box? In some prehistoric chambers, white quartz pebbles were placed with the corpses. The Apache Indians of America believed that quartz had healing properties; Australian First Nations healers were sprinkled with liquefied quartz in initiation ceremonies (Elkin in Lewis-Williams and Pearce 2009). They believed it enabled them to see the dead and move into another world. Numic shamans in North America used quartz as part of their toolkit for weather control (Lewis-Williams and Pearce 2009). Many of the British megaliths used stone that contained quartz. In more modern times, quartz pebbles are sometimes placed over graves in cemeteries, a practice that Lewis-Williams and Pearce argue was taken over by the Christian Church to provide continuity with the pagan past.

Quartz is a crystalline mineral. It has piezo-electrical properties. When it is put under tension or pressure it can produce an electrical current. Struck with another quartz crystal in the dark, it emits a red glow (triboluminescence). Today, quartz is used in many high-tech instruments, including in the radio, telephone and television industries. In watches and computers, it is used to keep time, as the quartz crystal vibrates or ticks an exact 60 seconds per minute when electricity is applied to it.

The excavators of Newgrange believe the front façade of the mound was adorned with a layer of white crystal, which has been restored today. It would have had an impressive effect as the sun rose each day. According to an official tour guide speaking at Newgrange 'on a bright morning, the front façade of Newgrange lights up with a golden glow that you can't imagine' (Sajo 2020).

It is possible the use of crystal related to rituals and trance experiences within or at the tombs. Other tombs were similarly aligned to celestial moments (e.g. Dowth, also in Ireland; Mae's Howe, Orkney Islands, northern Scotland; Atequera Dolmen Site, Spain) and some single standing stones and avenues are known to have astronomical relationships.

Symbology of the stones

How then, do these megalithic constructions relate to a tale of matrifocal culture? Megaliths are found all around the world. Goettner-Abendroth in her extensive study of matrifocal societies states that they appear 'whenever matriarchal, agriculture-base societies have settled'. Thus she feels it is probable that if there are megaliths, then there are, or have been, matrifocal cultures.

In their research, Ramirez et al. conclude that the stones represented ancestral beings. The meaning of each of the huge stones involved, 'goes beyond its appearance, weight, sculpting or durability'. They state that they are part of the symbolic story that justifies the building's construction and that they provide a link between different generations.

Goettner-Abendroth's analysis would support this. She points out that, as is still the case in matrifocal cultures, the horizontal stones of these sacred spaces are considered female. They embody the female ancestors, the clan mothers. The standing stones are considered to be male, embodying the male ancestors who stand guard as protectors of the original ancestress and her clan. It is usual in a stone circle to find a horizontal stone, and at the burial mounds there is usually one large stone across the entrance if it has not been removed over time (the exterior of

Matrifocal Megalith Builders

Newgrange is edged with 97 decorated horizontal stones). To us it is an illogical barrier to the entrance. What it means is that no-one can enter without taking pause here, at the 'mother stone', perhaps making an offering or speaking in prayer to her. This stone also occurs at the entrance to temples in Malta and to each of the rooms within a temple, of which we will learn more in Chapter 5.

There is another megalithic construction type, called dolmens. These are 'visually distinctive and impressive sites, landmarks in their own right' (Cummings and Richards 2016). The key characteristic is an enormous capstone or roof-stone, lifted up and displayed on smaller uprights in a tripod design. These uprights, usually still in place, comprise two taller doorway stones and a lower backstone, the heavier end of the capstone being above the doorway stones. Though the capstone was balanced on the narrowest possible part of the upright stones there are examples where these capstones weighed 60 tonnes, 70 tonnes or even, in one case, 170 tonnes in Kernanstown, Ireland.

Cummings and Richards argue that the dolmens were never covered over, like the long barrows were, except where adapted when later used for burials. They propose that the whole point was to display certain stones – the magnificent capstones. These were the most important part of the dolmen, constructed to 'seem to almost float above the ground'. It appears likely that these big stones were already noted or revered in the landscape and were simply dug up in situ, fashioned on the underside to some degree, and raised where they had always been. As the raised stone was horizontal, it would have been, according to Goettner-Abendroth's analysis, the female stone, representing the female ancestral beings. The male uprights which support her are essential to the success of the construction. Such an impressive landmark in those early times, the dolmen would have become a community focal point for spiritual expression.

Why was it important to honour the ancestors, particularly the female ones? These ancestors, who in their lifetimes had led the tribe to their current life and land, attained legendary status. They became Goddess figures, their stories told in the popular tales and myths. While holding this meaning, these large horizontal stones could also have other functions, especially when on the ground – as an altar, as a feast table, as a seat and as a stage to stand upon to speak to the community.

The sound of stone

In a new science called 'archaeoacoustics' studies are being undertaken of the sound resonance of megalithic stones, circles and constructions. Aaron Watson, an archaeologist at Reading University, found that ritually produced sounds can 'induce enormous stones to appear to shake and become alive'. What an incredible experience this must have been for the people of the megalithic world! They are likely to have perceived that some strange or supernatural event was taking place (Coimbra 2016), inducing a sense of awe for the places where such sound experiences could be produced (Watson in Coimbra 2016).

From studies of the human brain, it is known that, within a few minutes of exposure to 111 Hertz (Hz), an 'Alpha state trance' is induced in the listener. Stone age chambers, including those in Ireland, some dating from before 4,000 BCE, have been tested with results that fall within a very narrow band of acoustic wavelengths – 95 Hz and 120 Hz. Once 111 Hz is reached the effect is to immerse the listener in sound, and, amplified by the architecture, it filters out other frequencies, creating an acoustic standing wave; 111 Hz is one octave in a lower male baritone vocal range that can be comfortably hummed, sung or spoken (Chalk in Kreisberg 2014; Debertolis et al. 2015). It seems that within the stones the people were intending to create a sacred space where a trance experience could be undertaken. This would provide a feeling of having travelled into another plane of existence, 'to connect with the spiritual realm in order to gain a better understanding of life and the universe' (Narang 2015).

A few hundred years after the dolmen and passage grave constructions discussed in this chapter began, the people started to also build stone circles (3,250 BCE to 2,100 BCE). There are many hundreds of these in Western Europe alone. The collective effort involved was immense. If you lived in Britain you would probably have lived in a region where there was a stone circle. Many were small, but some were quite grand. You will easily bring to mind the dramatic stone circle of Stonehenge in England which includes 82 bluestone megaliths, each weighing over four tons. These are believed to have been brought from a circle in South Wales to England, following a land and water route of 320 kilometres (200 mi).

At Stonehenge the interior of some monoliths was intentionally polished to a concave shape in order to focus the sound inside the circle (Till in Coimbra 2016; Watson in Loose 2010). Watson concluded that participants in ceremonies inside the structure 'would have been immersed in a dynamic soundscape'.

When there is high wind at Stonehenge the stones give out a huge booming 'tune' from the vibrations created in the stones, 'like the note of some gigantic one-stringed harp' (Hardy in Coimbra 2016). It has been postulated (Mor and Sjoo 1991) that 'women/girls dancing in a circle at certain speeds, and all singing or humming the appropriate note, … might set up a vibratory resonance in the stone circle, subjecting each stone to a burst of sound energy as each woman passed it, … and this energy travelling from stone to stone … ! The ultrasound of the voices or music would act on the crystal structure of the stone.'

Today the stone circles at first seem like silent mysteries – or are they? Why did the populations of entire countrysides go to such trouble to build these circles? Certainly, social ties and cooperation were called upon and fostered by the effort. People worked in teams with their stone picks, possibly singing rhythmic working songs such as the stone-cutter songs that are still known in Easter Island folklore. The abundance of food produced through farming provided the surplus required to support the workforce. Spring and summer were the focus of farming, so most work on the megalithic structures would have occurred in winter and autumn.

Historians tend to agree that the circles were places for open-air ceremonies. These collective works in no way represent economic meaning, nor were they built to aggrandise one person. Together with the burial chambers, we are left to recognise that it was an inner, spiritual need that was being satisfied here.

Resonant healing from below

Guy Underwood, professional water diviner (or dowser) and amateur archaeologist, believes one answer to the mystery of the circles lies below the ground. He draws on earlier research of archaeologists, and his experience, to demonstrate how the circles stand above underground streams of water. He believes the sites were decided using water divining (the practice of locating underground channels with a forked wooden twig, still used today).

Matrifocal Megalith Builders

At the centre of each circle is a 'blind spring', where the water rises in a spiral but does not reach the surface. He claims the circle stones mark the radiating spirals from these blind springs and that the long rows of stones at Carnac in France lie on branching or parallel underground streams below them. He also suggests that the blind springs have a natural healing energy because of the water spirals. Cows, for instance, naturally choose these places to give birth. It may have been that Neolithic people found that blind springs were healing for humans as well and incorporated that energy into their sacred space. Debertolis (2016) studied the locations of the Temples of Malta (our next chapter), finding that they also were located above underground springs with detectable soundwave resonance.

Thus, we understand so far that the people expressed a deep connection to and understanding of the earth, waterways, properties of stone and celestial movements which they marked by the positions of megaliths. It was a natural world of which people were an intrinsic part, with a Goddess seen as the life-giving

21. Avenues of stone megaliths at Carnac, France
Alignments of local granite megaliths. There may once have been over 3,000, forming the largest collection in the world. Underwood claims they lie on branching or parallel underground steams below them. De Cleuziou argues for connections to sunsets at the solstices. 4,500–3,300 BCE. Photo: Kaalii Cargill.

centre 'their form, function and purpose reflected in Hers' (Carr-Harris 2011).

Megalithic sacred centres of the islands of Scotland

In the Orkney Islands remains of a megalithic society have been discovered, centred on the 'Ness of Brodgar' (see https://www.nessofbrodgar.co.uk/ for information about the ongoing archaeological excavation there). A stone circle stands at either end of an isthmus (or 'ness') – the Ring of Brodgar on the north-west end, and the Stones of Stenness at the south-east end, on the headland just before the isthmus. The Ness of Brodgar is a long narrow piece of land with water either side, in this case salt on one side, fresh on the other. If it was so in Neolithic times then this is a phenomenon that cannot have been lost on the people who lived there then. In the middle of the Ness was a sacred centre of large oval or sub-rectangular stone buildings within a wall, created from around 3,300 BCE. Archaeologists (Towers et al. 2015) clearly describe what they believe life was like in those times:

> Back then, the Brodgar peninsula drew people in from near and far, to honour the dead and to celebrate important events with feasts, to renew old ties and forge new bonds. When the broader world came together, many things were possible: the settling of feuds, competitions for renown, the exchange of goods, gifts and no doubt, gossip. And all of this woven around key moments of ceremony, through a sense of the spiritual that could be traced in the land and in the sky ... They have gone but the stones speak for them.

With megaliths found all across Europe this represented a shared philosophy, developed and exchanged through the travel and

Matrifocal Megalith Builders

22. Callanish Stones, Lewis Island, Outer Hebrides, north-west Scotland. Gneiss slabs. Showing the main circle. The stone avenue begins with the two stones to the left and two stones on the right point to the 'Sleeping Beauty' across the valley. 2,900 and 2,600 BCE. Photo: J. Cameron.

trade of the day, albeit with local variations. The culture lasted over two thousand years, so it was stable. The purposes of the stones were understood by a whole half-continent of people and the similarity of designs shows that their function was universal. There are many clues that these indicators of a megalithic culture pointed to a belief system based on an intimate connection of the people with the Earth and the heavens, and reflected in a female form.

On the Isle of Lewis, in north-west Scotland in the Outer Hebrides, is a remarkable megalith arrangement known as the Callanish Stones (built between 2,900 and 2,600 BCE) that illustrates this. Centred on the four cardinal compass points, a long avenue of standing stones leads up a steady slope to the stone circle – a wonderful processional way for ritual/ceremonial events. We can now only wonder what the processions looked like, the costumes or decorations, the music and human voices, villagers from near and far, all led perhaps by a priestess and a priest.

Small avenues lead in from either side of the circle. The circle itself is of thirteen stones with a monolith near the middle. The stones are on average three metres (9 ft 10 in) high. A row of five stones on the other side of the circle from the avenue lead the eye from the circle to the horizon in the south. There are numerous other megalith sites in the countryside around this main set of stones, which indicates that Callanish was an active site of religious activity for at least 1,500 years.

The focal point of the stones is the view to the horizon of a range of hills on the other side of the valley, popularly known as 'Sleeping Beauty', which gives the appearance of a woman lying on her back. If this 'Goddess in the landscape' were not enough, the site of the stones may well have been chosen for a phenomenon that can

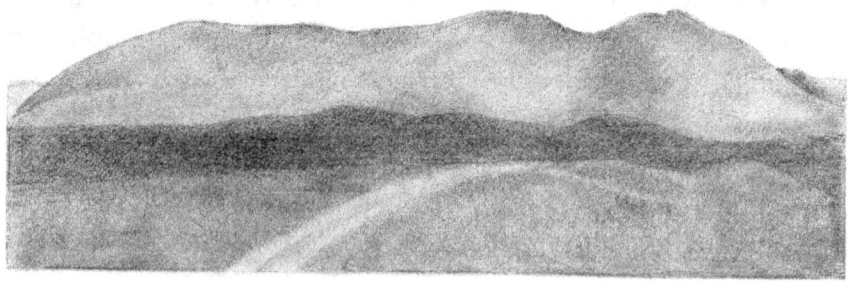

23. 'Sleeping Beauty' Isle of Lewis, Scotland
A natural formation of hills that are similar to the shape of a sleeping woman. It forms the horizon from the Callanish stones. The hills of Mor Mhonadh are the knees, Guainemol the body, and Sidhean an Airgid the head. Drawing: Kaye Moseley ©.

be seen from the stones, interacting with this landscape shape, in a lunar cycle of 18.6 years – it is known to astronomers as the 'major southerly lunar standstill'.

At this time, the low summer full moon appears to rise from between the legs of the female form on the horizon as if being born. As the night goes on, it moves along the line of her body, then disappears behind the 'hip' and appears again hanging low at the breast. Then, rising above her face, moon and Goddess appear to be gazing at each other for a while. At the Callanish Stones the last sighting is of the moon, as if inside the circle of stones, at the foot of the tallest central one (Streffon 2010). For most in Neolithic times, it would have been a once in a lifetime event, so it must have been witnessed with much awe and wonder. The Earth gave birth to the moon, nurtured her infant and gazed on the child with love.

There are also single standing stones in the landscape and these can be shown to align with astronomical events or point towards important spiritual landmarks. They can be plain; however, some seem to be chosen because of their similarity to animal shapes or to features of the land around them. Others have indicators that they are related to human anatomy. Avebury has the 'Vulva Stone'. Some are carved with breasts; others are clearly shaped as a penis. Some have both of these anatomical features. Again, this supports the proposition that females and males saw themselves in a collaborative connection in matrifocal cultures. It also indicates there was a sense of integration with the natural world for the megalith peoples.

Now we have two examples of the embodiment of the female within megalithic culture – one created in the long barrows, and the second seen in the landscape in relation to standing stones.

To complete this story in Britain we need to look to the Avebury Circle complex, in particular, Silbury Hill (probably built from 2,470 BCE to 2,350 BCE).

Another Goddess in the landscape

Several monuments make up the Avebury complex and archaeologists Gimbutas (1974) and Devereux (2000) see Silbury Hill as the focal point for all other constructions. The complex includes the great Avebury earthen henge (ditch and bank) and within it a stone circle – the largest circle in the world – so large (11 ha/27 ac) it once had a village built within it. It is encircled by a ditch 7–10 metres deep. The excavated soil was piled up on the outer edge of the ditch to form a ridge or bank, which is nearly 7 metres (22.96 ft) high from the original surface. The ditch was on the inside and so could not have been for any defensive purpose. The circle had 98 upright sarsen stones, some as high as 5 metres (16.4 ft) and weighing up to 40 tonnes (40.1 tons).

The Avebury complex is a comprehensive system of structures. It includes two avenues of standing stones – one heading west and the other south from the henge entrances. Significant among these structures is the great artificial mound of Silbury Hill, Europe's tallest prehistoric earthwork. It also includes the Sanctuary, which was a stone and timber circle multiple ring feature, now destroyed; a great timber enclosure at the Sanctuary, perhaps a temple or ritual preparation area (also now gone except for marks of post-holes); West and East Kennet Long Barrows; and various remnants of stone settings.

Silbury Hill (2,470–2,350 BCE) is an enormous human-made chalk and clay sculpture of a woman, who is in the traditional squatting

Matrifocal Megalith Builders

24. Silbury Hill and water
A seasonal spring fills the moat around Silbury Hill with water, creating a neck and head of water to the total shape. The water also sweeps around the hill outlining the pregnant body of the Earth Mother. Part of the Avebury group of megalithic constructions. Photo: ©Crown copyright. NMR

pose ready to give birth. This image of the pregnant Goddess has been found in sculptures in places as far apart as Scotland, Turkey, Bulgaria and Mesopotamia. To give birth in this position is still the norm in many parts of the world. In the aerial photograph here of the Silbury Goddess, you can see that the hill stands in a moat. The hill is her pregnant belly, and the water shows the outline of her body.

Once again, it would have taken the whole community to build this sculpture over many years. From head to thigh, this great Earth Mother measures 342 metres (1,122 ft). The moat, which framed the body of the Goddess, had a perfectly flat bottom and steep sides. In autumn, on the night of the full moon that occurred halfway between summer solstice and autumn equinox, a ceremony was

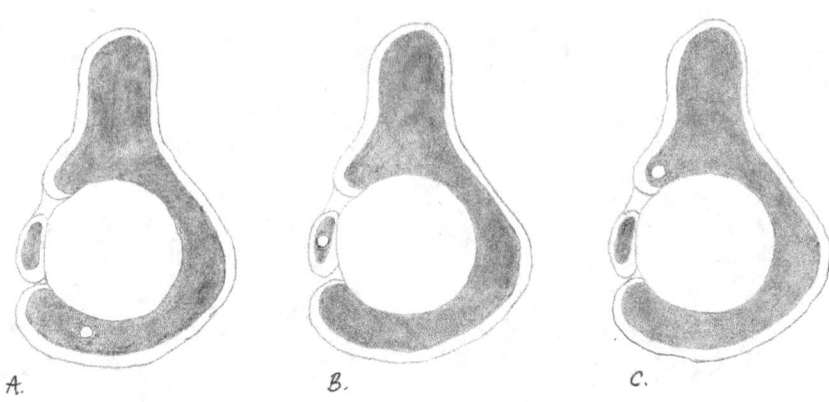

25. Silbury Hill, moon's passage
On a particular night in autumn the full moon appears reflected in the water of the moat, at the point of the vulva/birth canal (A). The moon child is born and travels along the moat to rest on the belly (B) and then travels on to be nourished at the breast (C). At sunrise the spectacle is over. Drawing: Kaye Moseley ©.

held, known in the ancient pagan calendar as Lammas Eve. The people gathered at Silbury Hill to watch the Goddess give birth to the harvest child. It must have been an exciting time. It is possible that the priestess and priest would climb to the flat area on the top of the hill and invoke, sing, dance and lead singing to encourage the success of the event.

Gimbutas states that the circular summit of Silbury Hill is the Goddess' navel or 'omphalos' in which her life-producing power is concentrated. She observed, 'In ancient Greece the omphalos, literally "navel", was held to be the centre of the world' and proposes that even earlier, for the people who created it, 'Silbury very probably was also considered to be the centre of the world'.

On a cloudless night the moon appeared in the reflection of the moat at the point which is the birth canal (vagina) of the Mother. This was the birth of the harvest child. The moon was the baby.

But the night did not end here. As the night progressed, the moon climbed in the moat's reflection until it reached the Goddess' navel. Based on what we know of later ritual, at this point the signal would have been given to cut the first wheat. This was symbolic of the cutting of the umbilical cord between the Earth Goddess and her child – the ripe harvest.

As the child's moon head travelled up the moat it reached the breast of the Goddess. For the next hour the breast swelled with white light from the moon's reflection in the moat. Gradually, the nipple was revealed. At sunrise the birth was successfully completed and the harvest began.

For a long time after the Neolithic period, Silbury Hill was still the site of harvest festivals, even into the 18th century. There is an old English nursery rhyme which may have its origins in Silbury:

'There was an old woman
Lived under a hill
And if she's not gone,
She lives there still.'

Why mace heads?

Before we leave the megalithic culture of Europe there is one last feature that needs to be mentioned. Polished stone axes and mace heads, that would once have been attached to a wooden shaft, are a persistent artefact. Axes were an essential tool to bring down trees to clear space for agriculture. A mace is used like a hammer and would have been useful in stone-cutting, among other things.

Ancient Ways for Current Days

26. Maesmor Mace head
Finely polished flint carved with lozenge-shaped patterns. Hole at one end for a shaft, probably of wood. Prestige item rather than a tool, with probable ceremonial role. Wales, United Kingdom. About 3,000–2,500 BCE. Drawing: Kaye Moseley ©.

Some of these items have been found with work marks on them, reground until discarded. But some show no sign of use. Examples such as these are artworks. Often the stone appears to have been carefully chosen for how it looked – the colour or patterns of it. Some are polished to an amazing sheen; some are carved with spirals, ridges and symbols that Gimbutas suggests represent the Goddess, such as the owl eyes motif and the 'V' symbol of the vulva (called a chevron), sometimes joined to create a diamond or 'lozenge' shape.

According to the Museum of Wales, these items could have taken the maker many tens of hours of work. Some of the stones used were sourced from over a thousand kilometres away (Schauer et al. 2020), for example, from the jadeite mine high on Mount Viso in the Italian Alps. It seems that the more remote and difficult it was to acquire the stone, the greater importance was placed upon the artefact (Barber in Schauer et al. 2020).

Throughout Neolithic Europe and the Levant (countries like Israel and Syria) the axe has been found drawn, carved in relief and created in the round, of stone, clay or later, bronze. Miniature axes of greenstone of exceptional workmanship and with no traces of use have been found in south-east Europe.

Those found further west were larger. At a size suitable to have been worn at the waist, decorated examples found in the west (which includes Britain), seem most likely to have had a ceremonial significance. Swedish archaeologist and religious historian Erik Rodenborg asserts that the axes 'were used during rituals of gift exchange'; this interpretation is supported by others (Cummins in Schauer et al. 2020; Lewis-Williams and Pearce 2009). We saw in the last chapter that rituals of gift exchange are a strategy of matrifocal societies. Exchange is undertaken as a statement of respect, a desire for collaboration and confirmation of continued friendship or social alliances (Sjogren 2011).

An object acquired through gift exchange was often held for some time within a clan, possibly for several generations. The object may have had stories attached, related to the hands it had passed through; they possibly had names. They may have thus linked different groups and places, providing connections to the past, with the gift-giving experience opening opportunities for the future.

The investment of time in the creation of these artefacts and the places the stone may have come from, together with any accumulated history, invested the objects with a social, even spiritual dimension. Some of these artefacts have been found in graves or other spiritually significant places, such as under a shrine floor as if guarding the entrance (e.g. Knowth burial chamber, Ireland; the possible temple or ritual house in Orkney at the Ness of Brodgar). This indicates they may, through ceremony, have been imbued with special, even supernatural powers.

In the late Neolithic (2,500 BCE) there was a marked increase in the incidence of the polished stone axes. It has been supposed that the axes and mace heads could have been used as weapons. They would work as weapons, but there is no evidence that they were used that way. The culture had been changing over a long period of time. Was what was once an item of reverence, an item of ceremony, becoming an item of threat?

It may originally have been an honour to wear the axe or mace, to indicate the respect in which the wearer was held by the clan. According to Pearson and Wills, '[mace heads] were generally emblems of institutional authority rather than personal status'. In this case perhaps it could be bestowed elsewhere if the current custodian of the item was found to be unworthy. With the passing of matriliny to a more male-orientated worldview, including lineage traced through the father-line, perhaps authority became embedded in one family within the clan and visibly expressed by one man – a Chieftain. This may have been the case even if the women still exerted strong influence on decisions (perhaps especially in the spiritual realm). The axes or mace heads may have become status symbols which showed their owner's power and prestige within their community – and potentially a warning not to dispute it.

Matrifocal Megalith Builders

Were they matrifocal?

A matrifocal culture centres around a Goddess in these earliest forms, and we have seen this from the megaliths in the birth canal and womb design of the burial chambers; the continued use of red ochre in sacred places; the ritual and Goddess design of Silbury Hill; the orientation of megaliths to natural formations in the landscape – including those shaped like a reclining woman.

The great burial chambers show veneration and care of ancestors, as do the practices of matrifocal peoples wherever they occur, yet burials were communal and egalitarian – there is no difference between gifts and adornments of different skeletons that might indicate rank. This is not about the individual, but about the group.

In the earlier part of the megalithic period in Europe we can say that it was a peaceful culture, with no weapons or depictions of war – at least until the prevalence of the axe and mace head in archaeological finds. Even so, these may have been kept as a symbol of authority and/or more of a warning than for use as weapons of war.

Finally, we can recognise the deep connection of the people to their natural world, to earth, the natural features of the landscape and the movements of stars, the sun and the moon. They had integrated into their lives an interconnected cosmology that recognised their dependence on the natural world that provided for them, and produced all life – the Mother.

These are all indicators of a matrifocal culture, certainly in the past, certainly in the spiritual realm in the megalithic period, and very likely evolving, to accommodate the more patriarchal tendencies that were appearing in Europe. Recent DNA testing and comparison (Reich 2020) shows that patriarchal peoples, known in archaeology as the 'Yamnaya', moved across Europe at different times from about 4,500 BCE and definitely in about 3,000 BCE from the Russian Steppes, their DNA found from Mongolia to Hungary, across Europe to England. They were mobile pastoralists who created rich burials. By 2,400 BCE they had arrived in Britain and they almost completely replaced the British farmers. An estimated 90 per cent of the population that created the megaliths was destroyed, with the women slightly more likely to survive.

In this chapter we have seen that matrifocal values were expressed by those who lived in the times of the megaliths. The people thoroughly understood how to work with the properties of stone and did so to embody and express their appreciation of the Mother Goddess, who nurtures all life, and so experience her in a spiritual way. In the following chapters we shall see that in spite of the aggression that brought the period to an end, the matrifocal way did not die out and is alive in some places, even today (Chapter 10). This matrifocal system was based on a very ancient evolution of ideas, possibly going back as far as 150,000 years. We will visit that period briefly in the chapters to come.

CHAPTER 5

The Maltese Phenomenon

The feminine holds the mystery of creation. This simple and primordial truth is often overlooked, but at this time of global crisis, which also carries the seeds of a global transformation, we need to reawaken to the spiritual power and potential of the feminine. Feminine qualities belong to both men and women.
Llewellyn Vaughan-Lee, Sufi mystic, author and teacher
(1953–present)

This is our last stop on the ancient megalith path in Western Europe. In a world of change, 'the Maltese islands appear to be one of the latest outposts of Neolithic culture' (Thompson et al. 2020). Of all the many countries engaged in megalithic building, only Malta created buildings we recognise as temples (stone circles were without doubt centres of sacred rituals, but they are not enclosed buildings for ritual). I invite you to come and explore …

Ancient Ways for Current Days

The great stone Temples of Malta, which are UNESCO World Heritage sites, are considered the oldest free standing roofed buildings on Earth. They are more than a thousand years older than the Egyptian Pyramids or Stonehenge (Kreisberg 2014). Who were the people who built them and what inspired them to create these monuments?

Neolithic people sailed the 80 kilometres (50 mi) from Sicily in about 5,000 BCE and may have joined some peoples there from Palaeolithic times, when there had been a land bridge to the present-day Italian land mass (Trump 2002). The newcomers were already familiar with farming methods and brought domesticated animals and tools to establish this lifestyle. From skeletal remains the researchers have deduced that these people had a good diet, ate flour that did not have stone grit in it that wears the teeth, and were about the height of people in Malta today.

Neolithic people who settled in Malta were apparently always in contact with the islands around them. Evidence of this is in the items found on Malta that have been traced back to their origins, such as obsidian (from Pantelleria and Lipari), flint (from north-east Sicily), serpentine (from Calabria) and the essential sacred red ochre (from south-west Sicily) (Trump 2002). None of these are naturally available in Malta. Even some broken pieces of foreign pots have been found.

The archaeologist David Trump proposes that rather than 'trade' this interaction should more rightly be seen as an economy of 'gift exchange'. This system is still practised among matrifocal clans in Polynesian cultures of the South Pacific (Goettner-Abendroth 2012; Trump 2002). Trump explains it in this way: one clan has a celebration and invites those from another. The host provides gifts of local produce to the guests. Before long it is the guests' turn to reciprocate and invite the initial hosts to a feast. Here gifts of similar importance need to be provided, in order to further enhance or solidify the connection. It is an exchange based on respect and reciprocity, rather than greed or profit.

At first, the people newly arrived in Malta inhabited caves; later some built simple huts above ground that consisted of a stone base with mudbrick walls. However, the caves were so commodious, light and airy, often with a water supply, that they remained inhabited until as recently as 1935, when it took a British government order to evict the people! Shortly after, the caves began to collapse.

A community of peace

The Maltese people enjoyed a period of peace which lasted for two and a half thousand years. The period between 3,600 and 2,500 BCE saw the greatest development culturally. Between 3,600 to 3,000 BCE the megalithic temples were built, and pottery developed to a high standard. It was a culture that appeared to have no concept of war (Kreisberg 2014; Trump 2002). Nothing found appears to depict fortifications, weapons, shields, warriors, armies or any other image of conflict or invasion (Trump 2002).

The Maltese archipelago abounds in limestone, which has a tendency to split both horizontally and vertically. This produced ready-made slabs, which must have sparked the imagination of the people with their potential for building. Over the two main islands, Malta and Gozo, there are about 50 megalithic sites of varying sizes. There are seven great temples, although there may once have been more. Overall the temples follow a similar basic plan. Like the 'Christ crucified' shape of Christian churches two and a half thousand years later, the Neolithic Maltese people built great Goddess sculptures to worship in.

27. Mnajdra Central Temple, Malta
Floor plan appears to outline the body of the corpulent Goddess of Malta. Thick stone and earthen walls replicate entering the Earth. It included an 'oracular chamber'. 3,600–2,500 BCE. Drawing: Kaye Moseley ©.

Goddess in architecture

This Goddess was large. Small sculptures of her found on the islands show her with big hips, big belly and big breasts. The design of the temples show this shape transformed into architecture. Like the later long barrows in other parts of Europe (described in Chapter 4), for the people, entering the temple meant they were entering the body of their Goddess (Gimbutas; Rodenborg 1991). However, the Maltese temples were not tombs, they were used for worship and associated ritual.

The Maltese Phenomenon

Though missing now, the temples had roofs, possibly corbelled with smaller slabs or made of lighter material than stone, or with some openings left for light and ventilation. In the temple at Skorba, that was destroyed by fire at some point, ashes of olive wood were found across the floor – perhaps here wooden beams had been employed in the roof. Inside the temples would have been pleasantly cool compared to the fierce heat of summer outdoors. The interior was dimly lit with lamps. The floor was of crushed and pounded rock called 'torba', which provided a smooth, solid surface (Trump 2002).

At the oldest temple, at Ggantija (pronounced 'ge-gant-tia') on the island of Gozo, the amazing rear wall rises six metres and some of the megaliths in it weighed 40 to 50 tons. Tradition held that the walls at Ggantija were made by a giant – a huge woman with baby at the breast. She bore this child from a man of the ordinary people. Perhaps this story was a remembrance of the powerful, large Goddess who was once worshipped there, who any person could approach without fear.

The outer shell of temple walls was formed with great blocks of stone propped up on their edges. The inner walls were either rough coralline blocks or well-cut slabs, arranged with tall vertical blocks then several rows of horizontal ones above (Trump 2002). The space between inner and outer walls was packed with earth or rubble. So once you entered you were, effectively, within the body of the earth (Mor & Sjoo 1991). For external doorways, two large upright stones were capped with a horizontal lintel. These doorways would have had wooden doors. Internal doors were often round holes carved into a large stone block. These may have been covered with patterned curtains of woven cloth, although no trace remains; all had a large stone block to step over, emphasising the act of entering and the specialness of the new space being

Ancient Ways for Current Days

28. Hagar Qim Temple, front exterior
Near Qrendi, Malta. A hilltop temple of Globigerina Limestone. Includes three 'pedestal' waist-high altars and once had a large Goddess as at Tarxien. Under a step into a side room a group of robust women statuettes was found. Includes the largest/heaviest Temple stone in Malta at close to 20 tonnes. 3,600–3,100 BCE. Drawing: Kaye Moseley ©.

entered. As discussed in Chapter 4, in matrifocal cultures horizontal blocks represent the female element.

All this work was done with hand-axes of flint and quartzite; knives and scrapers of imported volcanic obsidian; wedges of wood and stone; hammers of stone and levers of wood. The available stone used in construction was hard, grey coralline limestone, and a softer pale globigerina limestone which is still used to build homes in Malta today.

Astronomical links

Like megaliths we have explored elsewhere, these temples were also oriented with astronomical alignments; for example, Mnajdra South to the equinox sunrise and Hagar Qim (pronounced 'agar-eem') with summer solstice. At Mnajdra (pronounced 'eem-na-eed-rah') the sunrise at equinox falls directly down the centre of the entrance, projecting a spot of light into a small shrine in the depths of the Temple; other light projections occur there at both summer and winter solstices.

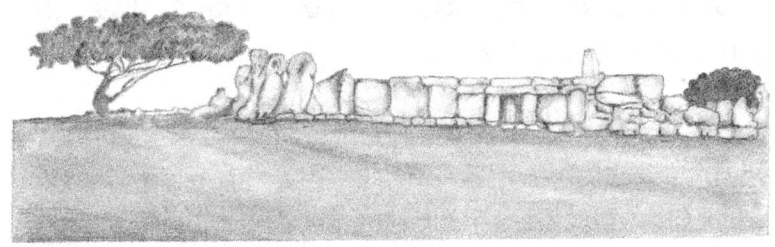

29. Hagar Qim Temple, approaching the entrance
Main entrance on the right. The large stones in the foreground have been weathered by sea winds. The Temple is based on the same plan as Mnajdra. Later a smaller similar planned temple was added joined to one side and then two other rounded additional rooms. Drawing: Kaye Moseley ©.

Also at Mnajdra one megalith has been referred to by some researchers as a Calendar Stone. Incorporated into the surface are numerous drilled holes. These holes have been placed in rows with various numbers of holes. The resulting configurations can be linked to seven different complex time periods determined by the movement of the moon across the sky (Ventura & Hoskin 2014). The moon is always associated with women because of its link to the monthly menstrual cycle (Mor and Sjoo 1991). There is room for much further astronomical study of the Maltese temples.

Temples as social centres

There were open courtyards in front of temples for group gatherings, which may have included singing, dancing, processions, contests, storytelling, speaking and discussion. They may have served as a marketplace, a venue for quasi-legal events like oath-taking, for dispute resolution (Trump 2002), and for gift exchange. But individuals could enter the temples as well. Recent study of the temples favours the view of an egalitarian social system, seeing the temples as communal gathering places (Thompson et al. 2020) where 'collective action was celebrated' (McLaughlin et al. in Thompson et al. 2020).

Some, Mnajdra and Tarxien (pronounced 'tar-sheen') among them, had a small special room on one side of an apse, now labelled an 'Oracular Chamber'. This chamber enabled an important part of the Neolithic ritual experience in Malta. A devotee could stand before a hole in the rock, while seated in the chamber behind, unseen, was a priestess, possibly in some sort of trance. Her response to the request or query of the devotee would have appeared to come from the rock, mysterious and clear. A corbelled roof would have provided an excellent acoustic arrangement, possibly with a special resonance or reverberation that we cannot now reproduce (due to the lack of roof). A screened room at the heart of Hagar Qim may have been used in a similar way. As time went on rooms seem to have been added to the temples that may have been storage areas and spaces specifically for the use of the temple personnel (Trump 2002).

At the Tarxien Temple (built about 3,150 BCE) there is an interesting low vibration from below ground (Debertolis et al. 2016) – probably from water moving through underground faults. This vibration appears to be transmitted through the megaliths, some of which have concavities or carved holes. The site may have been chosen for the temple as it was already recognised as a sacred place, where the Goddess spoke through the ground.

The presence of the Goddess

This Goddess was a visible presence at Tarxien in a stone statue, that would originally have been about 3 metres (9 ft) high inside the entrance, possibly as a guardian. Called by the original excavators

The Maltese Phenomenon

30. Malta Goddess – standing (Tarxien)
In the first court of the South Temple at Tarxien was a giant statue of the Goddess (originally 3 m/9 ft high). She may have also been painted in vivid colours. This reconstruction shows a dowel hole at the neck to fix different heads in place. She stands on a platform with a running frieze of eggs. When in the original site relief spirals adorn low, step-size horizontal blocks next to her. Approximately 3,150 BCE. Drawing: Kaye Moseley ©.

'The Fat Lady', the gender of the figure is debated. The heavy chest is not clearly demarked as breasts, and as the person wears a skirt, there are no exposed sexual organs, as in the other European Goddess figures we have discussed in Chapter 1. In Malta, other statues of a similar figure are clearly female, and I contend so is the one at Tarxien. So why the ambiguity of presentation?

Other, smaller, more complete standing statues (e.g. from Hagar Qim) show this figure has one arm resting across the ample stomach rolls and the other points down to the ground. It is possible that the expression of reproduction or sexuality were not the factors the Maltese artist sought to highlight in this stance. The aspect most emphasised in the ample proportions is abundance. In addition, she points to the earth from which food abundance comes. Perhaps this is what the people of Malta sought – the abundance of flourishing crops and domestic animals to ensure survival. Or perhaps the people had a truly egalitarian view of the human form and tried to show that the deity encompassed both female and male attributes.

Though the upper portion of the Tarxien figure is broken, we have smaller versions that show that the head was probably removable. It is likely that several heads would have been swapped for different seasons and rituals.

The earliest temple interiors were plastered and then painted in the sacred red ochre. In later interiors, the walls could also be decorated. There could be intricately carved spirals on steps and altars, friezes of farm animals, fish and snakes, and a simple pattern of pitted dots. There are indications of healing and fertility rituals; ancestor worship; and oracular practices, as part of the Neolithic spiritual belief system. All under the aegis of a Mother Goddess.

Large rectangular decorated stone blocks placed horizontally are designated 'altars', and at Tarxien, behind a slide-out section of the front, a long flint knife was found. Nearby are holes in the rock where an animal to be sacrificed could have been tethered. Holes in the floor were for libations and may have received offerings of all kinds of bounty from the Earth – water, oil, milk, honey and also blood collected from a sacrificed animal. There is usually a hearth where the sacrifice may have been cooked or, at other times, aromatic herbs burned to fill the space with healthy fragrances (Trump 2002).

Into the Earth again – underground burial temples

We have explored the temples of megalithic Malta, enjoyed by the living, but what of the dead? They were to be found in temples under the ground, returned to Mother Earth. The best preserved and studied of these is the Hypogeum of Hal Saflien, a remarkable monument constructed, it has been estimated, between 3,300 and 3,000 BCE, and used until at least 2,500 BCE. It was discovered in 1902 by chance, when a well was being dug. The Hypogeum was carved out underground from rock and caves, creating 34 interconnected chambers, through three levels down to water, at 10.6 metres (33 ft) deep. There was a light well from the surface down to this water, which also acted as a water well for those above.

The Hypogeum was a sanctuary, a healing space and a cemetery. In ancient times, people would enter between two, huge stones supporting a cross stone above for the lintel and walk into the hill along a narrow, descending corridor between smooth, stone walls, to get to the main area of the space.

Many small chambers leading off the entrance passage and each other, could be accessed through round-hole entrances. Often the chamber walls are painted in red ochre mixed with water. The internal design of the spaces replicates temple architecture above ground, following a simple geometric line and rounded shapes. Its beauty lies in its simplicity. Gimbutas regards the individual chambers, especially on the upper, oldest level, as replicating an egg-shape and sees this as a Neolithic symbol of regeneration. In the middle level, the central chamber has stone 'windows' replicated on all four sides, cut as if they had frames. The Hypogeum was dark and humid, and according to Gimbutas would have been lit by lamps burning fat or olive oil, the flame flickering in the dimness.

Ancient Ways for Current Days

31. Hypogeum at Hal Saflien, interior
An underground temple, healing centre and mortuary, carved from the natural limestone. Three levels, 34 interconnected chambers. Some chambers painted in red ochre, some adorned with painted red spirals. Constructed between 3,300 and 3,000 BCE, in use until 2,500 BCE. Drawing: Kaye Moseley ©.

There are others in Western Europe (Bueno-Ramirez et al. 2015), but the one at Hal Saflien is the oldest and the best preserved of the three known on the Maltese islands. The others are Xaghra Circle and Santa Lucija. Hypogeum literally means 'underground' from the Greek 'hypo' meaning 'under' and 'Gaia' – Mother Earth or Goddess of Earth. Within the Hypogeum at Hal Saflien some 7,000 human bones were found, mostly in egg-shaped niches on the lower level which Gimbutas (1999) claims 'suggest the symbolic affinity of these tombs to the goddess' womb'. With them were personal items of adornment, mostly beads of shell, and animal teeth but also tiny carved or modelled birds, animals and snails. The interments occurred over a 600-year period to about 2,500 BCE (Trump 2002).

Analysis of bones of 800 individuals found at Xaghra established that both genders and all ages from foetal to adult were interred

(Thompson et al. 2020), indicative of an egalitarian approach and recognition of the 'personhood' of the deceased regardless of age. To complete the interment, the descendants returned to the site at designated times to move the bones in different configurations. Thompson comments, ' … interacting with them would have been an emotionally charged process'. The ancient Maltese people returned the bodies of their dead to the Mother Earth, without particular recognition of role or contribution – it was an egalitarian approach (Thompson et al. 2020). It is likely the bones were brought here after the organs and soft tissue had decayed. They cared about their ancestors, storing their bones in specially carved out underground temples.

Earth healing

The Hypogeum of Hal Saflien was indeed a temple, a healing place, in addition to the resting place for the bones of those who had died. Here were held a range of rituals, for example at death, for the ancestors, animal sacrifices, initiation and healing. Priestesses used the sacred space for trance dreaming and possibly prophesy. Gimbutas states:

> … sick people sought health, barren women sought pregnancy, and devotees congregated and slept in womb-shaped chambers. Strengthened by the Earth powers and probably by a priestess's divination and acoustic conjuring reverberating through the vaults, the pilgrims were born anew.

As we explored in the discussion of the long barrows and the stone circles, the same sound phenomena has been found to be true at the Hal Saflien Hypogeum. Sound at the 111 Hz frequency is understood to directly stimulate the area of the brain that is a

Ancient Ways for Current Days

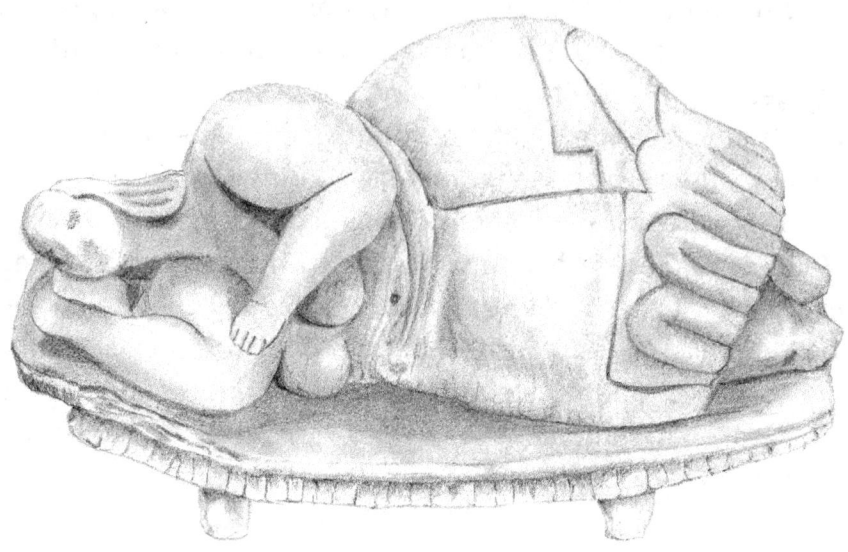

*32. The Sleeping Lady, or Dreaming Goddess
Found in the Hypogeum at Hal Saflien, Malta. Clay figurine, with traces of red ochre, of a sleeping woman lying on her side, naked from the waist up (12.2 cm/4.8 in long). She wears a skirt which may have had embroidery, and which ended in a fringe. The hair from the forehead to the crown of the head appears to be shaved and the remaining hair is shoulder length. Dates are contemporaneous with those for the Hypogeum. Drawing: Kaye Moseley ©.*

problem area for some mental health conditions (Chalk in Kreisberg 2014). It is also associated with endorphin release, a potential non-addictive panacea for pain relief, and with inducing a trance-state as explored below. Added to this information we have an insight into other healing practices in the Hypogeum, from two statues found there, both of a Sleeping Goddess/Priestess.

The centre of the sound effects at the Hypogeum is a space called the Oracle Room. It has two sound holes ('acoustic nodes') in one wall. If sounds or words are sung or chanted, directed to either of these, the sound is amplified through the rock and can be heard anywhere in the entire Hypogeum, causing a shift in consciousness of all present (Stroud in Narang 2015). Since there are two nodes, perhaps at times two voices combined at once.

This Oracle Room is on one side of a chamber that adjoins the Main Hall. The Oracle Room has a ceiling of red ochre drawings that have been likened to the 'tree of life', a symbol of life, health and longevity in many religions. The room it opens onto has red ochre honeycomb patterns and spirals on the roof. The two small sculptures of a woman were found lying on this floor, left when the temple was sealed and abandoned.

Made of clay, the sculptures bear traces of red ochre. In one, the woman is depicted as sleeping on her front, in the better preserved one she is depicted lying on her side, on a rush mattress on a bed, resting her head on a stone pillow. She has huge breasts, belly and hips; small, fine hands and feet; and shoulder length hair. The face shows a very high forehead – possibly somewhat shaven – with closed eyes and a peaceful expression. She is naked to the waist and wears a skirt with a fringed lower section. She is sleeping, possibly dreaming. Some sculpted figurines in ancient Malta were intentionally without sexual attributes but most, these included, are clearly women, their corpulence signifying wellbeing; their pose and place of discovery indicating a spiritual state.

'Temple sleep' was a phenomenon known to have been practised much later in ancient Greece, where it was called 'enkoimesis'. A person seeking help would fall asleep in the temple – in Greece with the assistance of a sleep drug – and dream of meeting a wise spirit or divine being who gave information and advice. Upon awakening, the experience was recounted by the person, discussed with and explained by the attending religious personnel/healers.

Ancient Ways for Current Days

In the Oracular Chamber of the Hal Saflien Hypogeum, sounding (e.g. clapping, clicking), singing, or chanting, creates a reverberation, that is greatest in the Chamber itself. It would appear that in Malta the priestess fell into a sound-induced sleep, or trance, although hallucinogens may also have been used. The priestess would have been regarded as the medium through whom the spirit world communicated with the human world. The priestess may have lain on beds in the room outside the Oracular Chamber; they may also have lain in some deep niches that would have worked for this purpose, in the walls in a room further on, named the 'Holy of Holies'. They were deep in the body of the Mother.

Today only 10 people at a time, per hour, are allowed into the Hypogeum. A few years ago, I was privileged to be in such a group. We were a group of women, friends who understood the nature of the place we were entering. The space is dimly lit and temperature controlled to preserve the ancient structure. Standing on the walkway deep in the Hypogeum, one of our number was drawn to begin to sing, and the rest irresistibly followed. It was a sublime experience of great peace, that created a sense of wellbeing in body and spirit. I felt both secure and ethereal as the sound swirled around the space – it was not an echo, but an amplification, and the female voices were uplifting, transporting, and the feeling was of experiencing something exceptional. A link to be sure, back all those thousands of years to the people who had designed and created this extraordinary testament in stone. We filed out in silence.

So, while the female voice may not be deep enough to induce trance, it can produce meaningful effects, and trance may not always have been desirable. A further possibility for ritual is that anyone using a steady repetitive beat on a frame drum, which the people used at that time, would 'sonically excite the chamber' (Narang 2015).

Kreisberg comments that the body shape of the priestesses of Malta reminds us of 'what we would expect ... of a modern opera singer' and he calls to mind that such opera singers have been known to shatter glass by producing the correct sound. A multitude of ways of using the resonance and amplification effects of the Hypogeum would have been understood and used, creating a skilled partnership of female and male shamans, or priestess and priests, in the spiritual world of this matrifocal culture.

Why did it end?

The megalithic culture in Malta went into rapid decline about 2,500 BCE. A cause, thought likely, was extreme deforestation by the population and soil loss that accompanied that practice (Trump 2002; Gray 2020). Famine may have been involved. About 3,500 to 3,000 BCE there was a considerable natural increase in population – Trump hazards an estimate of 10,000 people in total – leading to land clearing for further agriculture. In this scenario, unable to sustain its population, the megalithic people and their culture suffered. Perhaps their leadership ultimately convinced the population that the only option was to leave Malta completely (Trump 2002), until at last its monuments lay abandoned for several centuries.

Malta was then settled from the European mainland, around 2,400 BCE, by war-like people with formidable weapons – copper daggers and axes and sharp obsidian arrowheads (Gadon 1989) – and 'a lower level of culture, apparently owing nothing to what had gone on before' (Trump 2002).

The builders of the great temples vanished, their memory perhaps disguised in myths told by the conquering 'heroes', of monsters with supernatural powers (Kreisberg 2014). Perhaps the tale of Ulysses and the Sirens came from existing stories of women with extraordinary voices, with a range that took the sound out to sea (sound is amplified over water), as remembered from Malta. Kreisberg even proposes that, if a form of defence from the outer world was needed in Neolithic Malta, the ethereal priestess voices could have been used in this way.

Unfortunately though, they were unable to save their people from the internal challenges, consequences of being in the initial learning stages of an agrarian way of life. For example, they did not understand the potential long-term negative effects deforestation can have. Can we blame them? It is perhaps a lesson some are still not heeding.

Does the spirit of a place prevail? Malta today is a very Catholic nation (93.9% in 2018) yet 80 per cent of its many churches are dedicated to a woman, especially Mary. During a visit to Malta I was at dinner in a small, town square when the local community staged a drama, as was traditional in that village. The drama was about the presence of a Goddess over thousands of years in Malta – surviving in various forms in the face of many different invasions and challenges. The final words of the Goddess were 'I have been with you from the beginning, through all troubles and joys and I will be with you till the end. You will hear me in the laughter of your children'. This story of Malta, all these thousands of years on, still reflect the sense of being guided by a female spiritual presence, including, in the matrifocal way, a commitment to the wellbeing of children.

Archaeologists who come from a traditional (i.e. patriarchal) mindset find it difficult to conceive that a culture that built monuments, like those in Malta, could have done so without

The Maltese Phenomenon

a hierarchy of power that forced the people to do the work of megalith building. This reveals an inability to imagine a model other than the one we have now: an inability to imagine a society organised around consensus and mutual goals, 'without a hierarchic structure of decision-making in the hands of a privileged group' (Rodenborg 1991). Megalithic Malta tells us that these monuments were completed without having any force involved. Perhaps guided by the Council of Mothers (older women who were also priestesses), in consultation with the men (who carried out the engineering and construction), the people created something wonderful to represent and embody their beliefs. With a matrifocal organising system they could do it, and they did it because they wanted to.

CHAPTER 6

Continuity from the Deep Past

Both girls and boys could be raised to respect and value each other, with neither needing to resort to domination. The matricentric vision lodged by nature in our brains would be continuously reinforced and communicated by endless new forms of expression.
Liz Carr-Harris, psychologist, philosopher, researcher and writer (1936–2011)

Ancient basic values underpin the emergence of matrifocal cultures, and the origin of it lies in the mother/child relationship, the first relationship for primates. Humans are primates in a group that includes monkeys and apes. Starting millennia ago, from the many pre-human strains that initially developed in Africa, there eventually emerged the modern human.

In her book *The Descent of Religion*, the psychologist Liz Carr-Harris proposes a credible, if unorthodox (by her own admission) theory for how this occurred. We will explore this in the current chapter. Carr-Harris was strongly influenced by the work of Elaine Morgan who, in her 1982 book *The Aquatic Ape*, developed the Aquatic Ape Theory of evolution. Her work was based on the hypothesis of Sir Alister Hardy, an English marine biologist. While this theory is regarded as highly controversial, it has proven tenacious, with David Attenborough, the world-renown English natural historian and broadcaster, supporting it in a BBC radio series on the theory in 2016.

Morgan proposes in brief, that 7 to 8 million years ago, a pre-human form had developed, which has been called a 'Swamp Ape', a commonly used term in anthropology for an assumed ancestor to the human, that lived in swamplands. She proposes that it lived in North-East Africa on an island in the Danakil Depression, part of the Red Sea near the Gulf of Afar that leads to the Indian Ocean. Here, she contends, over millennia, many physiological changes occurred in this entity. Living in groups, bands of such 'proto-humans' would leave the island at differing points of physical development. Carr-Harris also proposes that the home base continued to provide conditions from which new forms evolved, and additional cultural behaviours were adopted in response to them.

Relationship – a form of female defence

Some examples of the changes in development and behaviours that Carr-Harris refers to include the increasing brain size of offspring. Among other things, this meant the baby could not fully develop in the womb and fit through the birth canal, at the size the birth canal was at that time. Consequently it was born early, less and less able to fend for itself. Offspring became dependent on the mother, so babies were inevitably 'matrifocal' creatures. The mother was the safe centre in the world for her young.

To diverge for a moment from the past to the present, we can say that the experience of the mother as the centre of a child's world, almost universally a safe centre, continues for humans to this day. Shelley E. Taylor, a professor of psychology at the University of California, undertook research with her team to explore how women in their caring roles respond under stress. Traditionally the received wisdom has been, for both animals and humans, of a 'fight or flight' model for response to stress, such as a threat. Proposed by Bradford Cannon in 1915, the 'fight or flight' options proposed are that we, like other animals, may choose to stay and fight the source of threat, or choose to run from it.

Taylor proposes that this model does not apply to women and throughout the process of evolution would not have worked for them. With one or more children to care for, flight would be unlikely to get a mother very far. If she were attacked and overcome, the offspring were left without the means to survive. If she stood her ground and was defeated the same would be true.

Instead, from her research, Taylor proposes that the 'tend and befriend' model operates. In a book by her co-researchers, Levine et al. state that 'people, especially women, evolved social means for dealing with stress that involved caring for offspring and protecting them from harm and turning to the social group for protection for the self and offspring'. Nurturing group support for mutual survival became a basic female skill, that males also shared to some degree.

In response to danger, oxytocin levels (which generate pro-social behaviours) go up in women; men generate increased testosterone (which supports a fight-or-flight response). In line with this, in Taylor's study, in times of stress men were more likely to withdraw from family life.

The maternal family

Let's now return to the story of slow evolution of the pre-human into the human form. As offspring became more complex and needed longer to mature, they were born unable to care for themselves. The need to care intensively for a child, for at least up to two years, led to the maternal family. As in Taylor's research, the mother turned to the social group to support her and the young offspring. This family/social group comprised the mother and her offspring – a matrilineal clan.

The need to care for dependent offspring necessitated having a safe home base, such as might be provided by a cave. It further required collaboration, for childcare to be undertaken. Some members took on the role of watching and protecting the young while other members of the matrilineal clan went out to collect food, especially in times of diminished resources. A female and her daughters and sisters and at least in their early years, her sons, created the first maternal family.

Male offspring and their family

It is not unusual in ape groupings that adolescent male offspring are ejected from the troupe as they become more boisterous – sexual maturity occurs earlier than social maturity. We can speculate that this may have been a behaviour in proto-humans, possibly continuing even later into human development. The adolescent ape males either go off and create bachelor bands – transitory, loosely formed, foraging groups – or they live at the edge of the matrilineal group, where they engage in rivalries with each other and challenges to the dominant male.

Being at the edges of the troupe these young ape males would be the first to be taken by predators, so that they consequently act as an involuntary protective line of first defence for the troupe. Ape offspring have a long dependency period on the mother, up to five years suckling and a further three years to continue learning. According to the Centre for Great Apes, once in their male groupings the male offspring hunt cooperatively together. They continue to recognise their matrilineal descent and even quite large, male chimpanzees will go to their aged mother to be soothed by grooming (O'Neil 2012).

According to Carr-Harris, in the emerging proto-human matrilineal society, compliant sons (those prepared to be child-focused and community centred) would have been retained in the group. Tasks would have been split along sex lines. As primary caregivers, the females were more tied to home base, where they could exploit local food resources – they became the gatherers. The males could forage further afield and became the hunters. But males were trained in child-caring and would also undertake such tasks. For early human groups, high female and baby mortality would have made the lives of mothers and infants very valuable.

On the journey to being human – physical changes lead to new behaviours

Carr-Harris proposes that, on the island in the Danakil Depression, which is her favoured locale of development from ape to human, many social and physical developments we still have today occurred. These emerged over eons of time and Carr-Harris mentions a variety of these physical and behavioural changes, extrapolated from the work of Morgan. The changes are real, the explanations plausible, in the agreed context of apes evolving into humans who walked upright, have frontal sex and several other features that beg an explanation. See what you think:

- Kissing began as a behaviour in which developing humans were replicating the comforting sound of breastfeeding.

- When pre-humans started to walk upright the angle of internal organs changed and sexual activity moved to the front of the body of the female, instead of rear sex as is the case for most other species. The 'g-spot' in the vagina, comprising a set of pressure receptors over a larger area than in women today, had been the source of pleasure for the female before walking upright. However, with frontal sex now required, this spot was no longer stimulated and intercourse for females could be painful. Since a female could experience painful sex, she might refuse. A male would not have understood why an age-old behaviour on his part was producing this undesirable reaction. In an act of frustration by the male, a female for the first time could be raped.

- Over a long period of time clitoris development, from the vestigial penis nerve, occurred in females to compensate for the loss of pleasure in sex when the apes started to walk upright. However, the clitoris also meant females were not dependent on sex with a male to experience the pleasurable feeling – rubbing against anything would achieve the desired result.

Continuity from the Deep Past

- Oestrus, or being 'in heat', is the recurring period of sexual receptivity and fertility in animals and birds, and does not occur for human females. Females moved to regular menstrual periods, rather than each female sending out aromatic signals when she was ready to become pregnant. In the animal world, these signals indicate to males when sex is appropriate. Without it, males do not become aroused. Without it occurring at all however, males could not tell when to refrain from requesting sex, or what should be the object of it, even children could be targets. In this environment, over time both sexes become responsible for decision-making about sexual activity based on thought and a range of social values, rather than on an innate drive alone.

- Menopause emerged – rare in the animal world. Most mammals can reproduce until death – female bodies exhausted by continuous birthing. Research indicates that male chimpanzees in fact prefer older females as mates, perhaps because of their proven track record of birthing and raising young (Muller et al. 2006). Research on monkeys indicates that they reproduce across 70 to 90 per cent of their potential lifetimes, while human women cease just before 50 per cent of their potential lifetimes (Walker and Herndon 2008). Menopause enabled females to live to be mature adults. As such, with their knowledge and experience, they were respected, to teach and hold wisdom and support their biological line to survive.

We can therefore see that our physical development produced a range of areas that were once automatic, but now required thought, cooperation and understanding. A challenge that couples today confront as they try to navigate their way to create successful permanent relationships.

Thinking beings …

Modern brain size was reached 500,000 to 300,000 years ago. What did we do with all that brainpower, represented by the increasing size of the brain? It allowed us to think.

Because of the caring role of mothers, learning is primarily passed on by them, which expands the mothering role from just the practical to cultural mothering as well. Rituals, myths and ideals were passed on through this innate, constructive relationship of love, and bound the social fabric together.

As Carr-Harris points out, modern humans are not the evolutionary top of the tree. There were many versions of the 'human' – ours was but an incidental spin-off. Our survival was very marginal at many points in the human network of descent. For example, there was one form of human that had bigger brains than we do, but due to environmental factors they died out.

Neanderthals (Homo neanderthalensis) were also a successful human variant for some 350,000 years (Wragg Sykes 2020) and they became well spread within Europe out to the edges of Asia. Research by Whiting et al. (2018) suggests that Neanderthals possessed high-level cognitive abilities, which supports the Carr-Harris contention that they had a strong visual and symbolic language, before the kind of human who could speak arrived from Africa.

Speech is due to developing the capacity to hold and control our breath – other animals cannot do this. Rigby reports that a study at the University of Madrid (2020) identified that humans and Neanderthals had a similar sized hearing bandwidth, something that had not evolved in any other ancestors for the human to that time. No research has yet identified a Neanderthal ability to control breath, however. They could certainly make sound, and if they were without speech, Neanderthals had to develop alternative forms of communication such as hand signals. We can see how practical this would have been by recalling the sign language used very effectively in modern deaf communities.

Modern humans (Homo sapiens) emerged from Africa later than the Neanderthals and on some of the occasions that they encountered each other, they had offspring together. Carr-Harris proposes that the modern humans (who definitely could speak) respected the Neanderthals as wiser, more spiritually aware, than they were, and that they learned much of their culture from the Neanderthals. Wragg Sykes in her comprehensive work on the Neanderthals draws strong parallels, for example, between funerary practices of Neanderthals and early Homo Sapiens. Carr-Harris believes that the earliest cave paintings were a way for Neanderthals to communicate the basic symbology of life to these modern humans. Such contentions are becoming more plausible as more information and new ways of analysing Neanderthal sites come to bear (e.g. Hoffman et al. 2018; Wragg Sykes 2020).

Foundations of a spiritual consciousness

'Organic religion' is the Carr-Harris term for the basic values that developed in these matrilineal, matrifocal clans. She proposes that it emerged organically, partly from our evolving physical biology, and from our growing understanding of both ourselves and of the natural world around. 'It sprang entirely from our earthly experience, with no concern for anything above or beyond nature.' This organic religion is extraordinarily ancient, started all those millennia ago in Africa. It is based on the need for survival, on the drive to have our species' genes continue, which we, as modern humans have retained. It is 'hardwired' information that is about life. These thoughts from within became the reliable source of enlightenment – the 'higher power' of organic religion, according to Carr-Harris.

The ways of being described in this chapter developed essentially to hold together what Carr-Harris calls the child support communities, and they strengthened behaviour patterns intended to lighten the maternal load, e.g. caring, feeding, protecting. In return, for those individuals following the matricentric mammal behaviour patterns, this activated the oxytocin (sometimes called the 'happy hormone') hormone reinforcement system. This produces a long-lasting, positive emotional state for the individual (Blaffey Hrdy in Carr-Harris 2011). In further research undertaken by Feldman, this has been found to be true today for human parents both female and male equally. In her research, enhanced oxytocin showed high stability in each individual for the first six months of parenting. Based on this it can be said that most child caring situations (whether of your biological offspring or not) will produce happy feelings.

This does not deny that up to 80 per cent of new mothers experience the 'baby blues' in the first few days after giving birth (Wright 2018). If it lasts more than a couple of weeks the depression and anxiety may come to be regarded as Postnatal Depression. More than one in seven new mothers and almost one in ten new fathers experience this (Wright). The increase in oxytocin in the first six months may be a survival adaptation humans developed, to get through this time of huge change that occurs with the arrival of a new baby into a home, impacting on each of the parenting adults and the relationship between them.

Continuity from the Deep Past

Carr-Harris proposes that the development of a religious impulse was also based on principles to further protect the mother and child. She holds that initially organic religion had nothing to do with the supernatural. For Carr-Harris, beliefs about the supernatural were added to the social framework of organic religion, and were established later.

The development of language provided a way to externalise information. This built on the ability to think internally. Humans could go into their own inner world using the capacity for introspection (self-awareness), which, along with empirical observation 'separated their brain's centre for social wisdom, or Higher Power, from cognitive "background noise", it would have become increasingly manifest' (Carr-Harris 2011). Carr-Harris claims we were in awe of our own inner consciousness and from there extrapolated to a 'Higher Power'.

I would contend that, as central as the mother-child bond was, the next most important relationship for humans of both sexes was with the natural world, which, like a mother for a child, provided sustenance for life and fertile grounds for learning. Given the strong mothering model shared, even by proto-humans, it was an obvious framework to then place on the natural world. It proposed the world as mother, Mother Nature, constantly giving new life and rebirth, just as plants returned again in spring.

Whether you are convinced by the details added by Carr-Harris (and before her, Morgan) or not, in this chapter we have considered a plausible development of the human through a long process that embedded love, respect and the need to protect the mother into the human psyche. Deep and innate, it provided a foundation for the cultural and religious developments that we first saw emerging in tangible forms at least 40,000 years ago – as explored in Chapter

Ancient Ways for Current Days

1 of this book. It was a value system strong enough to survive for at least a further 36,000 years, to about 4,000 years ago.

I have made reference in this chapter to the 'bachelor bands' of outlawed, non-compliant males. We will explore this more in the next chapter. As a central part of the Carr-Harris theory, in her view it held the basis for the emergence of a new and destructive system, one that eventually became patriarchy.

CHAPTER 7

The Onslaught of Patriarchy

> The people of the West want to live 'better'. Accumulate more money, gain more power, become famous. Just a few people hoard the power while causing the suffering of millions … We don't want to live 'better', we want to live 'well'. Living well means return to balance, return to natural harmony.
> **Fernando Huanacuni, Bolivian Aymara leader (1966–present)**

We have seen that the Palaeolithic period and the Neolithic were peaceful, creative, productive, innovative periods over huge amounts of time, in Europe and in the Middle East, in what I am calling matrifocal cultures. Why would they have chosen to move into a patriarchal system that introduced hierarchies, inequalities in resource distribution, warfare, the subservience of women?

The answer of course is that the matrifocal peoples never chose any of it. They were forced into it. Not without resistance though, and that slowed the pace. Here is how and why.

Ancient Ways for Current Days

Two natural factors need to be taken into account – drought and flood.

Biaggi records the transformation of the Black Sea Lake around 6,600 BCE. Well-established matrifocal settlements flourished on the shores of a huge lake, which was to become the Black Sea. A huge natural dam wall of glaciation debris kept the fresh water of the lake from mingling with the Mediterranean Sea. With the melting of the glaciers the level of the sea began to rise, such that its waters began to trickle over the top of this barricade. A stream became a river and soon a total of about 42 cubic kilometres (10 cubic miles) was pouring from the Mediterranean into the Black Sea Lake. No doubt psychologically devastating, the famous flood was recorded in a number of stories from ancient civilisations in the region, such as the story of Noah. The Flood had begun.

The Lake began to rise by 15 centimetres (6 in) day after day. Without pause it came. It took two long years for the level to rise by 100 metres (330 ft) to the same level as the Mediterranean. It removed the stable lifestyle of the Lake people from them and sent them on the search for new land. They fled towards lands by then occupied in Russia, adding stress to the limited resources of those already there.

Later, sustained drought in Central and Western Asia (5,000 to 4,000 BCE) again forced entire settlements and groups to move. On the steppes of Russia and possibly Ukraine, in their homelands between the Dnieper and Volga rivers, was one such group who, in all likelihood, were agriculturalists whose ancestors originated from the area known as Anatolia – where Çatalhöyük is located. They were named the Kurgans by Marija Gimbutas, and their adopted home had an animal that had become extinct elsewhere: the horse.

As in much of her work, the reality of an influx of new people from the Russian steppes has now been confirmed in genetic studies by Reich and his colleagues, who use the title 'Yamnaya' for these mobile pastoralists. Their studies also showed that they were a tall people. Unlike the earlier influx of peoples from Anatolia during the Neolithic in Europe, which were groups balanced equally with both women and men, the Kurgans/Yamnayans show a 'dramatic male bias' in their numbers – possibly one woman to every 14 men (Goldberg 2017). By 2,500 BCE they had reached as far as Spain and Portugal. Miguel Vilar, a genetic anthropologist, says the DNA suggests a 'massive influx of men from the steppes [of Russia] ... the influence was very male dominated' (Blakemore 2019).

The patriarchal emergence

Perhaps the Kurgans/Yamnayans didn't set out to be patriarchal, but became so from separation from a matrifocal base.

Some theorise that one method of dealing with unruly males within dislocated matrifocal groups was to eject them from the clan, just as our ancient pre-human ancestors had done. Carr-Harris proposes that these marginalised young men formed groups – bachelor bands. She proposes five important male behaviours that must have developed at that time:

- Conventions of exclusion (who is in the 'in-group' versus those who are not)
- Dominance hierarchies (leaders, deputies, rank and file)
- Creative display (this could be shows of anger, chest thumping, exaggeration of size and strength, speech-making, use of equipment and adornment/dress to impress etc.)

Ancient Ways for Current Days

- Brotherly love
- Male bonding.

Prior to 5,500 BCE there is no evidence of defensive weapons. Men were mentally prepared for self-sacrifice, to protect women and children in situations of threat (wild animals, natural events like storm and flood). Men had diversions for their aggressive tendencies through displays of strength, hunting prowess, competitive display, public games and other contests. After this, if the Carr-Harris theory is correct, marauding bachelor bands came into play, and if so, the exile of miscreants had been a big mistake.

Other researchers suggest that it was just small groups of unruly young men who departed their clans and forced their presence on the ancient matrifocal culture to the south. As described above, their orientation was more patriarchal than the groups they left behind. Some of the traditions in their area of origin to this day still indicate a respect for women and expectation of equality between the sexes.

According to Carr-Harris, previously childless male bands began to reproduce, possibly first with stolen females. They became a tribe. As poorly socialised young males, their groups built around volatile, aggression-based hierarchies, they were at first much more unstable as groups than their mainstream counterparts. Rejecting the values of the Mother Goddess culture, they came to attain absolute male control over children as well as their mothers. Eventually, in some expressions of their social system, women were property, vehicles for baby-making, baby-sitting, sexual pleasure and trading. It was a social model based on single competing males, rather than on a collective child-care network.

The Onslaught of Patriarchy

Did it happen like that? Perhaps it started as a different reaction to stress. Goettner-Abendroth proposes that to survive in the increasing dry, men could have returned to hunting and left the women to support themselves through their agriculture. This, she states, is a matriarchal solution – that in times of stress the men leave their clans, so as not to be a burden on the women and children, who are regarded as more important for clan survival.

Perhaps the women did not survive, the matriarchal system broke down; perhaps the men found it impossible to come back. Thus, uprooted and undisciplined groups of men migrated, in the process perhaps developing the social systems identified by Carr-Harris above. Robbins Dexter in *The Rule of Mars* informs us that information about these young male groups is found in ancient Germanic, Gaulish, Celtic, Greek and Roman myth 'and probably society as well'.

It is claimed that eventually these people tamed the horse (by about 5,700 BCE). This was the key to their success in Gimbutas' view. Flood makes a strong argument that horses were not domesticated until the Iron Age (1,200 BCE) and before that horses were rather small animals – oxen were used instead to haul wagons, for example. If the Yamnayans had tamed the horse, the speed and distance they could travel would have been phenomenal and probably exhilarating, compared with traditional tribes. Very effective raiding parties were possible.

Either way, as population increased the Yamnayans sought food and new lands, trying to escape the aridity and cold of the steppe. In an arid world, the agricultural skills of the women became of minor importance.

These groups on the move encountered already established groups in their way. The green and flourishing lands of Europe must have been very desirable to them. Others moved west and also south, some reaching as far as northern India, others over centuries moving down around the top of Africa and then back up to Spain. Over time they learned to turn their hunting tools into weapons, and use them to remove the existing people, whose matrifocal ways would have given them no chance of survival in the face of this murderous intent. Joan Marler (in Biaggi 2005) states that during that period so many late Neolithic/Copper Age sites throughout Southeast Europe were consumed by fire, that this level in archaeological digs is called the 'Burned House Horizon' (5,900 to 3,500 BC).

This Burned House phenomenon attracts a number of theories but no definitively accepted solution at this point. It might, however, have been the case that the way ahead was cleared for the Kurgan/Yamnayans. Traces of an ancient form of the plague – a pneumonic (rather than bubonic) version, which takes hold in the lungs – has been found in the teeth of a woman who died in western Sweden (Sample 2018). She was buried in a megalithic passage grave with 77 other people. Did a plague sweep across Europe and people burned the infected buildings to the ground, in an attempt to counter it? If so the Kurgan/Yamnayans may just have been able to slip into the emptied spaces. It is also possible that the people burnt the houses as part of a ritual cycle. They did then rebuild on top of the burnt-out walls. These are the conundrums that archaeology can present.

Provisions of violence

Over time the invaders learned to use bronze for their weapons. Once they had domesticated the horse, developed bronze (and later iron) weapons, they were unstoppable. Perhaps they became

The Onslaught of Patriarchy

proud of the destructive new lifestyle, their minds changed to enjoy domination.

According to Gimbutas, pastoralists, especially if they adopt a nomadic life, develop different cultures due to a lack of connection to the earth. It is a very different experience than for those established in one place or area for generations, working with crops and the soil, identifying their spirituality with the landscape.

The transformation to patriarchy took a long time. The first wave of the Kurgan invasion, Gimbutas claims, was about 4,500 BCE. Adoption of the new way was of course resisted by the matrifocal, Mother Goddess people they encountered. As the invaders intermingled with existing people they found they had to modify their ideas and hybrid cultures emerged. Often to be recognised as the leaders the invaders had to marry the main priestess. Women, as well as their men, learned warrior skills as part of the need to deal with the violent male-centred raiders next time, or to stand up to those in their midst.

There was another wave of these invaders about a thousand years later, more destructive, and probably a third wave five hundred years after that, each one bringing a more entrenched patriarchal system and developed religion. Each resulted in massive movements of the existing people in Europe, intermingling of the gene pool and dilution/redefinition of the ancient culture. These invaders have become known as the Indo-Europeans and the horse and the violence of the men gave them the power to impose their language and social structure upon the Neolithic Europeans, out of proportion to the actual number of them that arrived in Europe.

Strongly impacted by aridity, theirs was a Sky God, as far from the Earth Mother as they could go. The sun and the broad skies as they travelled were their inspiration. Carr-Harris claims the new theology was crude and simplistic compared to the ancient religion of the Goddess. Temples on high places with altars, were now required. Animals were sacrificed to these gods, administered by priests. Male gods, who lived in the sky and were equipped with weapons, now appeared in the iconography of the arts and weaponry. Heroes dominated the storytelling. Rape appeared in the tales. Walled encampments and towns developed, tombs were built which included grave goods, which showed clearly that some were rich and others had very little. Even family members and animals were 'sacrificed' to die with the chieftain in the grave. A class society emerged.

Mor and Sjoo comment about this change: 'The patriarchal God has only one commandment: *Punish life for being what it is*. The Goddess also has only one commandment: *Love life, for it is what it is*'.

In a matrifocal, Goddess-centred world, women who were no longer menstruating had lived a long life, learned many things that were valued and were deemed wiser than others, especially as, instead of bleeding, they retained the magical powers of their blood. We have seen that these were cultures linked to the Earth and sea that worshipped the Great Goddess, the Earth. They saw that just as plants went through a cycle of birth, death and return to life again, so did humans. The Earth was the mother who enabled this. There was no separation between the sacred and the everyday.

Could it be that male domination of the horse and other animal herds, led to a lack of empathy, a loss of the old sense of oneness with other creatures? Instead they were to be controlled, killed when past their usefulness, slaughtered in blood sacrifice, disposable. With that separation established, perhaps it was possible to transfer that emotional distance to people not of your clan, and women – people not of your gender. A key component of patriarchy.

Ways of resistance

It can be noted though, that Australian First Nations people, who came to Australia at least 65,000 years ago, also experienced extreme weather and climatic shifts, without establishing patriarchy as an overall ideology. We can trace a shift in power and influence into the hands of men, but women retained strong and balanced roles. They were people who were able to avoid wholesale slaughter over this.

Two factors should be considered – Australian First Nations people developed methods of birth control very early and never allowed population to build up to a point where they needed to take over the land of others. Also, there was no animal in Australia suitable to domesticate at all, let alone for riding or hauling. The horse and the wheel could not play a role.

The people developed a way to live cooperatively, no doubt building on the old matrifocal ways. Patriliny became recognised as part of the social system alongside matriliny. Strong identification with tribal lands through mythology, the Dreaming and ancestors, removed interest in living in lands other than those in which you were born. (This topic is explored more fully in Chapter 11.)

In Europe, there are glimmers of how women pushed back against the new way. There's the tale of the Jewish women in Jeremiah, retold later in this chapter. A story recounted by Vicki

Ancient Ways for Current Days

Noble, comes from the ancient Greek historian, Herodotus (484 BCE?–430 BCE?). In this, a group of Greek raiders had captured some Amazon women in a battle in Turkey. Sailing for home in three boats, while they were on the Black Sea, the Amazons broke out, murdered their captors, and took over the ships. Since the Amazons were warriors we know that they were already exposed to patriarchal ways and had learnt the skills of self-defence. They were not, however, a seafaring people and were actually then adrift at the mercy of the tides.

Eventually they came aground on the eastern coast of the Sea of Azov (modern Ukraine). There they set up camp, seized horses and plundered the countryside. The locals were Scythians, also formidable warriors, and did not realise their foes were women until killing one of them. Then they wanted to mate with these women as 'they wanted to breed children from them'. Some young men camped by the Amazon camp, and when the women saw that the men were not dangerous, they let them stay.

The men saw that the women went to the bushes to relieve themselves at midday, so the men did the same. One man approached a woman and rather than fighting him, she enticed him and they were intimate. Afterwards she indicated to him that he should return the next day and bring a friend and she would bring one too. Clearly a first principle of marooned women's groups was to find ways to reproduce, for before long every woman was mating with a young man.

Soon the two groups combined their camps, each man with the woman he had 'first lain with'. The young men wanted the women to live with them in their village, and be monogamous wives. But the Amazons declared that they could not be housebound women. If the men wanted them as partners, and to be honourable men, they should go back, receive their allotted share of their property, and come and live with the Amazons (basic behaviours of matrifocal cultures), which the young men did. Their language and ways became different from the Scythians due to this admixture of the two.

Women in any culture are the custodians of traditions; they teach the children. The matrifocal women of the past worked together and kept their beliefs going, within these changed times. Obviously, there were men who still held to the old matrifocal ways, and in cultures to come, strong Goddess temples were built and the traditions taught alongside those for the new male gods.

There is a glimmer of the ancient matrifocal past in traditions of the Jewish people, such as to be Jewish you must have a Jewish mother (matrilineal descent). The Israelites were continuously including the Goddess Asherah in their worship, known as 'The Queen of Heaven' and represented by a stylised pole, or a tree growing at the temple entrance. In the texts an exasperated God often tells them (e.g. Deuteronomy 12) not to recognise the Goddess and worship only Him, for fear of dire consequences. Jeremiah (7.1), written between 650 and 570 BCE, records:

> *The word which came to Jeremiah from the Lord ... 'Don't you see what they are doing in the towns of Judah and in the streets of Jerusalem? The children gather sticks, the fathers build the fire, and the mothers knead the dough, to make cakes for the Queen of Heaven, and they pour libations to other gods, to vex Me ... My wrath and My fury will be poured out upon this place, on man and on beast, on the trees of the field and the fruit of the soil. It shall burn, with none to quench it.*

A different world for women

As the role and place of women was steadily diminished, the Goddess came to be represented in roles as mothers, wives and daughters in the patriarchal mythic stories, with diminished powers. Indeed, women gradually lost their freedoms and became minor players in the men's game, eventually not much higher than the slaves – a new category of person created from the spoils of war, the new attitude of racism, and the victor's desire to dominate. If you viewed those you conquered as lesser, you could kill them, you could make them slaves, and certainly create yourself as a class above them, to be served by them.

Some of these invading groups of men came into Greece and were the forerunners of the famed Greek civilisation. The word for wife in Greece came from the root word 'to subdue' or 'to tame'. Women in the ancient Greek world, particularly Athens, had few rights in comparison to male citizens. Unable to vote, own land, or inherit, a woman's place was in the home and her purpose in life was to manage the household and to bear and raise children – preferably boys. She was under male guardianship for life.

The Roman approach to their women was based on Greek practice, although Roman women were citizens – but like Greece, were unable to vote or hold political office. In both cultures girls could be married as early as 12 years of age – a device designed to ensure that the husband received a virgin, untouched by any other man. The deal was between the father and husband, usually to advance the interests of one or both of them, certainly not the young woman.

Ironically, in the first century, Christianity preached preserving matrifocal values. But the alliance with the Roman Empire ended

The Onslaught of Patriarchy

that. By 380 CE in Rome, the last Goddess temple was closed by the Christian Emperor Theodosian. In 391 CE he burned down the library at Alexandria, famed compendium of the knowledge of the world. Eighty years later the fall of the Roman Empire is considered to be complete. Thus began what has been termed the 'Dark Ages', which we can note was a time of a world without respect for matrifocal values or honouring the female divine.

CHAPTER 8

The Battleground of the Female Body

The people who could do most to improve the situation of so many women and children are in fact men.
It is in our hands to stop violence towards women.
Patrick Stewart, English actor, director and producer
(1940–present)

Sometime between 300 and 400 BCE Christian monasteries were established across Europe and from then came to control knowledge. They taught only what Carr-Harris calls 'the androcentric heresy', that included an all-male ruling elite, defined by a combination of patrilineal descent and male ownership of private property. It is a heresy because it contravenes the most basic of principles of the matrifocal way. The male Christian officials railed against Goddess worship – an attitude enshrined in the Bible (and even more in the Apocrypha, an adjunct book to the Bible, that in the past was often published with it).

The Old Testament is full of accounts of blood-thirsty massacres of the 'enemy', leaving no adult or child alive e.g. the story of the defeat of Jericho (around 1,400 BCE). Scouts sent out to assess new lands returned describing the people they met as peaceable, trusting and productive in their agrarian lifestyle – typical descriptors of matrifocal people. This made them easy to conquer and kill, which is what the Israelites then did, according to the Bible.

Such tales, characterised as heavenly retribution, were well-exploited in the preaching of the Romanised Christian Church as it emerged. The religious hierarchy of the Christian Church became very rich, but their wealth was never enough. They tithed the peasants and converted 'pagans', frequently less out of Christian zeal than to increase their income base.

Witch-hunts

Then, for 300 years, from about 1,200 CE there were witch-hunts in Europe resulting in deaths of at least 40,000 to 60,000 women and men, although the number is widely disputed. Some estimate 500,000 and others claim 4 million or more. The witch-hunts reached an hysterical level of hunting down, persecution, torture and murder of people. The period is referred to as the Witch Burning, but the victims were also drowned, attacked with swords, tortured in a prison hellhole, as well as those who were burnt, tied to a stake on top of a pile of dry wood and set alight. To speak against it would have been to suffer the same fate.

The women revered in the community who were the midwives, herbalists and healers, were the focus. They came under suspicion for refusing to comply with the patriarchal social system in some way, including for heresy. Indeed, they were in fact the quiet, careful keepers of the ancient customs and herbal knowledge.

Though these women were traditionally relied upon for medical aid, they were outside the male medical system that was developing, and so, disparaged for the unchristian act of using magic and spells. But there were also whole groups of people labelled witches and heretics, executed for holding different religious beliefs from the Church of Rome, or for adhering to traditional practices, such as group resolution of issues, and an attitude of independence, with disregard for the laws the rulers imposed. The Church feared losing its grip in the face of the strong undercurrent of matrifocal customs still in play.

Hearth and home

The Industrial Revolution (from 1760 for almost 100 years) broke down the extended family into the nuclear family, reducing clan ability to socialise the young. In what was known in Scotland as 'The Clearances' peasants were forcibly evicted, dispossessed of food-producing land to dedicate vast areas to sheep for wool for the mills. Sometimes this cold-hearted capitalist push went too far and governments intervened to prevent wholesale revolution.

Between 1893 (New Zealand) and 1920 (America) after long and sometimes violent struggle against them, women got the right to vote, and suddenly hearth and home were on the agenda. Male-centred power moved into the world of commerce as its major base, where the values are clearly evident to this day. Just when national governments realised they should be curbing the power of big business, it went transnational (Carr-Harris 2011).

Modern capitalism

Modern industrial states are as dependent upon wealth from transnationals as any individual worker is. Research by Global Justice Now, reported in 2018, showed that corporations, not governments, now account for 157 of the world's 200 largest entities. The income of the US mega trader, Walmart, was higher than all but the top nine countries on the list. At this point the UN started to seek to hold transnational corporations responsible for human rights abuses around the world. However, Nick Dearden, who at the time of the report was Director of Global Justice Now, claimed that through trade and investment deals, it is corporations that are able to demand that governments do their bidding not the other way around.

Carr-Harris put forward the idea that as the concept of patriarchy gained traction, rulers realised that the key to power was to hold control over food. In the current day control over wages has the same effect, limiting access to the ability to acquire food. According to the Food and Agriculture Organization of the United Nations (2019) the world produces more than one and a half times enough to feed everyone on the planet. Yet in 2018, 820 million people did not have enough to eat. How can these two realities exist on the same planet? The chances of being food insecure are higher for women than men in every continent. In a matrifocal system resources would not be dealt with in this way – the needs of women and children would be placed above power and control, profit and capitalism.

As far back as 1995, the research analysis in *Women, Men, and the Global Quality of Life* (Eisler in Biaggi 2005) reported that in significant aspects the status of women can be a better indicator of general quality of life than Gross Domestic Product. It verifies a strong correlation between gender inequality (e.g. low female literacy rates, high maternal mortality, low female participation in government) and a generally lower quality of life for all. The report further found that when the prevalence of contraception increases, life expectancy overall in the society increases. Overpopulation does not benefit any of us.

Today people are alienated from the Earth, religions often emphasise escape from the world to another place and state of being – Heaven, Nirvana, Paradise. Women of course, are taught that they will find it harder to get there than men.

In First Nations cultures of Australia, you disturb nothing on the Earth and recognise the food that is given to collect from it. If you are alienated from the Earth you will have no reverence for it. Mining and agriculture are done without a sense of collaboration with the environment or First Nations custodians, and companies are not obliged to rejuvenate the places they have mined as they leave. Only the scars remain.

The expressions of patriarchy – attacks on women

In our everyday life we live in a patriarchal society. In that world our jobs, our politics, and our mainstream religions are mainly based on values recognised as masculine: domination, hierarchy and control. Different societies around the world differ in the degree to which this male dominance occurs. The tools used to enforce it are systems of beliefs, laws, discriminatory practices, and cultural norms (including direct or indirect male violence). Patriarchy places social, political, and economic power in the hands of men at the expense of women. In Australia one in two women report that they have experienced sexual harassment in their lifetime;

Ancient Ways for Current Days

one in three have experienced physical or sexual violence since the age of 15; one in five have experienced violence by a partner since the age of 15 (Australian Bureau of Statistics).

As I have mentioned earlier, women perpetuate culture, sometimes a subversive culture to patriarchy, to remember old, women-centred ways. But mostly such knowledge is lost, and the rules of the patriarchy are taught from mother to child – originally this would have been to ensure children would survive in a violent world. Relatively recent history of this includes the tradition of the 'foot-binding' of women in China. Although now ceased, there remain some surviving older women who suffered from it and live with the scars.

Here girls between the ages of two and four years had their feet bound by the older women, their toes forced under the foot, so that as they developed bones bent and broke, thus the women were hobbled. But the shape of their bound feet was regarded as beautiful lotus-buds and very sexually erotic to the male. Apparently, Qing dynasty pornographic books list 48 different ways of playing with a woman's bound feet. What they were really enjoying and celebrating was the excess of their power over women.

The bandages used were three metres (10 feet) long and only changed every couple of weeks, producing a highly unpleasant smell when unwound. To have 'golden lotus feet' was the passport to marriage into upper class families, so that by 1912, when it was first made illegal, 40–50 per cent of all women and 100 per cent of upper-class women had their feet bound. In some places the practice continued in secret. It was part of the enslavement of women, turning them into commodities, even though walking would forever be painful and difficult. They could certainly never run away.

The Battleground of the Female Body

In recent times the practice of genital mutilation of girls (Female Genital Mutilation or FGM) has served the same purpose. While it originates today in Islamic communities in Africa, it has spread to the Middle East and parts of South East Asia – 30 nations worldwide. It is now understood that it is not a requirement of Islam but originates in isolated traditions that have spread. Where the idea came from is unclear – mummies from ancient Egypt (500 BCE) with FGM have been found. It is recorded that female slaves in ancient Rome suffered FGM to deter unwanted pregnancies. As recently as the 1860s in England the practice was recommended as a cure for epilepsy to prevent masturbation. From that time, for 100 years in America, removal of the clitoral hood was regarded as a cure for women who were not enjoying sex with their husband. Under patriarchy the failure of a woman's pleasure could never be the male's responsibility!

What is Female Genital Mutilation (FGM)? In the current era girls aged five to nine, sometimes before age four and up to age 15, have been held down by the women of the clan and had their inner labia and clitoris sliced away. This is done by a midwife or trained woman, without the aid of anaesthesia, antibiotics or sterile equipment. In some cases the outer labia is then sewn across the vaginal opening so that the husband can be certain he is the first to sexually penetrate his young bride. When the time comes he will have to force entry, ripping the area open to gain access. The most extreme cases of FGM result in infertility – which of course will be blamed on the woman. It is estimated by the World Health Organisation that over 200 million girls and women alive today have undergone genital mutilation. This is in spite of the fact that 59 countries have passed laws against the behaviour.

Suffering for beauty is a concept familiar to most Western women as they slip into shoes that cause pain, or undergo painful and costly cosmetic treatments and surgery. Under patriarchy the social system is set up so that women are conditioned to think poorly of their own sex, themselves and other women. It happens every day that women criticise themselves, and each other: online for example, and through various social media, TV, streaming, books and magazines. There is a clear message about what weight you should be, that age is a disadvantage, what clothes you need to wear, what products to use on yourself, the attitudes and possessions you should have, how your face should look and surgery to reach an 'ideal'. Very little of this enhances a sense of self-worth or power in the world for women. What it does do is get women to cooperate in their own subordination, to feel unworthy and inferior.

This is the world created under a patriarchal system. Patriarchy is at the base not only of obsession with body image and of eating disorders, but misogyny, co-dependency, sexism, racism, homophobia, religious fundamentalism, alcoholism, addictions, wars, genocide, greed, pornography; violence against women, children, men of colour, lower classes; domestic violence, child abuse, rape, incest, crimes against humanity, false imprisonment, and many other abuses. The emergence of many of these is followed in Chapter 9.

Rape and murder

Young women (aged 15–19 years) are raped more frequently than any other age group but one, and that is children aged 0 to 14 years. Both statistics are shocking. In Australia, 98 per cent of sexual assaults are perpetrated by men, the highest offender rates being among those aged 15 to 19 years. For adults, most rapes are perpetrated by a man known to the woman. The effects at any age are wide-ranging and lifelong (Australian Institute of Health and Welfare 2020). It is a confronting reality that just being known by some men is enough for them to take the opportunity to sexually invade a woman. It would seem that the traditional Australian First Nations prohibition against young men having sex at all, while they learn how to be responsible men, is a wise precaution.

The economist, Jane Gleeson-White (2021) points out that 'one in every 130 women and girls on the planet – 29 million people – lives in modern slavery'. This is a term that includes forced labour, forced marriage, debt bondage, domestic servitude and human trafficking. This is only possible in the combination of patriarchy and capitalism – economics of 'systemic magnitude' played out on the female of the species.

On average in Australia one woman a week is murdered by her current or former partner (Bryant & Bricknall 2017). These occur primarily in the home (63% – Australian Bureau of Statistics) where a person should feel safe. Humphries reports that between 2000 and 2019 an estimated 1,038 Australian children were bereaved by domestic homicide, meaning that the child's mother was murdered. The term 'femicide' is being increasingly used and literally means murder of a female because she is female.

The Middle East and South Asia have higher rates of so-called 'honour killings' where women are killed by male family members because the woman is perceived (whether actual or assumed) to have committed a transgression, as the male social system defines it – usually sexual intercourse, adultery, or even being the victim of rape (which is seen as sex out of marriage). These are viewed as bringing 'shame' to the family, as can refusing an arranged marriage or seeking a divorce or separation. However, even simpler things like flirting or failure to serve a meal on time might also be seen as shameful. The United Nations Population Fund estimates that over 5,000 women are murdered as 'honour killings' annually worldwide (Singh and Dailey 2016).

Trying to stem the tide

Australia is now into its fourth National Plan (2010–2022) to reduce violence against women and their children (and is developing its fifth). The goal is for 'people in our community to learn that violence is not acceptable and that women have the right to feel safe', making improvements that 'will last for a long time'.

Enhanced outcomes for women are achieved with the support of increased numbers of women in parliaments. Research indicates that it reduces the likelihood of human rights abuse and conflict abuse. Increased female participation in peace processes makes peace deals more likely to be implemented and endure (Smith & Cockayne 2020). As of February 2019, of 190 countries considered, only three had at least 50 per cent of parliamentary seats filled by women (Inter-Parliamentary Union). These countries were Rwanda, Cuba and Bolivia. This group was joined by Australia in 2020 when the number of women in parliament reached 50 per cent. With such a skewed set of values towards the male perspective, represented in law-makers worldwide, it is little wonder that so much is spent on war and so little on the welfare of the people across the globe and the lack of laws created to protect women, which would be the focus of a matrifocal system.

Although we still live in a patriarchal society, in the last 150 years, women have battled for political, civil and legal rights and also managed to get religion to take a second look at the feminine role within the churches. In careers there is no doubt now that women can successfully undertake any roles that men can do, and on the flip side, this has opened some careers (e.g. nursing) to men, who previously would not have considered them.

In 2001, Adler (Pepperdine University) shocked the male establishment by findings tracked over 19 years of 200 Fortune 500 companies. This showed that the 25 firms that most actively promoted women into executive positions had 34 per cent higher profits as a share of revenue than the industry median. Following this, research conducted by Catalyst (Carter and Harvey 2011) showed that having three or more women on a company board produces consistently higher results for the company than those without, and their representation has been consistently rising.

However, Uribe-Bohorquez found that these 'successful' women tend to adopt stereotypical male values and behaviour. Excelling in the values of the patriarchy is, no doubt, one way for a woman on a company board to survive, and prove that she is as good as her male colleagues. It's understandable, but not too helpful for the direction of the world generally at this time.

We can still see that men are favoured for promotion – optimistically, the fact that we can see it is the point. We have now developed the analysis to tell us about these things and the commitment to call it out. Though women can now obtain tertiary qualifications, in the job market they are still paid less (in the U.S. women earn about 79% of the male wage). Though women comprise more than 50 per cent of the world's population, they only own 1 per cent of the world's wealth.

A woman's working life can be interrupted by child rearing, often followed by part-time work. In this circumstance, and on lower wages anyway, their opportunity to accumulate superannuation is reduced, compared to most men. Currently in Australia, the group most at risk of homelessness are women over 55 years, through lack of financial reserves, including superannuation. According to statistics released by the Association of Superannuation Funds in Australia, by age 60 to 64 a woman only has 58 per cent of the money that a man has in his superannuation.

Women and girls make up half of the world's population. Without their participation, we lose half our potential. Globally, women still have fewer opportunities for economic participation than men, less access to basic and higher education, greater health and safety risks, and less political representation. In Australia for every dollar earned by a woman, a man will earn 13.4 per cent more (Workplace Gender Equality Agency 2021).

Can we do better?

Some may say this is unbalanced as a picture of the outcome of patriarchy. Much has been achieved of benefit it is true; construction, huge medical advances, scientific research, the most recent being in information technology. Does such advance have to be at the expense of women, children, First Nations peoples and the natural world? Surely not?

In the early matrifocal cultures radical new technologies were invented, often by women, that included the creation of thread and woven goods, pottery, metallurgy, deep understanding of the nature of working with stone, astronomy, navigation. All sorts of arts developed starting with sculpture and with cave paintings showing a detailed appreciation of the animal world. Then came understanding of how to live together in larger groups, writing, theological exploration, city construction with sanitation.

The Battleground of the Female Body

Women's initial role as the gatherers brought them increasing understanding of the way that plants worked and what benefits or dangers different plants had. They pioneered medicine and worked out how to plant cereal crops and become farmers. Why would we not assume then, that knowledge and advances would have continued to occur under matrifocal cultures?

'Average figures from Europe, the United States and Australia have shown that men stand charged for between 80 and 90 per cent of all violent crimes.' (Breines et al. 2000). In Australia, 75 per cent of men breach an intervention order taken out by a former partner. They just won't leave the woman alone.

Matrifocal society provides physical safety for women and exposes the myth of the uncontrollable sexual urge of the male. Breines et al. for UNESCO states that men must become involved in building a culture of peace that does not include violence as part of the definition of masculinity. It would include to be caring, sharing, moderate, flexible and communicative. We need, they say, to develop an active disgust for war. To that end UNESCO proposes supporting women's initiatives for peace, promoting women's political participation, gender-sensitive socialisation and providing education, particularly for boys and men on non-violence and egalitarian partnership. You could say, a return to matrifocal values.

Brienes et al. also reports that 'in one of the more than 3,000 UNESCO's Associated Schools, in Tronso, Norway, the teachers decided to avoid reacting to negative behaviour and disturbances from the pupils and instead give feedback only to positive behaviour. After four years they report a changed school environment, more gender-sensitive and less violent'.

Ancient Ways for Current Days

It seems that men need the intention to change – why would a focus on women and children help, as in the matrifocal model? A Millennium Cohort Study commenced in the UK in 2001, tracked 13,000 married and cohabiting couples from nine months after the birth of their first child to the child's 14th birthday (and have just gone to the 17th). It discovered that a mother's happiness is nearly twice as crucial as a father's when it comes to keeping the family together. It also found a happy mother meant that the children would be less likely to develop mental health problems and more likely to enjoy stable relationships of their own in adulthood. Instead of control and domination of women, men should be focusing all their attention on having a happy relationship with their partner. The whole social structure should be focused on what will make the woman happy and fulfilled. Men and children then will be happy too.

The matrifocal model gives the lie to the idea that men are innately violent. For thousands of years, men appreciated living in a peaceful, matrifocal world. Modern research informs us that men can get as much pleasure from a new baby in the family as can women (Feldman 2010). Oxytocin is a hormone that produces warm, positive feelings and aids bonding. It is often associated with 'falling in love'. The study showed that while mothers and fathers interacted differently with a new baby, their release of oxytocin over the first six months, was similar for both.

The matrifocal model exposes the myth of the uncontrollable sexual urge of the male, discussed above. In matrifocal cultures men could and did engage in respectful and mutual sexual relationships with women. Matrifocality provided safety for women and satisfaction/fulfilment for men. Flexible 'marriage' arrangements meant that if a partnership was not working, then no-one was stuck in an unhappy situation. They could agree to part and move on.

The Battleground of the Female Body

All the appalling statistics of male violence and oppression of women represent the acts of the degraded masculine, the destructive masculine. We know that women increasingly alert us to the occurrence of these crimes against women, and to call out bad behaviour – as occurred in the #MeToo movement exposing the sexual assault of women by famous men. #MeToo broke the resounding silence surrounding the behaviour of men in influential positions in all areas of society. It exposed that the appearance of respectability can mask a depraved (patriarchal) male internal dialogue of the right to power over women – it is not just the product of poverty, drugs/alcohol, or mental illness or any of the other excuses.

It was courage that enabled the women who responded to the MeToo hashtag to speak up. They spoke from the whole heart, with fierceness, and the togetherness of women unified. The struggle for right treatment of women has been going on for a long time, at least 200 years. There is now some good support from men. We all know men who are not represented in these statistics. It is men who can and should now help each other return to a sense of self based on positive worth, constructive social contribution and respect for the female – both in themselves and as expressed in what they do and say in the world. Women will continue in their struggle, but they have been seeking that change alone long enough.

CHAPTER 9

What's Civilised?

Another world is not only possible, she is on her way.
Suzanna Arundhati Roy, author, political activist in human rights and environmental causes (1961 – present)

As groups of humans moved out of Africa, they would have found a place with ample foodstuffs to gather or capture; they would make a seasonal pathway across the landscape and back again in that area. If they prospered, some in the next generation or so might pack their few clothes, utensils and tools on their backs, and move on to explore again. At some point their wanderings through Palestine, Jericho and Lebanon and further north led them to the left or the right, the west or the east, decisions which, unbeknownst to them, had unimaginable ramifications for their descendants in the vast future of time.

Matrifocal flourishing on Crete

We have explored the matrilineal, Goddess-worshipping city of Çatalhöyük in Anatolia, in Turkey from the Neolithic period. When the people abandoned that site, they moved on to find new settled experiences. It is suspected that some of these were early inhabitants on the island of Crete around 5,500 BCE (Douka 2017). They came in family groups, mainly of women (Goldberg 2017). From these Neolithic origins, on this island arose the fabled Minoan culture, in the following Bronze Age (from approximately 3,200 BCE). The Minoan culture is regarded as at its height from c. 2700 to c. 1450 BCE until, after a late period of decline, it finally ended around 1100 BCE. These were cultures based on technologies that nourished people's lives, in contrast to the patriarchal focus on domination (Gimbutas 1975) that came after them.

The English archaeologist, Arthur Evans, famously excavated the site that was to reveal Knossos, the temple complex at the heart of this culture. He identifies sacred symbology of the upright wooden pole and stone columns, sacred stones and trees and the religious symbol of the double axe, as cult objects of the early Minoan mother goddess, whom the Greeks later called Rhea (Goettner-Abendroth 2012).

Double axe-shaped artefacts were made of soft material (e.g. thin-sheet bronze; soft stone) – not an item that could function as an axe. Gimbutas contends that the double axe shape was originally the hour-glass shaped Goddess of Death and Regeneration, and it is usually now interpreted as a butterfly regenerative symbol of the Goddess.

What's Civilised?

33a. Agia Triada sarcophagus decoration
Of limestone, it is the only known painted Minoan sarcophagus. Scenes of burial and sacrifice. This image is a procession of two priestesses with a priest playing a lyre, to make gifts at the altar which has a double axe (labyris or butterfly axe) standing either side. Approx. 1,400 BCE. Drawing: Kaye Moseley ©.

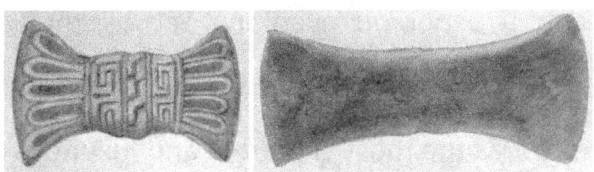

33b. & c. Miniature Double Axe or Labyris
Baked and painted clay. They are likely to have had a haft of some perishable material, like wood and may have been a votive offering, part of a home altar, or possibly worn around the neck like a charm. Drawing: Kaye Moseley ©.

The achievements of a Goddess culture

Major published academics accept that the female divinity had the highest place in Cretan Religion. As Goettner-Abendroth tells us, male gods did not yet exist, although the Goddess was shown at times with a (very small) young male companion – her partner, lover or son. Priestesses are shown centrally in depictions of rituals. Sometimes holding snakes, the priestess figures are always in the foreground (French 2008), with strong and healthy male attendants behind. Some have suggested that young Cretan men within this culture were required to serve for some time at the Temple community.

As an aside, snakes were always sacred in Goddess temples. They actually lived in the mother earth and their annual shedding of skin was a symbol of regeneration. It should be no surprise then that in the Bible it was a snake in the Garden of Eden that offered a woman knowledge (symbolised by the apple). It was knowledge which was her historical birthright, from the Mother Goddess. When she accepted, it made the patriarchal god Yahweh furious, because it challenged his supremacy. Without women's knowledge to assist women in childbirth, childbirth of course became the painful and more dangerous event that Yahweh threatened that it would. But I digress.

Minoan Crete was the most elaborate and luxurious Neolithic-based society (continuing through to the Early Bronze Age) found so far (French 2008), with infrastructure that included paved roads (a first), lookout posts and roadside shelters, aqueducts, sanitary and drainage systems. Then there were dockyards that supported a massive network of trade. They built temples, including using sacred caves and mountain-top shrines. The Minoans built light-filled architecture. Confronting the demands of living in an

What's Civilised?

34. Minoan Snake Goddess
Original artefact was multi-coloured and had the head missing and half her left arm. In the reconstructed version (29.5 cm/11.5 in high) the head, hat and cat were added, though the cat and 'hat' were found elsewhere in the area. Priestesses were known to work with snakes, which lived in the Earth and were seen as messengers from the Goddess. Minoan Crete 1,600 BCE. Drawing: Kaye Moseley ©.

earthquake-prone area, their use of wooden beams and columns was both attractive, and probably designed to make buildings more earthquake resistant (Jusseret and Sintubin 2017).

They buried their dead in communal graves, called 'tholos' tombs, with no distinguishing feature of hierarchy or rank. It has been estimated that in one tomb in Kamilari, 400 to 500 people may have been buried over time. The tombs were shaped like a womb and faced the east – the rising sun of new life and rebirth.

The people of ancient Crete developed an exquisite form of art celebrating life which was displayed in their pottery, weaving, metallurgy, engraving and frescoes. Gimbutas says the images are 'full of life-affirming grace'. Colourful murals have been found, which can be on walls, floors or ceilings that depict all sorts of land and sea creatures, plants, and human undertakings such as ceremonies, daily life, celebrations and activities, including the athletic young women and men bull-leaping.

Life in a Minoan town

> Imagine, if you will, a Minoan township. You wander in through sometimes meandering streets, the houses on either side rise up as mudbrick or stone walls (depending on local availability) to two or three stories. Occasionally the space opens up into a plaza, not vast, but a crowd could gather there. Some children run by with shaved heads, with certain ringlets left to grow long – once initiated into adulthood both women and men grow their hair long, curling in locks down their backs. In one building there is a low opening – a kind of servery, and some citizens are queuing. It seems that they are receiving their allotment of the communal goods, one gets flour, one beer, another clothing. If you followed

What's Civilised?

35. Minoan Crete Bull-leapers fresco
Fresco from the east wing of the Palace of Knossos (reconstructed). 78 cm (30.7 in) high. A woman at the front may be about to leap, a man is vaulting on the back of the bull and the woman at the rear steadies to land and/or to assist the vaulter to do so. Background is blue, the bull is brown and white. Approximately 1,400 BCE. Drawing: Kaye Moseley ©.

one such person when she or he departed, the person may arrive at a complex of rooms, one of which is clearly hers/his. There is a communal kitchen area, and here those in this community share meals.

But our Minoan doesn't stay long; there is a ritual soon in another square that is a special event. We follow and arrive there to see a procession and hear music, perhaps of a lyre, sistrum and recorder-like instruments, as a priestess and a priest arrive at a ritual house, followed by others required in the ritual.

*36. Minoan Goddess and Procession of adorants
Fresco (reconstructed) where young men in devotional pose face the
Goddess figure in the centre, followed by others carrying gifts/offerings
to the Goddess. 1,700–1,400 BCE. Drawing: Kaye Moseley ©.*

Like all Cretan women, the fully naked breasts of the priestesses celebrate the life-giving nurturance of the Goddess and illustrate their special connection to her. Some uninitiated young men wearing loincloths and initiated men wearing 'kilts', are carrying offerings.

The procession moves inside and up the stairs to the ritual chamber on the first floor. This room has a large window opening onto the square and those below could readily observe some of the action in the chamber, and hear words and music from the sacred event. Often a meal will be involved in the shrine rooms for those participating in the ritual.

Were we present at other times, we may witness festivals, such as the celebration of seafaring, with Minoan boats arriving in the harbour festively decorated with flags and the passengers wearing colourful clothing.

In spring, villagers would make the pilgrimage up to the regional Peak Shrine (seven of these have been found) on a mountaintop.

What's Civilised?

They would bring flowers (such as crocuses – which produce saffron) to the Goddess there, and a large feast, with a bonfire, and ritual would be held, with singing and dancing. They may also bring and leave small clay representations of body parts, for which they sought medical aid from the Goddess. The villagers return home the next morning.

Among the festivals was also the bull-leaping festival where the crowds would cheer as young women and men took turns. An athlete would run at the bull, grasp its horns and as it tossed its head, somersault onto its back and flip over down to the ground behind, where a teammate waited to support the leaper to safely land. Meanwhile another leaper held the horns of the bull. Some have suggested that these bulls must have been trained to work with the athletes – or maybe not.

As in Çatalhöyük, the bull and its horns symbolised the Goddess. On the larger Minoan buildings a u-shaped, stylised set of 'horns of consecration' (named by Arthur Evans), would have been found. Larger ones may well lead the eye to view a sacred item in the landscape, as at Knossos where one frames the Peak Shrine of Mount Juktas. At temples and shrines, libations (liquid offerings) and other gifts to the Goddess were poured or left before the horns.

Rituals and festivities relate to the season; there is one lovely rhyton vase (black steatite, 1500–1450 BCE) with a carved scene of men marching carrying their harvesting implements over their shoulders. They are happy and their mouths are open as they sing a harvest celebration song, accompanied by a sistrum – a percussion instrument associated with religious festivals. The scene displays the grace and vitality typical of Minoan art. This vase also tells us that farming work was done communally, not individually, a feature of a matrifocal culture.

Ancient Ways for Current Days

37. Horns of Consecration
Reconstruction at Knossos, Crete (2.2 m/7.2 ft tall, 2 m/6.6 ft wide). The horns symbol is found throughout Minoan culture e.g. lining the roofs of buildings, and is thought to represent the sacred bull. Here, Mt. Juktas, where there is a Peak Shrine, is framed between the horns, now obscured by the trees that have grown up. The bull was sacred to the Goddess and to the Minoans, who also practised bull-leaping sports. Drawing: Kaye Moseley ©.

Another communal activity on Crete was the circle dance – a group of four clay figurines from late in the Minoan period depicts women holding each other's arms at the elbow dancing as another plays the lyre. Professor Mara Keller recounts her modern experience of such dancing on Crete, where she felt 'the exhilaration and thrill of the dance, the flowing power of the repeated rhythms … as one's very being transforms, trancelike, enchanted … body and spirit slip and soar over the edge of everyday reality into ecstasy'.

The life of the natural world in its seasons is recalled often in temple rooms decorated with friezes. Colour, movement, plants, birds and

What's Civilised?

38. Harvester Vase
The harvesters sing loudly together to the rhythm of a sistrum as they travel between fields and home. The 27 men carry their implements, which may be olive harvesting poles. Found near Phaistos at Agia Triada, in a substantial home in the south of Crete. Minoan, black steatite (i.e. soapstone) vase or rhyton (drinking container), 11.3 cm/4.5 in diameter. 1,450 BCE. Drawing: Kaye Moseley ©.

animals in action, abound. The Minoans celebrate life and situate their Goddess in an abundant natural world. Priestesses adorn themselves and become living representations of the Goddess on Earth (Gadon 1989; Keller 1998). There is a joyful and unashamed appreciation of life, the body and the natural world.

People obviously feel safe in their island existence, relying on their extensive fleet to protect them. There are sailors and warriors but they are not the central feature of art and expression; the spiritual world is. There is no adulation of a particular figure such as a pharaoh or king, as occurs in patriarchal cultures, where

Ancient Ways for Current Days

39. Swallows and Lilies fresco
From Akrotiri – a Minoan influenced settlement on the west coast of Santorini (or Thera), facing Crete. Green-blue rock hillocks sport vibrant lilies in deep red shades that seem to bend in a breeze. The swallows are black. Part of a composition that covers three walls as a backdrop to ritual action. It depicts the reawakening of nature in spring. Drawing: Kaye Moseley ©.

nature is stiff and diminutive compared to conquest, killing and the dominant male.

A temple community

Cretan society was based upon a temple community ethos. The so-called 'palaces' were sacred and administrative centres. Gimbutas points out that there are two distinct areas at Knossos: the west and east temples. The west contains what Gimbutas calls 'crypt-shrines'. These are small, dark, pillared spaces – 'womb-like' according to Gimbutas. They were for ritual, where offerings of grain and animals were made and precious sacred items stored.

What's Civilised?

The ritual, she tells us, was about regeneration – from death, or winter – rising earth energy, and seasonal rites of renewal. Over time, imagery shows that a young male god developed, as a vegetation god. He died annually, as the vegetation did over winter.

In the eastern section of the Knossos precinct, in contrast, there are no basements or darkness – here it is all 'light and gaiety and extravagant colour'. Here Gimbutas believes was celebrated birth and life. Writer, activist and educator Carol Christ further suggests 'that gratitude for the gift and gifts of life was not only a focus, but a central focus, of religion in ancient Crete'. Gimbutas reports that a giant wooden statue of the Goddess measuring about 3 metres tall and adorned with bronze locks of hair stood in the great East Hall, where she was worshipped in her life-giving aspect.

These sacred centres included reception halls, meeting rooms, a plaza for sports and festivities and extensive storage, especially of food. This food storage may have been to support the crowds attending the large festivals held there, or as a base for distribution. If this were a palace, you would expect grand private apartments but it is disputed whether there were any residential rooms. If there were, they were small suites.

There is one beautifully decorated room at Knossos that has a special chair built into the long wall; on either side of it, painted on the wall, a large recumbent griffon faces this seat. This is called the 'Throne-room', a description that disregards that there is also a bench running around the room for other people to sit upon. Such a configuration is much more representative of a think-tank room, a room of group discussion, than a royal audience chamber. No doubt the head priestess did use the 'throne', and her inner group of priestesses and other advisors probably sat around with her, to discuss the issues at hand in managing the Cretan world.

Ancient Ways for Current Days

Interestingly, a contemporaneous culture which also had women as leaders, similarly had an elaborate building with a room that has been dubbed the 'parliament' by the archaeologists there, with benches for 50. Buried in the centre of this room under the floor was a woman adorned with jewellery and a silver diadem with a central disk, worn across the brow and downwards to cover the nose. This is the Argaric culture that flourished between 2,200 and 1,500 BCE in South-Eastern Spain (Metcalfe 2021). They used bronze long before neighbouring tribes and the women had a strong role in the economy through their work in metallurgy, linen and wool textiles.

The culture of Minoan Crete was originally based on an egalitarian matrilineal clan structure (French 2008; Gimbutas 1974, 1999), but over time social stratification did occur. A noble class based on religious function developed, but respect for all trades and roles existed, and there is no evidence of poor living conditions. In the township of Gournia neat rows of stone houses of one or two storeys had flat roofs for residents to seek the cool night air after the heat of the day, as well as for viewing public events below. Clearly not all people would have lived with the kind of elegance portrayed in the larger homes. Walls there might be lined with marble or with plaster which was often painted with frescoes.

The main city was Knossos which covered an area of about 80 hectares (200 acres), and had about 100,000 residents. The sacred centre itself was so large, with interlinked rooms, several levels and joining passages, that it would have been very confusing to visitors accustomed to the simpler architectural designs of the times. The double axe adornment was everywhere, it was called a labyris, so that the place was known as the Labyrinth of Knossos. It entered mythology as a place only the bravest could enter, find their way and return unscathed (as in the Greek tale of the patriarchal hero Theseus, and Cretan priestess Ariadne).

What's Civilised?

40. 'Palace' at Knossos as labyrinth
This section of the complex at Knossos has been reconstructed at the site and illustrates the interplay of stairs, light wells, passageways in the expansive building. May indicate why outsiders said there was a 'labyrinth' there that you could get lost in. 2,000–1,100 BCE. Drawing: Kaye Moseley ©.

Depictions of women show them in many occupations – farmers, merchants, chariot-drivers, dancers and hunters. They are portrayed as strong and capable. Some tombs of women contain expensive items – jewellery, gold, copper artefacts, precious stones; no male equivalent has been found. Unlike women living under the more patriarchal territories in Greece, women on Crete lived longer than men.

All this indicates a culture with huge respect for women, and as Platon (in Foster 2013) claims, ' ... women and men appear together in Minoan art ... as partners in relationship' citing the shared bull-leaping as one example. Men are engaged in all aspects of life, as are the women. If anything, the male is an idealised form in much of Minoan art, manhood expressed particularly in athletics, hunting and seamanship.

Nevertheless, people were not constrained by their sex in their life-choices. In the Minoan frescoes, women were painted white, men brown. So it is clear that some women were bull-leapers and wore male attire to do it; some men were religious personnel and wore long dresses like the priestesses to do that. As in many matrifocal cultures, in Crete the task was gendered not sexualised. The rich, stratified, female-centred Cretan world that developed, seems to have evolved while retaining the old values of sharing, peace, pleasure, nature and sex (French 2008).

The creeping influence of patriarchy

As time passed, Crete was in contact with a wide range of people through their trading activities; for example, Egyptian influences in some paintings can be seen and Minoan in some Egyptian work (Marinatos 1984). The world around them, as we will explore in later chapters, was becoming increasingly patriarchal, through the influence of the 'Indo- Europeans', and the Cretan culture was not immune to these more patriarchal influences. Over time, role divisions between the sexes began to emerge – women to the domestic and religious domains, men to the outer world of soldiers, farmers and metal workers (French 2008). Even so, these are divisions seen commonly in matrifocal cultures.

What's Civilised?

41. Minoan-Mycenaean Poppy Goddess
Approximately 1,350 BCE, when the Mycenaeans from Greece dominated Crete. Gimbutas calls this terracotta figure 'the rising young Earth Mother'. She wears a conical hat with three removable opium poppy seed-heads at the front. Opium may have had a ritual or health purpose; the seeds could be a symbol of fertility. (79.5 cm/ 31 in, in height). From Gazi, Crete. Drawing: Kaye Moseley ©.

Around 1,450 BCE the Minoan culture, at its height, faced several disasters, from which it was unable to recover. There was an earthquake and possibly tsunami, perhaps caused by the volcanic eruption of the nearby island of Thera (Santorini). It has been suggested that the Minoan fleet in the harbour was smashed to pieces by the tidal wave that would have resulted.

While the Minoan society was reeling from the damage, the patriarchal Mycenaeans moved in from Greece. Using fire, they destroyed every 'palace' on the island and established themselves at Knossos. Ironically, in the prior centuries, the Mycenaeans had already adopted almost all of their artistic and religious forms from the Cretans (Hawkes 1979). Artistic works on Crete, such as pottery, became more stylised and less vibrant. Boar-tusk helmets from Mycenae were introduced and battle imagery appeared. Individual burials become more common. Residences, presumed for the royal family, were added to the Knossos complex. The Priestess-Queen was replaced by the King. As in Egypt though, the King was only legitimised by taking the High Priestess of the land (in Egypt at least, usually his sister) as his wife (Goettner-Abendroth 2012).

After about a century of partial recovery, decline set in, with Knossos surviving as some sort of administrative centre until about 1,100 BCE. Possibly the highest expression of matrifocal culture in Europe disappeared with the Minoan culture, and only pockets of mother-centred societies persisted, surrounded by patriarchy.

Crete, however, was not the only centre of a highly-evolved expression of matrifocal culture. At about the same time, far, far away …

Flourishing matrilineal culture in ancient India

We have been following the action for the Near East and Europe. But what happened for those who went east and passed through ancient Iraq? Crossing through land that later became

What's Civilised?

Mesopotamia, where the Sumerian civilisation would one day flourish, and on into India? Did the Goddess religion go with them? Could they maintain the egalitarian social system that excluded war and bloodshed?

Across the deserts and arid plateaus of Iran and Afghanistan, these groups stayed in the foothills. They found small valleys of fertile growth and over generations continued their passage east, until they came across the lush river valleys of the Indus River and its tributaries (Northern India and Pakistan). By 10,000 BCE we find sickles for harvesting and, on a rubble-built platform, is a triangular coloured stone. The triangle has long been accepted as a symbol of the Goddess – her pubic triangle from whence new life emerges. They brought the Goddess with them.

By 7,000 BCE the first farmers had arrived. They planted the grain they had brought with them that is native to Turkey, Iraq and Iran. At a place now called Mehrgarh (in modern Pakistan), and soon in other places, they flourished. Over time they domesticated animals and castrated oxen to turn them into draft animals. They developed their own wheeled carts to harness them to. The monsoons brought floods and they learned to tame and manage these as a watering system, to their advantage. They grew grains, fruits (like dates and melons), and green vegetables; kept chickens and other domesticated animals, and went fishing; and developed various meals, including curries (Shinde 2016).

There were no apparent hierarchies or leaders or weapons. They had large granaries to store the surplus produced, which they probably shared by communal agreement, led by the women, as is the custom in matrifocal cultures. Their village became a town, then a city. Then some new cities were started in new locations, at previously unbuilt-upon places, utilising their best thinking for a practical, clean and functional place to live to accommodate large numbers of people. Indian tradition has it that villages organised by clan councils were linked to central cities (French 2008). As we have seen elsewhere, clan councils are collective events, usually led by the oldest woman and/or her brother.

42. Indus Goddess figurine, Harappa
Terracotta statuette, 5 cm tall. Heavy jewellery up the neck and hanging in long rows to the waist. Such a necklace was recovered from Mohenjo-Daro with seven strands. A hip belt holds up a short skirt. Wears a high headdress (broken). Some figures like this were accentuated with black or white pigment, others were completely painted. Such figures are still made in some places in India today. 2,600–1,900 BCE. Drawing: Kaye Moseley ©.

What's Civilised?

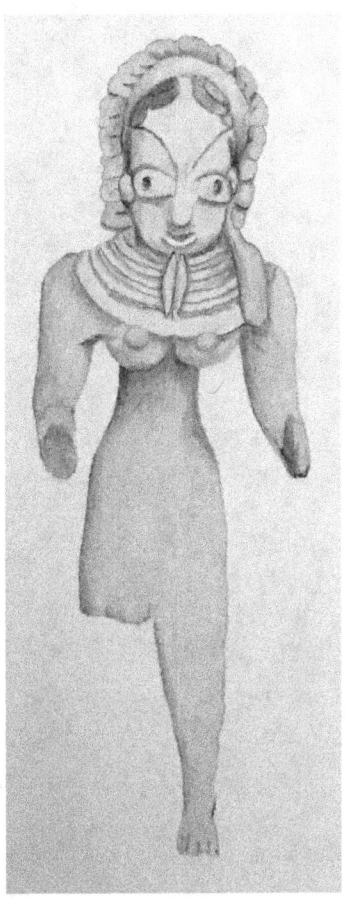

43. *Indus Goddess figurine, Mohenjo-Daro*
This standing sculpture wears black hair in large rings, topped by a yellow (gold?) 'crown'. A heavy red neckpiece of eight rings and two vertical bands of 'gold' down the middle front, comes up to the chin and down to the nipple-line. She may also wear a red bracelet and is otherwise naked. Approximately 2,700 BCE. Drawing: Kaye Moseley ©.

In the remains of the city at Mehrgarh (and then later in the other Indus valley cities) the ubiquitous female figurines have been found again. About 13 to 18 centimetres high (5 to 7 in), with prominent naked breasts, these fascinating versions from India, often feature elaborate hairstyles and necklaces. These images appear to have

Ancient Ways for Current Days

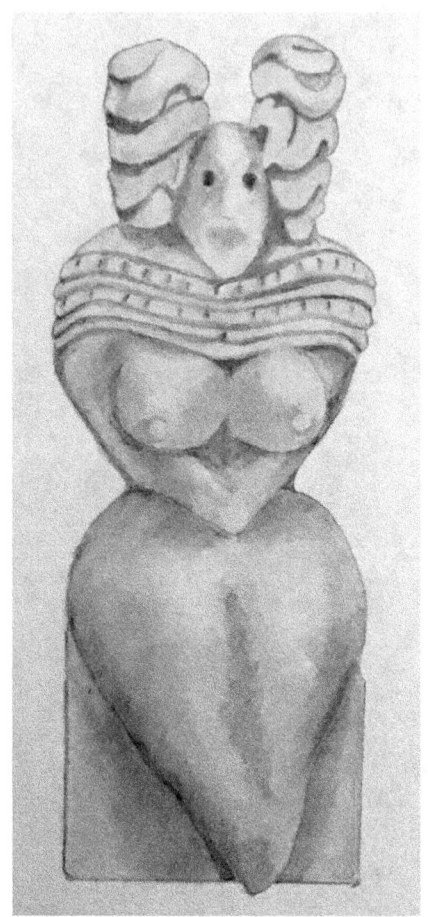

44. Indus Seated Goddess, Mehrgarh
A terracotta figurine (9.5 cm / 3.75 in) which was probably painted in brown ochre. Abundant hips and breasts suggest links to her gifts of fertility. Five rows of heavy necklaces (probably yellow) cover the upper arms and chest. Her once-black hair is in an elaborate hairstyle, typical of statuettes in the region. 3,000 BCE. Drawing: Kaye Moseley ©.

been made for a temporary ritual purpose and then discarded (Ratnagar 2018); some have cups on the sides of the head-dress where oil may have been burned.

What's Civilised?

Women, Goddess and communities of peace

It appears then, that these people continued worship of the Mother Goddess – the artefacts, in particular delicately decorated steatite seals, depict women, bulls and other animals, fertility symbols, geometric patterns and figures in a difficult yogic position (in modern times called the Moolabhandasana or Root Lock Pose). In particular, there is an intriguing Goddess shown with tigers, and as a part tiger. The images and seals are kept in the homes, there is no temple complex. Pots with food buried in graves indicate a belief in an afterlife. The very earliest elements of Hinduism were probably in place in the Indus River valley.

45. Woman who dances with tigers moulded tablet
A Goddess holds a ferocious tiger upright with each hand, or holds them apart, above an elephant. Above her head is a symbol from the Indus script, of a spoked wheel. Harappa. Terracotta, 3.91 cm/1.5 in long, 1.62 cm/0.64 in wide. 2,600–2,400 BCE. Drawing: Kaye Moseley ©.

Ancient Ways for Current Days

46. Seal of Goddess with upright tigers
This repeats the theme of Goddess and tigers (Fig 45) that may represent a story known to the people of the time. Perhaps a 'Mistress of Animals' theme. A number of script symbols are above. Seals are about 3.3 cm square, usually of steatite and seem to have been used in commerce. Harappa. 2,500–1,500 BCE. Drawing: Kaye Moseley ©.

47. Seal of Goddess and beast
A ferocious mythical creature turns fiercely to the Goddess figure under a tree, who reaches to the animal with her right arm and seems to be attacking using her bull horns. The creature has upright feathered antlers, a striped tiger body, a tail, sharp claws and with teeth bared. The Goddess is part animal, with tail and horns and appears to have cloven feet. Four script symbols are above. Mohenjo-Daro. 2,500–2,000 BCE. Drawing: Kaye Moseley ©.

What's Civilised?

Studies of burial sites at Mohenjo-Daro and Harappa (Harappa Archaeology Research Project) have shown that a man was often buried with his wife's family. This indicates the matrifocal tradition of a man moving in with his wife's family, rather than the woman going to his. Supportive of this are DNA studies indicating that most women were local while the men arrived from outside the Indus Culture (Robbins Schug 2019).

At the Harappan burial site at Rakhigarhi there were special brick-lined graves where each of the individuals in the graves were women. The archaeologists there stated the grave evidence showed 'the status of women in Harappan society was high' (Shinde 2016). These factors, plus the female figurines of Harappa, Mohenjo-Daro and Mehrgarh, point to the important role of women in the social system. The culture was matrifocal and remained so throughout its long history.

The Indus Valley people had woven cotton and wool cloth and eventually, even silk, locally produced. Handcrafts included jewellery, children's toys, dice and board games, stringed musical instruments, sculpture, painted pottery, writing, and metallurgy (bronze, copper, gold). They produced and exported wooden furniture, inlaid with bone, shell and ivory patterns. They created fine pottery, in plain red or with a rich variety of simple patterns in black. Commerce and construction benefitted by the use of standardised weights and measures. All of these are markers of a sophisticated lifestyle. What the culture did not have were weapons (other than hunting tools), representations of great leaders, or of warfare.

Mehrgarh shows us the beginning of the Indus Valley culture that existed peacefully for about 2,000 years (3,300–1,300 BCE), and grew to over 1,400 towns and cities, that have so far been identified. Estimates

Ancient Ways for Current Days

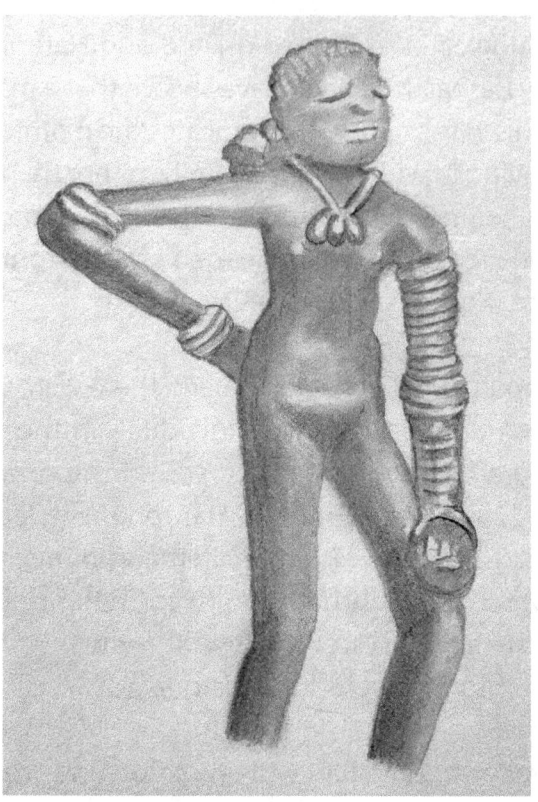

48. Bronze statuette of a girl.
Usually referred to as a 'dancing girl'. She stands in a relaxed, confident pose, clad only in bracelets (25 on the left arm, four on the right), and a necklace with three pendants. Her heavy hair is in a loose bun twisted in a spiral fashion pinned to the back of her head, and sweeps from the left back down to the right shoulder. Right hand on her hip, the left is on her thigh and once held something. She has a sense of personal autonomy and self-respect. Bronze, using the lost-wax technique. 10.8 cm/4.25 in tall x 5 cm/2 in. Mohenjo-Daro. 2,300–1,750 BCE. Drawing: Kaye Moseley ©.

of the total population vary from one to five million people. At its height, the Indus Valley culture stretched for more than 1.5 million square kilometres (1 million sq. mi) across the plains of the Indus River from the Arabian Sea to the Ganges, over what is now Pakistan, northwest India and eastern Afghanistan. This is an area larger than ancient Mesopotamia and Egypt combined (Flood 2019).

What's Civilised?

Sophisticated cities and international trade

Harappa, Mohenjo-Daro and Rakhigarhi, the main cities, were laid out on a grid pattern with large main thoroughfares where two elephants could pass between the tall blank brick walls of the buildings. Such planning was unknown in other contemporary cities (in Mesopotamia or Egypt). Early Harappa had high walls to protect from floodwaters. The solidly built fired-mudbrick houses, up to three stories high, were built

49. Mohenjo-Daro archaeological excavation
Taken from a rooftop level, before the viewer is part of the ancient city of Mohenjo-Daro, UNESCO World Heritage site. It is similar to the site of Harappa. The roofs were flat and used by the residents in daily living. Just over the parapet is one of the straight long paved roads of the city, where the typical high blank walls show patterned brickwork. Other homes and rooms are beyond with inner courtyards where a door would open onto side lanes. Built on a planned grid-pattern layout, around 12,500 BCE, in a central position between two rivers in Pakistan. 300 hectares, at its peak Mohenjo-Daro is estimated to have had a population around 40,000. Photo: ALexelA / Shutterstock.com.

around a courtyard with an entrance that blocked the view of the interior. Homes had bathrooms and a water supply and the world's first known sanitation system. There were dams constructed and wells placed throughout the town, one for each city block of houses. On the streets, there were communal bins for non-liquid waste, which historians have presumed was collected and taken outside the city.

The town plans included markets and large grain storage facilities. The area lies at the confluence of two major weather systems so that it benefitted from two rainy seasons, one in summer, one in winter. Thus they could have two crops a year – with winter crops like wheat, barley and some pulses, plus summer crops like rice, millets and tropical pulses. No doubt they could use this variety within the internal trade system.

The city of Mohenjo-Daro included what is now called 'The Great Bath', that appears to have been a large square pool for citizens to use in ritual cleansing. The city had paved stone streets and megaliths along the roads into the city. The Indus cities would each have held 35,000 to 40,000 people.

These people were gradually joined by others from Iran and the Middle East, diversifying their genetic base and cultural inputs. It was a quite multicultural place (Robbins Shugg 2019). Eventually, with the development of boats made of planks and with a mast and sail, and impressive dockyards, the civilisation was trading back into Mesopotamia, to Sumer and Akkad on the banks of the Tigris and Euphrates Rivers. They traded for raw metals from Oman and there is some evidence of trade contact as far away as Crete and Egypt. This vibrant economy underpinned prosperity of the citizens of the Indus Valley. Between 4,000 and 3,000 BCE the Indus Valley civilisation was developing a script

What's Civilised?

(as yet undeciphered), just as the Sumerians did slightly later (around 3,200 BCE).

Like most Neolithic matrifocal cultures, the Indus culture shows no evidence of kings or armies, and similarity of living conditions indicates it was egalitarian. As in Crete there is some evidence of social stratification – it is possible that geographically there was an upper and lower part of the cities that may reflect social stratification. There must have been a process of decision-making and agreement in place to produce the uniformity of measurement and grid design of streets. With no evidence of a single leader we are left to consider a very different, shared but consensual approach to group decisions – in the matrifocal tradition. The cities may have operated as centres where decisions for the communities were proposed or ratified. As Dr Vasant Shinde (2016) explains:

> The available evidence indicates that they were getting a lot of wealth from the West through international trade. This wealth was used by the Harappans very practically and wisely to create world class cities and basic amenities for all classes of people in the society. Probably they thought that creation of monumental architecture or burying huge wealth along with dead bodies could be wastage of the resources as they were not beneficial to the society. They use this wealth or prosperity for sustainable development not only within cities and towns but all over the Harappan region. It also enables them to create some sort of uniform culture over a vast territory.

In this context, the common use of seals is likely to represent a tool for commerce (Shinde 2016) while also honouring the spiritual in the symbols and images used on them. With no temple spaces and small figurines, especially of women/Goddesses found in the homes, and spiritual figures painted on the pottery, it is likely that the spiritual was very integrated into life in general (Shinde 2016). Robbins Shugg suggested, 'the entirety of the city was a space for ritual'. The archaeological digs display wide differences in burial practice (Robbins Shugg 2019) that would indicate that people were attracted to come to live there by the certainty and prosperity of the non-militaristic Indus world, where they were also free to retain their own beliefs and personal religious practices.

Patriarchal influence arrives

Images on seals seem to indicate that dancing, singing, storytelling and sharing forms of wine were among the pastimes of Indus people. Dogs and cats were kept as pets. Burial sites of women held more (though modest) grave goods than those of men. However, by about 1800 BCE in an Indus town called Sanauli there is a large burial that includes two chariots of wood and copper – usually representative of an implement of aggression/warfare. Perhaps things were beginning to change. Then the arrival of a large migration of Indo-Europeans from Iran, around 1,500 BCE, marked the beginning of the destruction of the female principle in the Indus.

These invaders called themselves 'Aryan' probably meaning 'nobleman'. They were nomadic cattle-herders, with a good knowledge of astronomy and mathematics. Flood postulates that they were from a mining tradition, giving them better understanding of metals than the Indus peoples. According to Basham their daggers were stronger than those of the Indus Valley people, having a central rib to reinforce them.

What's Civilised?

50. Statuette of a bearded man, torso
Later called 'Priest King' this man may once have been seated. His hair and short chin-beard are neatly combed and he has a disk emblem tied to his forehead and a smaller one on the right upper arm. The ties of the headpiece fall neatly at the back of his head. He wears a wrap-around garment that falls across the left shoulder, and is covered in circle and trefoil designs, once filled with red paint. His deep narrowed eyes, which would have been inset in shell or stone, and downturned mouth, make him appear rather severe or superior. 17.5 cm/6.9 in high x 11 cm/4.3 in wide. Statue in white low-fired steatite (soapstone), Mohenjo-daro, late Mature Harappan period, 2,200–1,900 BCE. Drawing: Kaye Moseley ©.

Male figurines began to become more numerous, Goddess figurines less so. Hinduism originated in India from the Vedic religion of the Aryans. It is a patriarchal religion that supports a caste system where Brahmins are at the top. A genetic study (Narasimhan et al. 2019) has proven that the Indo-European ancestry in the area today is primarily from males and is disproportionally high in the Brahmin caste.

Was this an invasion? Perhaps. The local people may have adapted to develop warrior capacity in response. If the Indo-European arrival was not a military one, it was certainly a cultural one. The Indo-Europeans met with a society more advanced than their own, and adopted aspects of the Indus Culture, but they also kept their own belief and social systems. Groups of mainly men (Silva 2017) led ox-drawn covered wagons with families inside them. Potentially there were five to fourteen more men to every woman with these groups (Goldberg 2017). These men were on, or with horses (Flood 2019), an animal previously unknown in the Indus Valley. Horses were quite small at the time. The Indo-Europeans also had the chariot – a vehicle with two solid wheels and drawn by two horses (Flood 2019) or bullocks. They believed in their superiority and right to rule, and bred within their cohort as much as possible – hence the gene transmission mentioned above.

Deterioration and the climate changes

It seems most likely that the Indus culture was already in decline when the Indo-Europeans arrived (from about 1,800 BCE), due to a drying event that affected Europe as well (Flood 2019). There was a major drought in about 2,200 BCE. With this climate change came reducing monsoonal rain, increasing soil salinity, the land drying into desert, and earthquakes. Earthquake was the probable cause of a change in the course of a major tributary river to the Indus Valley system, causing the river in the east of the system to dry up; and there may have been a destructive monsoonal flood. Leprosy appears for the first time in the archaeological record and possibly tuberculosis.

Over a period of about 200 years the vast international trade network set up from the Indus Valley fell apart. Around 1,900 BCE the seals used in commerce disappear. These catastrophic events had disrupted the trade routes that underpinned the prosperity of the culture. It is a symptom of social disintegration, a loss of faith in the economy that had served so well until then, and nothing the matrifocal system could do could stop it.

Without adequate water, there was not adequate food, the variety in the diet diminished, and the towns could not survive. At the end of the period the incidence of cranial trauma (being hit on the head) increases to 50 per cent of all skeletons found. The ancient tradition in such times was for the family matriarch to lead the clan in search of another safe place to live.

It appears there was indeed a movement of people (Narasimhan 2019) from here both north to the Ganges, or migrating in ships south to Kerala, also in India (Goettner-Abendroth 2012), where a matrifocal culture survived into modern times (Kurup 2014). Everything that remains today in India of this pre-patriarchal society is called 'Dravidian'. These people were all placed in the caste system by the invading Aryan Brahmins as low caste (Reich 2020).

Matrifocal 'Commonwealths' and patriarchal 'civilisations'

The Indus culture was the last matrifocal example we have from ancient times in a city format. Its social conditions were comparable to early Sumer, and superior to the contemporary Babylon and Egypt (Violatti 2018). Haarmann (in Biaggi 2005) proposes that this form of state should be called a 'commonwealth' (or an 'oecumene'). He applies this term to Çatalhöyük, Halaf and the Indus culture (as well as in Europe, to the Danube society).

Different from the stratified model of states, this model offers equality of the sexes, little to no class distinctions, shared authority and overall egalitarianism. These are aspects of a matrifocal culture (Goettner-Abendroth 2012). Haarmann states that 'in these cultures, egalitarianism evolved through lively trade relationships of villages that exchanged goods among themselves or with towns'. The villages adopted positive aspects of the prevailing culture for example, standardised weights and measures, but basically managed their own affairs, ensuring equitably shared resources (the common wealth).

Dr Vasant Shinde claims the Indus culture contributed much to world history. He calls the Indus society the first empire in South Asia, which probably represents the result of the 'oecumene' model discussed above. The Indus people used a scientific basis for construction in the uniform ratio of brick sizes and pattern of one row of bricks placed horizontally alternating with one placed vertically; the 'outstanding' drainage feature of the cities; pioneering water management and water harvesting for both agriculture and domestic uses; the dockyard at Lothal; the earliest silk production in Eurasia; the trade strategy of obtaining raw materials and then trading finished articles back to these suppliers;

What's Civilised?

a new subsistence strategy of two agricultural zones of multi-crops with two annual harvests; and pioneering basic technology to enhance their craft work (pottery, metal artefacts, stone beads, ornaments and domestic objects).

At the same time, elsewhere, a new form of human organisation was emerging that represented the slide into patriarchy. The height of civilisation was past – although what historians have called 'civilisation' was emerging. The tradition of Western historians (until recently mainly men) to see history as a steady upward climb, with modern Western culture as the apex, comes from the patriarchal ethos of superiority over others, that we still live with. It also justified the horrendous things the invading Westerners did to native peoples worldwide. It led to the colonisers of Australia declaring the country 'terra nullius' – uninhabited land and listing the First Nations people as fauna. This was indicative of an utter incapacity to understand the complex First Nations' culture; their knowledge and management of the Australian landscape; systems of agriculture, kinship, mythology and the knowledge encoded therein (see Chapter 11).

The 'cradle of civilisation' is a term generally applied to the area of the Tigris and Euphrates rivers (now mainly in Iraq) because of the patriarchal city states that developed on these alluvial plains – Sumer, Akkad, Mesopotamia, Babylon, Assyria. Here the first writing we understand began.

Under this definition of civilisation war was almost constant, taxes were introduced to fund standing armies, slavery and bondage was everywhere and new laws introduced that gradually took the position of women from revered, to little more than a trading commodity. Women became property that a man (father, brother, husband, or merely owner could buy, sell and control). New laws were introduced that created crimes that applied only to women – wives could be divorced for childlessness under Hammurabi (1,800 BCE), who also instituted the veil for 'respectable' women; King Urukagina (2,400 BCE) was the first to codify adultery (for women not men); in Assyria abortion was punished by the woman being impaled and unburied (men however had the right to commit infanticide).

The point was to gain control over fertility and to establish a reliable way to trace fatherhood. To do so a woman's sexuality had to be controlled. When obligation, inheritance and food distribution came through the female line such control was not required – everyone knew who the mother of a child was. But fatherhood was less clear, and that had not been an issue in matrifocal cultures.

Free choice of sexual partner/s was over for women. Prostitution was invented as part of this trade and control formula. Priests prostituted female captives to attract men to the temple. As Marilyn French states, 'From the first, prostitution was designed to profit men'.

Domestic violence was extreme and assumed. In Assyria a man had the right to whip his wife, pull out her hair, bruise her and destroy her ears. But if he wanted to do worse, he had to do it in public – flog her, tear out her breasts, or cut off her nose or ears.

Horticulture had been in the women's domain and they had stored and distributed the produce for the benefit of the community. Under 'civilisation' no members of the lower-class had enough land to support themselves and were forced to sell their labour. They had to pay taxes to support the upper class. If they couldn't do it then sometimes they had to sell themselves into slavery to pay the debt.

What's Civilised?

51. Seated couple 'Old Married Couple of Sumer.'
A gypsum statue found underneath the floor of a shrine in Nippur, Iraq. The huge eyes are typical of Sumerian sculpture and would have been inlaid with shell and lapis lazuli held in place by bitumen. The man does not look happy and the woman looks despairing. He holds her around the shoulders and his left hand reaches across to hold her by her right wrist, as if restraining her. She looks away from him. 2,500 BCE. 14.6 cm/5.7 in high, 8.9 cm/3.5 in wide at the bottom. Drawing: Kaye Moseley ©.

Those who had land, were not permitted to grow diverse crops, as they had in the past self-sustaining matrifocal cultures. Monocrops meant that no one area could set up as independent from the ruler of the total state. This was a worldwide strategy utilised by states as far away in time and geography as the Aztecs in Mesoamerica (approximately 1345 to 1521 CE).

Ancient Ways for Current Days

Mono-crop regions would find surviving hard without access to the state-controlled food distribution system. Workers were paid in food and women were paid the least. When the state malnourished females, women became less strong, smaller, and more dependant.

This scenario for women differed from region to region. In some regions, some women had rights with varying degrees of autonomy, in others there was none: King Urukagina mentioned above, also created laws to protect widows; in some cities women could be plaintiffs and witnesses; in others, women with property retained some rights over it.

Some senior soldiers were rewarded with grants of land and wealth. As they gained it, the old kinship groups lost it – it was their land being given away – and with it, women in particular had their rights and community roles and status removed. As French points out, the soldiers felt they had earned their status, not inherited it by descent from a goddess through their mothers. They felt justified.

By the end of Sumer the old life-worshipping world of the mothers had been forgotten, says French, except that the word for 'freedom' was 'amargi' – 'return to the mother'.

CHAPTER 10

The Survivors – Hidden Matriarchies

*We must strive to build valuable ways of being for society.
Mother Earth energy is the force that grows in our spirit.*
**Noemy Blanco Salazar, a Bribri matriarch of Amubri,
Costa Rica, 2018**

It is clear from the research of Goettner-Abendroth and others, that matrifocal cultures occurred worldwide. There are even some which continue today, although they are under increasingly great pressure from a variety of sources.

In this chapter we explore some of the individual cultures in more detail, to provide insight into how they may have lived. Goettner-Abendroth is again the major supplier of the research information shared here. In her work, she details 27 specific cultures worldwide and mentions many more, however, this is by no means inclusive of all that there are.

Ancient Ways for Current Days

The Nayars of Kerala

The matrifocal culture of the Nayars from the state of Kerala in India, was abolished by law under the British, and finally disappeared with independence in 1949. Thus, there are still elderly women whose formative experience was of the matrifocal ways and who spoke of it in 2014 to a Nayar woman researcher, Rekha Kurup. From her recounting, the following picture emerged that I share with you now.

> This story from Kerala begins with a birth. All children are welcome, and if it is a boy the branch of a certain tree beaten on the ground announces it with a thud, if a girl, a bell is rung. In this case the family will particularly celebrate because the line, the motherline, will continue – a daughter born of a daughter and so on back through time.
>
> As the child grows she, like any girl or boy, can run freely about the huge compound of her extended family and out into the streets. Children are highly valued and no-one would dream of hurting them. They live in complete safety. In the evening, the girls gather at the special pond or swimming pool dug in the ground and swim naked together, laughing and telling stories about their lives, joking and promising to meet there again the next night. The men and boys have their area at the other end of the pool and out of respect do not look at the girls.
>
> Both male and female wear a skirt only – consequently, with puberty girls do not cover their breasts but go without clothing on the upper body, as do the boys. The women are completely comfortable with their breasts and young children can play with them without reprimand. They are not naked for men, or to attract men, but for themselves.

The Survivors – Hidden Matriarchies

At home, the children live with their mothers and maternal family all of whom engage in their care and upbringing. Their father is known, but has little to do with them and no responsibility for them. He comes from his maternal home at night to sleep with his partner. The adults have a private room and their sexual/erotic activities are their own private affair; nevertheless the woman has her relatives near at hand if she did need them. In the morning, the visiting man goes home to his mother's extended family, where he has responsibilities relating to his nieces, nephews and elders there.

The bond between brother and sister is strong. It is stronger than with their sexual partners because they are of the same matriliny. The whole family is headed by the eldest woman of the line, who inherits all property on behalf of the family. She determines everything. Her brother or uncle deals with matters of the external world, such as money, trade and agriculture, but makes no major decisions without discussion with the matriarch.

How are these women described? The Grandmothers remember that such a one walks like a queen, her bright eyes shining with enthusiasm. She knows each person and her sweet, soft and gentle tone makes one feel loved unconditionally, at the same time knowing she can be fierce and stern when necessary. She speaks with passion and exudes deep knowing, strength and wisdom. She is held in esteem, loved, and ensures the safety and wellbeing of the whole clan.

Growing up, there are special holidays and rituals. One involves the erection of special huge swings in the trees on which the girls swing and do acrobatics; another at the pool that involves a song and then slapping on the surface of the water with much laughter; another of creating a mud deity and adorning it with flowers for nine days.

Ancient Ways for Current Days

Somewhere between 13 and 16 years of age the girl begins to menstruate, which is a sacred event with various rituals over several days – she is excited, and is treated as someone very precious. The girl is asked to stay inside; the extended family are informed and the women come, sometimes with gifts, to prepare a room of seclusion into which the girl is led and will stay for three days. Sacred objects are there. They make jokes with erotic undertones with the girl. The girl receives teaching about sexuality, eroticism and what to expect with a man. After three days she is paraded through the village with singing and happy banter. When the group reach the river she bathes and further ritual honouring ensues.

Then there is a feast to conclude. Ever after the woman will take three days of seclusion whenever she menstruates, she rests and is free of all responsibilities for the time. As there are many people in the extended family group, her labour can be covered to facilitate this.

According to Kurup, the Nayar matrifocal system 'was based on values of simplicity, cooperation, living within one's means, and respect for life generally'. It should be no surprise that in December 2018 the women of Kerala came together in a protest for women's rights – not just a few women, five million women! They formed a 620 kilometre line in support of gender equality – not spread arms' length apart, but shoulder to shoulder, sometimes in two rows. The ostensible issue was the right to enter a temple that had a ban on entry for women of 'menstruating age'. The courts had upheld the right of the women to attend the temple, but male right wing resistors were preventing women from exercising this right. The Kerala women knew that menstruation was wondrous, rather than an unclean thing.

The matrifocal people of Kerala represent three distinct cultural traditions. Chapter 9 included the Indus Valley civilisation where

The Survivors – Hidden Matriarchies

we noted that when the Aryans, with their iron weapons, moved into the Indus Valley, they displaced the matrifocal people who were already there. Goettner-Abendroth proposes that this was resisted and that the matrifocal people learnt combative skills at that time. However, these original Indus people eventually took the path of many matriarchal peoples and departed for new lands. Some sailed away down the west coast of India, eventually finding the lush and lovely world of Kerala on the Malabar coast and deciding to settle there.

This is unusual in matrifocal behaviour because there were already other matrifocal people in residence who the Nayars, with their military skills, defeated. These people were the peaceful Pulayan and Parayan who found themselves caught between the sea and the mountains. With nowhere to go they became servants and field labourers under the Nayars, which created a class system – again very unusual in matrifocal traditions.

The Pulayan were probably the original, or indigenous people, and they worked the soil with bamboo tools. Even today they observe inheritance through the female line, girls' puberty rites, sexual freedom of women and burial in the earth.

The Parayan are much more numerous than the Pulayan and have a matrifocal culture much like the Nayars, but probably traced from the north-east of India, not the north-west. Eventually the Brahmin culture of the Aryans made its way to Kerala and, while never able to subjugate the Nayars, they placed the Parayan into the lowest caste possible in their caste system, so extreme was the distaste for their ways – and also to counter their numbers which could have provided resistance. The Parayan became the 'pariahs' (a derivation from their clan name) and 'untouchable', scorned and considered 'unclean'. They could not lift their eyes for even their glance was deemed polluting. Such were the ways of the patriarchy in stamping out the women-centred cultures.

Yet I have included the Nayars as recent matrifocal survivors. They continue their traditional body painting in henna for women, based on flower and plant imagery (Foster 2013), especially for celebrations. Kurup searched her own experience for any trace of the matrifocal past that was part of her Nayar inheritance. Among her thoughts she says:

> I recognise matriarchy in the auspiciousness and beauty associated with being a girl or a woman. Any festival or occasion, women led the way. I remembered during vacations when I walked through the fields with my father, older women from other homes would approach my sister and me, telling my father how fortunate he was to have been blessed with such beautiful goddesses, and I personally saw it in their eyes - a deep appreciation of me as a girl.

The Khasi of North West India

This lived experience would also be a part of the experience of Khasi girls, living far to the north on the other side of India. These people were part of the movement from East Asia of matrifocal peoples, travelling east 58,000 years ago along the valley waterways of the vast range of the Himalayan mountains. In the Khasi Hills of Assam they settled large tracts of land which they farm to this day. They are part of the Wa peoples now found only in pockets from China to India, and the Wa are considered the indigenous people of the area.

Goettner-Abendroth describes the traditional Khasi women as wearing long colourful garments and arriving at festivals in precious robes and filigreed silver and gold crowns. Like the women of Tibet they are incredibly strong and carry burdens that would defeat the men of the lowlands, let alone any European visitors.

'Kha-si' means 'born from a mother', so this totally defines the people. In typical matrifocal tradition one mother is the head of the clan, custodian of all clan property to be used for the welfare of all in the clan. She distributes surplus according to need in a form of 'gift-economy'. It is a challenging role. If she comes from a clan of poor means the consequences can be that she may have to seek help from distant relatives to support the aging, or any clan member who is in difficult circumstances. She exerts a natural authority that develops from family respect, rather than power over others. There are no enforcement officers. She provides advice but the choice to accept it is voluntary.

The Khasi recognise their line of descent through the mother and inheritance passes in that line as well. If no girls are born, one is adopted to carry on the responsibilities. For sons, brothers and uncles, their home is in the house of the clan mother. A man's self-definition is as a son, and as a brother to his sisters.

Husbands reside in their mother's home and visit their wife for the night hours, known as a 'visiting marriage'. Divorce is simple and there is no prohibition on the number of times one can marry, this can be called 'serial monogamy'. Where the clan house becomes overcrowded, older daughters may extend the clan house or erect new houses nearby, creating a new matriliny.

Over time, the most ancient clans accrued the greatest respect and developed as an 'elite' level of Khasi society, although it is not a 'class' system of privilege and power as other cultures know it. Rather, it is expressed in the high respect and honorary status paid to members of these oldest clans.

The eldest brother is the protector of his sisters and the social father of his sisters' children, with whom he shares the clan name, while the biological father does not. The clan house is the basic political structure, where decisions are made by consensus. Senior male clan members are appointed to represent the clan at clan council meetings. In turn, this body sends male representatives to a local council. The British introduced a district council which effectively took away from local councils the power to settle matters by consensus.

These gender-based roles create a functional balance where no-one personally 'owns' the clan property – its use is determined by firm clan rules. And no-one accrues power in a personal sense as a political leader. The combination of the two (ownership and political power) in one person has had very different results in the patriarchal system, but the separation brought peace within matrifocal ones.

The matriarch of the family is the clan priestess, and accorded the highest dignity, holding all the sacred objects required by ritual. She always undertakes the first sacrificial act in the household and then hands over the tools and animals involved to her son who continues the ritual outside, before the gathered clan. He and other men decapitate the goats with a single swift blow of their long knives, dedicating the sacrifice to the highest goddess, who they believe protects them from troubles in life. Death and harvest attract the most ritual activity.

The Khasi believe in honouring nature, the rivers and trees in particular. Each village has a sacred grove of trees, usually of oak,

The Survivors – Hidden Matriarchies

52. Khasi living bridge
The Khasi people make living bridges like this one by training tree-roots over years to knit together. Meghalaya, India. Photo: Alexander Mazur/Shutterstock.com

where no tree may be cut down. They are the manifestation of the divine on Earth and to damage nature, tree or river means severing ties with the divine. Rather than damage anything in the jungle, for thousands of years the Khasi made living bridges – and still do. Their bridges are made of nothing but the living roots of rubber fig trees and hollowed out trunks of the betel trees (Julia Watson in her book *Lo-TEK Design by Radical Indigenism*).

Elaborate ceremony is dedicated to honouring the ancestors and the dead, underpinned by the belief that one will be reborn in one's own clan. The Khasi are one of the groups who erect megaliths to this day and this provides clues about how and why it was done in the past. Each assembly of megaliths is centred on one huge horizontal stone, which the Khasi identify as the female stone – the ancestress who brought them to their land. They say she deserves to lie down after all of her hard work.

Behind this stone is the largest upright stone and either side of this are at least two other upright megaliths (totalling three, or five or seven). These are male stones. The largest is the brother of the mother stone, who continues to guard and protect her eternal peace. The rest are other brothers or sons of the ancestress. Some observers have assumed they are penis symbols, but this is not the case, they represent the whole person, who is believed to reside within them, as is also the case for the mother stone. These beings can be asked for help. Sometimes the upright stones have human features carved on them.

53. Khasi megaliths
Showing the typical male uprights and female altar stone, this setting is next to the Mawphlang Sacred Grove in the East Khasi Hills of Meghalaya, India. Such megaliths are still erected by the Khasi today. Photo: Samuel Antony Shots/Shutterstock.

The Survivors – Hidden Matriarchies

In ancestor festivals, the stones are decked in greenery and a feast laid out upon the mother stone. The mother stone serves as altar, table and podium. At other times the ancestors, as divinities, can be offered sacrifices of male goats or roosters which are decapitated upon the mother stone and their blood painted across the stone. The ancestors are thus fed by the living and also enjoy their company in the festivities. The mother stone receives all the gifts given to all of the ancestors. As she had in life, she receives and distributes.

In Chapter 3, I also referred to the ancient tradition of sacred male sacrifice and the Khasi are one group who used to practise this. The men were not forced to take up this role. They were from a highly-regarded clan and went voluntarily to their meeting with the goddess of death, in the firm belief that she would swiftly give them an honoured rebirth.

Later however, captives of war were the victims of beheading before the stones and this was an atrocity of war, indicative of the effect of the need to develop a warfaring capacity.

This, the Khasi certainly had to do. Though they retreated further into the hills in the face of the Aryan invasion and Brahmin patriarchy, they resisted their impacts, as they did also with Hinduism and Islam. They were finally defeated and disarmed by the British in 1924. Following the British came Christian missionaries. Today there are almost 1.5 million Khasi people and 85 per cent of them are Christian – the remainder still practise their traditional ways. Nevertheless, even if Christian, the Khasi believe it is a goddess who protects them from the troubles of life. In addition there are four other male gods.

The introduction of colonial practices and rules of landholding and inheritance were disastrous for the matrifocal system. It was especially so for women. When the effect of the nuclear family isolation and men leaving their families was felt by women it was/is not the Church, which had promoted this system, that comes to help them – it is still the matrilineal clan that does. The Khasi Social Custom Lineage Act now protects the traditional Khasi, and their women enjoy a security unlike women in the rest of the country. Women are supported in education and business by their clan.

The Mosuo of China

The Mosuo were part of the same Tibetan-Burmese cultural group that also gave rise to the Khasi and many other matrifocal cultures. There are approximately 40,000 Mosuo people and 60 per cent (Foster 2013; Goettner-Abendroth 2012) are still practising traditional ways today. They live in China (Yunnan and Sichuan provinces), high in the spectacular landscape of the Himalayas, close to Tibet. They are the indigenous people who were there before the Han Chinese. The Mosuo were pushed into marginal areas when the Han Chinese arrived, bringing patriarchal and racist attitudes with them.

By now you will not be surprised to know that the Mosuo are matrilineal and practise walking marriages, where the man visits his wife in her home at night, returning to his matrilineal home in the morning (Goettner-Abendroth 2012; Marsden 2018). There can be no sexual liaisons between people from the same clan or if too closely related. The Mosuo practise easy divorce and serial monogamy, leading to the Chinese thinking that they were promiscuous. This attracted male tourists to such a degree that a red-light district was created in an effort to keep them away from the Mosuo women.

The Survivors – Hidden Matriarchies

In the 1960s the Chinese government tried to break up this ancient way of life, but within a few years of the end of the Cultural Revolution (1976) the Mosuo had returned to the old way of visiting marriages. There are some families where children receive the clan name of both parents, but it is the female line that is counted. There are some patriarchal families but they remain very unpopular with the Mosuo and are resisted by the women who object to moving into a house of strangers when they marry.

Property is passed down through the female line (Goettner-Abendroth 2012; Marsden 2018; Garrison 2012) and the matriarch, the most capable woman, is elected to be head of the household. She is chosen as the one who cares most for everyone (Goettner-Abendroth 2012). The matriarch is responsible for the family wellbeing, care of guests, distribution of the family wealth, food and goods and business decisions. However, no decisions are made without discussion within the family. The matriarch arbitrates in clan conflicts. Until recently, matriarchs of different clans were included in the village council (Goettner-Abendroth 2012). This is a typical matrifocal society of peace, suicide is rare, there are no murders, and no word for 'rape' in the language (Blumenfield 2009).

As in all matrifocal groups the home and family is the female domain and the outer world of trade, building, herding, fishing, animal slaughtering and politics are the domain of the men (Goettner-Abendroth 2012; Garrison 2012). However, based on aptitude, the roles can be taken up by either gender if desired. The men represent their group in political forums as is the case in other matrifocal societies. A balance is kept between work and time to relax.

The brother-sister relationship is the most important one as the brother is the protector and social father to his sister's children

(Mattison et al. 2014; Goettner-Abendroth 2012). These days most children do know who their biological father is, but they always reside in the clan home of their mother (Garrison 2012; Goettner-Abendroth 2012; Marsden 2018). If there are no offspring of one sex in a clan, it is common to adopt a child who may come from a large family or a line too small to continue. These adopted children are fully integrated into the lineage of the adoptive family (Blumenfield 2009).

Everyone lives communally in a beautiful, spacious, double-storied clan compound built of whole logs, with many generations (12 to 20 people) within the same household. There is a central large hall for the clan to gather in and a sacred hearth there where the ancestors are venerated. Here the communal meals are prepared and eaten. The elder women sleep here by the fire with the children. Men have a communal men's room though they may also sleep at their partner's home. Women between certain ages have private rooms.

The most important ceremony is the coming of age ceremony at thirteen. Children all wear the same attire, but at this ceremony they are given their first adult clothes, a skirt for girls and trousers for boys. The belief in rebirth is strong and at the initiation ceremony the whole clan recognises which ancestor has returned, the young person is then regarded as the personification of that ancestor and that name is given to the young person. The ceremony is particularly important for young women because by giving birth a woman directly carries on the line of the clan. At this time the girls are given the keys to their own bedrooms ('flowering rooms') and once they begin menstruating they can invite a partner to join them in a walking marriage. Menstruation occurs late for the Mosuo and sexual activity may not begin until late teens or early twenties (Blumenfield 2009). It is always the woman's choice.

The Survivors – Hidden Matriarchies

Until recent times the Mosuo practised marriage where all the young women of one clan had as suitable sexual partners all the young men of another clan. Now the choice has widened. There is no word in the Mosuo language for 'spouse' (Goettner-Abendroth 2012), 'husband', 'father', or 'jealousy' (Marsden2018; Blumenfield 2009).

The Mosuo basically follow their ancient religion, though other influences have impacted (e.g. Tibetan Buddhism). In typically adaptive matrifocal style they have integrated aspects of Tibetan Buddhism into their own religion. Often if a family has more than one boy they will send one to be a monk (Mattison et al. 2014).

The Mosuo relate to nature as a sentient being: mountains, springs, gorges and fields are all sacred and alive. Their lands lie around Lake Lugu, which in Mosuo language is the Mother Lake. A beautiful mountain rising from the lakeside is their highest Goddess, Gan Mu, a Goddess of rebirth. A mountain dance festival is held at summer solstice. Thus they adhere to the matrifocal principles of seeing the deity as female, a Goddess, and experiencing a sacred connection to all aspects of nature.

There are a number of threats to the Mosuo way of life, which is now thousands of years old. In the modern world, the destruction of their forests for wood resources, with the logs choking the rivers is one of these. Chinese mass tourism has brought with it a money economy and increasing conflicts in a traditionally peaceful society. Young people are attracted through television and the internet to the cities, threatening the viability of the matrifocal family. The lure is money and goods, although they come to understand the cost they pay, in terms of added stress, constant work and loss of lifestyle.

Ancient Ways for Current Days

The Minangkabau of West Sumatra, Indonesia

The Minangkabau heartland is in the fertile hill country of Penang, West Sumatra. Some 3 million Minangkabau live there engaged in rice cultivation on terraces; another 3 million live outside the heartland, including in all the major Indonesian cities, making them the largest existing matrifocal culture group in the world.

They operate within a living law known as their 'Adat'. It is a matrifocal tribal law, originating in reflection of the way in which nature operates. Goettner-Abendroth states that it was the original social form of all Malay peoples. The Minangkabau still see Adat as their cornerstone – they have strongly resisted the impact of patriarchal influences across the centuries, and are proud of their 'matriarchy'.

The matrifocal tradition of men travelling for trade and external clan relationships has situated the Minangkabau well to expand peacefully as participants in the dominant culture. The Minangkabau strongly value education, opening to them all work pathways, including politics, where they are well-represented. According to Goettner-Abendroth, 'In Indonesia they are regarded as well-educated, highly cultured and cosmopolitan, with great business acumen ... there is not one modern profession that the Minangkabau have not taken on'.

Minangkabau living in the wider world face patriarchal influence daily, but adhere to Adat as best they can and also frequently support the homeland financially. Under inheritance law anything they acquire privately from their work in the wider world can be held for a single generation then it reverts to the ownership of a man's mother's clan.

The Survivors – Hidden Matriarchies

54. Minangkabau Ceremony
Dressed in red with gold trim Minangkabau women and daughters carry out traditional ceremonial activities to confirm the title of 'progenitor' for adult men of the tribe. West Sumatra, Indonesia, 2020. Photo: taufik imran / Shutterstock.com

Adat is strongly held and nurtured in the homeland – it is the law of the land. Under Adat the culture is matrilineal, the people practise visiting marriage, they live in communal long houses and each clan has a female clan elder or matriarch. The property 'belongs' to the women but it cannot be sold, so it is really a custodianship role.

Biological fathers are recognised and their role honoured, but the brothers act as the social fathers for the children of the women of the house. Goettner-Abendroth reports that in this role a man must be 'mild and friendly, patient, tolerant and dignified; he must be like a good mother'.

Originally there were four clans with one ancestress, whose name means 'our own mother'. They used a system of paired marriage clans, also used in other matrifocal societies. This system is about maintaining the strong relationships that tie the groups together.

In the large clan meeting hall the people can gather and discuss, seeking consensus. The matriarch, respected as she is, maintains the equilibrium, and when she speaks her words tip the balance. The next organisational level is the village, regarded under Adat as a politically self-determining republic.

As we would now expect, the matriarch is assisted by one of her brothers who is the clan liaison with other clan houses of the village and the outside world. It is one of the highest honours a man can achieve – to represent the clan of his mother and sisters. He can be removed from this role if the women feel that he has failed to fulfil his duties. He must reflect their decisions and speak in an eloquent way. He has a role as an Adat scholar, reinterpreting the old wisdom and presenting it to the outside world and the younger generation. Adat is based on 22 rules, never written down, relying on transmission through an oral tradition.

Under Adat, solving conflict is to be through negotiation and conciliation, with the primary goal being to achieve peaceful consensus. The process is still used today. Some in the West see consensus as impractical in the modern world, taking too much time. When there arose for the Minangkabau the question of whether to have a new, larger airport or not, the consensus decision-making process took three months. In the end consensus was achieved – the Minangkabau reached a decision that everyone could live with.

In ancient times the Minangkabau saw all plants, animals, rocks, rivers and weather systems as animated and alive. In the landscape there are megaliths, thought to have been put in place by the first

Minangkabau people to arrive. At that time, the first ancestress established the system of Adat.

Though adapting to influences from both Hindu and Buddhist beliefs and then later Islam, which particularly took persistent negotiation (Sanday in Foster 2013), the Minangkabau still keep the basis of Adat strong. Adat values good deeds and kind-heartedness (Foster 2013) – motherly values. Everything can be reflected by the model provided by the natural world where nature provides. Goettner-Abendroth gives the simple example of rice: the tender sprouts when first planted are quite weak, yet with proper care they grow to feed the human population. So too, people must nurture and care for the small and weak (the younger generation) and thus society can grow strong. The benign aspects of nature are included in Adat, the destructive aspects are excluded (Sanday in Foster 2013) as not contributing to a peaceful, successful society.

Nagovisi of South Bougainville

In the south of Bougainville Island, the easternmost island of Papua New Guinea, live the Nagovisi people. A couple of the tribes around them have similarities to them, but the Nagovisi display a complex of features that are distinctly matrifocal. The research into these people was undertaken over several years by the anthropologist, Jill Nash.

Nash recounts that, for the Nagovisi, there are two most prominent spirit beings, their ancestresses, Poreu and Makonai. Everyone in the tribe can trace themselves to one of these two sisters-in-law, who are credited with giving rise to the Nagovisi people. This defines each person's place within the total clan. So here we have again the foundation story of, in this case two

Ancient Ways for Current Days

women, who moved from elsewhere to establish their own tribe, a matrilineal group.

The village revolves around matrilineally related women, their unmarried siblings, their imported husbands and all children. The husband works the land of his wife's clan, not that of his own clan. Women hold shared sexuality and gardening in equal importance. Nash describes the Nagovisi as 'emphatically egalitarian'.

Clans and lineages own shell valuables, which are used today, even for the payment of state-incurred fines. Some of these objects are kept as heirlooms and some used in gift exchanges – an aspect of matrifocal cultures explored in Chapter 3. A matriarch may even destroy some of these to show sorrow or displeasure. There are eight different types of shell valuables, varying in length, colour and other features. Though the husband will work hard to acquire these, they are clan property inherited by the daughter.

These shell valuables can be used in exchange for other goods, such as the purchasing of pigs, which will be needed for major ceremonies. The man undertakes this purchase under clear instruction from his wife, who has the right to reject any offered or purchased pig. In the matter of pigs and shell valuables the woman cannot be disobeyed.

In the adaptive way of matrifocal cultures seeking to survive, the Nagovisi are for the most part now Christian, but some of the old matrifocal rituals, which were based around life events, continue, especially those for death. Men are responsible for the death ritual and women for matters of the living. The life stage rituals are held during the day when women can easily attend and most of those present are women, with men in the background. The women

The Survivors – Hidden Matriarchies

will decorate the honoured person with the shell valuables and act as priestesses to invoke the ancestresses.

With the death ritual, the woman determines the size of the gathering, with consideration of the food, such as yams, that can be provided for it. Women as wailing mourners are essential to the success of the ritual. The man organises the event, creates the songs required and provides expressions of thanks. Though women are in the background here, the matriarch has funeral obligations both to those of her lineage who have died, and returning obligations to others where there are family ties.

The interdependence of two plays out in the social system with the balance of roles between women within the domestic and tribal sphere, and men in the clan arena where various clans consult, do ritual and trade. Women's powers and men's powers are seen as complementary. Clan property belongs to the women and what is produced because of it – even coin from the cash economy – is given to the wife. Once childbearing years are past women are freer to engage in a wider sphere and the clan head is a woman, usually an older woman (at least over 40 years), preferably with a forceful husband who can play an influential role in inter-tribal and inter-clan politics.

So here we see that the husband fulfils the role that in other matrifocal groups, the brother or uncle does. His interests are strongly identified with his wife's group and they share the everyday concerns and tasks. There is no traditional ritual for marriage. He brings to the union labour and managerial abilities, she brings shell valuables and the land needed for survival. She is responsible for the home and children, relationships inside the kin group, and etiquette. He has a freer schedule that allows travel. A man's success in the outer world depends on having an effective wife. She supplies the resources and shares the garden labour which is essential to his leadership aspirations.

The spokesman for the village becomes a 'big man' – one whose personal talents provide leadership over dissenting groups and a wider sphere of influence than available to a woman. He is the person Westerners considered the chief. His role includes giving advice on community matters, supervising cooperative work projects, organising feasts. He emphasises compromise, thoughtful weighing of all points in a discussion. 'Big men' have ties with other 'big men' in distant villages, which link them in trading relationships.

Nagovosi women freely attend all events and spaces of the tribe. The men make an art of discussion and decision. If women, used to speaking to children, choose to speak in these forums, it is brief and to the point.

In modern times it has been assumed the westernising of tribal cultures will bring greater equality for women. For the matrifocal Nagovisi this does not seem to be the case. Being matrifocal meant the women already had power, complementary to that of men. Nash comments that in asserting 'equality' (rather than 'complementarity') women are required to act more like men – 'to speak in public, to be mobile and travel from home, and so on … [it] means alienation from people and from other women in a way that it does not necessarily have to for men'.

The Bribri of Costa Rica

The Bribri are a small indigenous matrilineal group of just over 13,000 people (but possibly up to 35,000), living in the Talamanca

The Survivors – Hidden Matriarchies

canton in the Limon province of Costa Rica and in northern Panama. Each person belongs to a clan, determined by their mother, and all land is the property of women. They have made a firm decision to continue the ancient ways, to live out the matriarchal vision in alignment with the Earth Mother and have their traditions recognised by law (Garrison 2012). They have 'made some truly groundbreaking strides in areas such as land conservation and standing up to the mining industry' (Parker 2014).

Bribri legend has it that the cacao tree was once a woman, who was turned into a tree by the gods. Thus only women can prepare the traditional cacao drink used in sacred rituals. Noemy Blanco Salazar, a Bribri matriarch (quoted at the start of this chapter) says of women that 'we are the heirs of life' (Parker 2014). Knowledge and tradition are passed down through the grandmother. Salazar states that: 'Our close relationship to our Grandmother is a pillar of knowledge … We transmit the value of life in our approach to Mother Nature as an experiential space every day; in work in the kitchen, at the ceremony, and in the upbringing of our children' (Parker 2014).

There is currently a Bribri matriarch-centred movement to generate new avenues of revenue for the community. This is in part an effort to bypass involvement in large corporations, such as the fruit-picking industry, that offer work only to men and, by unrestrained use of pesticides, pollute and endanger the health of the people. The clan efforts include eco-tourism, organic agriculture, crafts, food and traditional beverages, community radio and educational opportunities (Parker, 2014). Salazar is directly involved with facilitating the opportunity for a graduate level course, 'Indigenous Rights Law in the Field'.

In a world in need of answers Salazar says women in subsistence economies who produce 'wealth in partnership with nature, have been experts in their own right, of holistic and ecological knowledge of nature's processes' (Parker 2014). Understanding the ancient matrifocal traditions may provide indicators of the way forward that we need.

CHAPTER 11

The Oldest Continuous Living and Thriving Culture

The land is my mother. Like a human mother the land gives us protection, enjoyment and provides our needs – economic, social and religious. We have a human relationship with the land: Mother, daughter, son.
When the land is taken from us or destroyed, we feel hurt because we belong to the land and we are part of it.
Djinyini Gondarra, Senior Yolŋu Elder and Law/Lore man
of the Dhurili Nation of Northeast Arnhem Land, Australia
(1945–present)

Cultural sensitivity warning: This work contains information which may be regarded as secret and which some Aboriginal women and men may not wish to see. It also mentions some people who are now deceased.

The tragedy of isolation destroyed

First Nations Australians have been in Australia for approximately 65,000 years. Some First Nations people claim that they were always here. Before British colonisation there were over 500 different clan groups or 'nations' and over 250 language groups. Today there are 649,200 First Nation peoples of the 23 million inhabitants (2.8%) of Australia (2016 Census). Culture and lifestyle loss is a real and current grief for First Nations people of Australia.

The original Australians suffered terribly by the arrival of the British colonisers, who first arrived in the south-east in 1788; in the north they suffered from diseases brought by visiting traders, like smallpox and malaria from the Makassans from Sulawesi (now part of Indonesia) and leprosy from Chinese visitors to the north.

Contact with the British brought various diseases, including influenza, tuberculosis, small pox, measles, typhus, typhoid, diphtheria, venereal diseases, and finally the 'Spanish' flu, all of which were unknown in Australia previously, and ran rife through the population of the traditional owners (Chaloupka 1993; Flood 2019). Flood believes that disease was the biggest killer of First Nations population as a result of the arrival of colonists (Flood 2019). Yet massacres, planned and carried out by the new settlers, contributed considerably and are mentioned later. By the 1930s, the First Nations population had decreased by 80–90 per cent from pre-contact times (Flood 2019).

The newcomers introduced tobacco, causing cancer, and alcohol – which proved highly addictive and destructive for the First Nations people as they confronted the misery of the destruction of their traditional life and sense of self-worth.

The Oldest Continuous Living and Thriving Culture

Colonial people wanted to set up fences and boundaries which interfered with the movement of the original people across their traditional pathways and hunting grounds. Sometimes First Nations people hunted and took a sheep roaming on lands that were traditionally theirs to hunt. It was rare that the settlers would tolerate this.

For reasons mainly to do with settler greed for land (Rintoul 2021, quoting Sutton), it was not long before some among the incoming colonial peoples consciously undertook genocidal activities towards the traditional owners, like poisoning waterholes, putting arsenic in 'gifts' of flour and shooting whole clans where they lived or had camped, or in waterways and swamps as they tried to escape. Reprisals from the remaining traditional owners occurred. Early colonial newspapers contained news of the 'war' with First Nations people (Pascoe 2018).

There was little attempt by the newcomers to understand the rich and complex living culture of the First Nations people, and fundamentally they were viewed by most colonials as a low form of life. For their own sense of rightness it was necessary for settlers to do this, to justify their takeover of lands which were clearly already occupied, by large numbers of the traditional owners (Pascoe 2018). Indigenous attacks were more like reprisals – fair punishment for those who shot their people. But the colonials generally wanted the original Australians to be gone.

Fruitful custodianship of the land

Yet the early settlers commented on the 'park-like' aspect of the Australian countryside, groves of trees with little build-up of debris interspersed with open areas of grasslands – never dreaming that this was maintained by the careful management of the landscape by the traditional custodians (Pascoe 2018). Only now, in the time of catastrophic bushfires created by humanly induced climate change, are the 'cultural' or 'right-way' slow burning fire techniques of First Nations peoples being turned to for help (Allam 2020).

Once crops were domesticated in Europe matrifocal people were always agricultural, rather than herders. Australian First Nations peoples took this in a different direction and managed whole landscapes (Griffiths 2018). They determined where cropping occurred, allowed rest areas and encouraged regeneration; they never took all the plants growing in one place and replanted the parts of plants they had taken that would grow for the following year; in places they redirected water to ensure growth of particular plants (Pascoe 2018).

According to Peter Sutton, one of Australia's leading anthropologists, First Nations people were 'ecological agents who worked with the environment', (Rintoul 2021) rather than farmers as understood in the West. Sutton and his co-author, archaeologist Keryn Walshe, emphasise the complex skill and knowledge required for the hunter-gatherer lifestyle which should be respected in its own right.

In talking of First Nations people working with the landscape, Sutton and Walshe emphasise the spiritual and ritual connection of traditional custodians to the land and their nurturing of the land through these means 'the greater part of aboriginal traditional methods of reproducing plant and animal species was ... through spiritual propagation' (Rintoul 2021).

The Gay'wu Group of Women include five Yolŋu women from North East Arnhem Land and in their book *Song Spirals* they report that 'We don't use the land, not in that way (Western agriculture); we sing the land so that new trees grow, new plants come, animals flourish'.

According to First Nations author Bruce Pascoe the writings of early settlers (mainly in the south-east) mention First Nations people 'building dams and wells; planting, irrigating and harvesting seed; preserving the surplus and storing it in houses, sheds, or secure vessels; and creating elaborate cemeteries and manipulating the landscape' (Pascoe 2018). They let trees grow on rocky and less fertile land and encouraged food crops (e.g. yams or cereals) where the soils were better. Their practices enhanced the soil quality by techniques such as digging for food, thus aerating and mixing in ash from their controlled slow burning.

We should note that Tyson Yunkaporta (2019) Apalech man from Western Cape York and university lecturer states that First Nations tradition meant 'females [had] control of nutrition in our communities. They directed most of the harvesting, production and distribution of food, giving them considerable authority …'. This is entirely in line with the pattern in matrifocal cultures worldwide.

Pascoe also documents the round, dome-shaped houses grouped as villages and noted by colonialists in various parts of Australia. Some were of a size suitable for 15 people, and lined with mud or clay, they were dry, clean and warm homes. These were seasonal dwellings occupied when food was plentiful in that area (Rintoul 2021). The usual understanding of Australians who are not First Nations people, is that the original Australians were constantly nomadic people who built temporary 'lean-to' structures. Where a sparse environment required constant movement in search of food, these were certainly the shelters used by the traditional owners. However, in other places Pascoe indicates that First Nations villages existed and were often burnt down by settlers soon after they took over the land, so perhaps then the lean-to was the option most available to the remaining traditional owners in those places.

The widescale practical and spiritual landcare of the traditional custodians (which in some cases included waterworks such as fish races, that could direct a whole river flow to harvest the fish), rather than just privately owned plots, was outside anything the new arrivals from Britain and Europe could imagine. The Gay'wu Group of Women report that incoming colonialists and missionaries:

> … did not see rows of manmuna (long yams), they did not see orchards of larrani (bush apples) and munydjutj (plum trees) and dingu (cycad palms), they did not see a plantation of baladay (yam) and balkpalk and wunapu (types of fruit), they did not see a field of rakay (edible water reed) and dhatam (waterlily), and therefore they said the land was empty. They didn't see our songspirals*, our clan designs, they ignored our milkarri*, our relationships and connection to country.
> (*milkarri are songspirals as cried and keened by Yolŋu women)

Within a few years of the arrival of hooved animals and Western agriculture, the friable soil created by First Nations' practices with the earth, was compacted and unproductive. This was something the settlers noted as they observed it occur before their very eyes (Pascoe 2018).

Sharing traditional law/lore

First Nations' belief systems were, and are, learnt from childhood in gradual additions over a lifetime (Flood 2019; HR Bell 1998; Andrews 2019; Gay'wu group of Women 2019). Knowledge is not to be taught before the appropriate physical, psychological and intellectual development of the person concerned. The teaching comprises the traditional law/lore, encapsulating culture (Andrews 2019) which contains the correct social and religious practices (Flood 2019). Only the knowledge available to young children was at first told to colonial people (Andrews 2019).

As the old law/lore women and men are passing away and new generations have not been able to grow up in the traditional law/lore, there has been increasing concern among the senior law people that the law/lore will be lost. There is now a greater willingness to share knowledge with interested, respectful non-First Nations Australians. David Mowaljarlai, Ngarinyin Elder said, 'If we share the stories of our country with gudia (whitefella), then they will have our country in their hearts as we do, and they will understand and love it, and never damage it' (Bevis 2016).

Mowaljarlai and other Elders have recognised that for the First Nations culture to survive the Western systems of thinking, learning and law must work in hand with traditional thinking, teaching and law/lore, and this is being called two-way or both-way thinking. One outcome can be bi-lingual/bi-cultural education. There are efforts to create systems of learning for all developmental stages, for example, the Bush University initiated by the Ngarinyin people of the central and northern Kimberly (Western Australia) for non-First Nations people, and the Batchelor Institute of Indigenous Tertiary Education based on Kungarakan and Warai country in Batchelor, Northern Territory.

A matrifocal origin?

It is generally accepted that the First Nations people came to Australia across a land or land and sea bridge to the north (seas were low between about 160,000 and 140,000 BCE and again between 70,000 and 55,000 BCE [Flood 2019; Foster 2013]). Some links have been made to the Dravidian people of India who may share ancestors with First Nations Australians, and who tend to be matrifocal in their behaviour (see Chapter 9) (Flood 2019; Pike 2013). The original Australians brought aspects of the matrifocal culture, from which their culture continued to develop, with them. Their oldest myths record their arrival.

In the Arnhem Land area, the principle Ancestor, who became a mythic being – a transition typical of matrilineal societies – was a woman named Warramurrunggundji (and various other names depending upon language group). The earliest recorded version says that she came at a time when there was no water barrier (as was the case at times, noted above) and arrived at the Coburg Peninsula. She brought bags of yams with her and travelled the land leaving groups of people and yams at various places, and telling them what language to use (Chaloupka 1993).

This paints a picture for me of a matriarch leading her clan to new lands, as we have learnt occurred in matrifocal groups. The clan brought with them some of the foods that had supported their survival (yams). Over time her descendants moved out across the land, their language diverging, but with the oral history retaining the common ancestor who shortly gained mythic stature in the belief systems of her descendants.

There is an abundance of intricate paintings in rock shelters and caves across Australia recording the ancestral beings and

The Oldest Continuous Living and Thriving Culture

associated stories; fish and animals (some now extinct), as well as ships of various eras seen at sea. Some of these drawings are still maintained with new paint layers, as part of ritual obligations.

Speaking of Arnhem Land, art historian and rock art expert George Chaloupka reported that 'Some of the paintings are said to be of non-human origin – paintings where the given being has placed its own image on the shelter's wall'. Author and cultural advisor Hannah Bell reported the same view among the Ngarinyin of the Kimberley – that the ancient spiritual beings themselves created the paintings. In her book *Journey Into Dreamtime*, author Munya Andrews recounts that 'Some beings walked through rock walls as portals into another dimension, leaving their imprint behind' which the traditional custodians painted over, resulting in rock paintings.

On the north coast of Western Australia, on the Murujuga (Burrup) Peninsula of the Pilbara, there are extensive carvings (petroglyphs) made into rock surfaces. In association with them, there are standing stones and rock arrangements, moved there by people, that reflect actions of ancestral beings. In south-western Victoria, at Wurdi Youang a low stone circle has been identified, created by traditional custodians in times past. It marks the movement of the Sun throughout the year, and Venus, Jupiter, Saturn and Mars through one line of vision (Yunkaporta 2019). Other stones provide alignments to features in the landscape that no doubt have Dreamings associated with them.

Author Alice Duncan-Kemp recounts a circle in South-West Queensland that she observed in use in about 1920. It was a holy place made of a circle of stones, including about 15 upright stone pillars (1 m/3.3 ft high, 50 kg/110 lb each). In the centre was a stone altar on which was a smooth stone engraved with sun, moon and stars. A path led from the circle in each of the four compass directions (in Pike 2013). We have seen before the association of such rock formations with matrifocal cultures – the uprights being male, the horizontal altar, female (e.g. in Sumatra, and the megaliths in Europe and Malta, explored in Chapters 4, 5 and 10 in this book).

The culture of First Nations Australians has an exceptionally long continuity, to the current day, and has been adapted to changes over 65,000 years of First Nations' custodianship of the land. Some tribes are matrilineal and some patrilineal, and some both, depending on what is being transmitted (Andrews 2019). It is difficult to talk of 'inheritance' in either system when, like many matrifocal societies, the Australian First Nations' culture is not based upon acquisition of possessions. In her book, *Wise Woman of the Dreamtime*, author Johanna Lambert asserts that 'there is no grammatical form to express possession of anything in Aboriginal language'.

For the original Australians, the 'wealth' is knowledge, myths, rituals, artwork, the skills of daily living/bush survival, and most importantly relationships between all of these, all imbued with sacred meaning. What is passed on is the obligation to care for a place – one's 'country', a clan totem/dreaming animal and a personal totem/dreaming animal (Flood 2019) and nurture special relationships with different related people. These dreamings 'foster a strong sense of kinship and kindredness that serves to unite us.' (Andrews 2019). Deborah Wurrkidj, a Kuninjku woman of North Central Arnhem Land and a leading textile artist spoke of 'country' in a quote at the Piinpi Contemporary Aboriginal Fashion exhibition, in Bendigo, Australia in 2020:

> We are always thinking of our Country. Every time. Every single time.
> It doesn't matter if it's for our fabric or for bark,
> We are always thinking we are at our homeland, thinking about our Country.

The Oldest Continuous Living and Thriving Culture

Andrews tells us that First Nations law/lore is 'in tune with natural law'. She recounts that the Yolŋu people of the Northern Territory use a tree as the symbol of their law/lore, and their word for the Dreaming means 'the foot, footprint or root of a tree'. The footprints 'allude to the early Tree Ancestors or Dreaming Beings as having *walked* over the land, leaving their footprints behind'. This link between the land and nature as the basis for law/lore, is true also of the 'Adat' or 'Law' of the Minangkabau people of West Sumatra, Indonesia, a matrifocal culture who were described in Chapter 10. For them, Nature and the natural world provides a model for human behaviour. For the Yolŋu the 'humanising of tree-roots reflects the Aboriginal worldview that we are One with nature, *not* separate, …' (Andrews 2019).

Colleen Wall, a Senior Woman of the Dauwa Clan of the Kabi Nation of South-East Queensland, speaks of traditional gender roles 'Grandfathers look outwardly, protecting the camp. Grandmothers look inwardly, nurturing new generations …' (AIATSIS website). This represents the traditional matrifocal roles, with women concerned with local and family affairs and men concerned with a wider external sphere.

A culture of relationships

As much as any matrifocal culture, maybe more so, that of First Nations Australians is a culture of relationships. Thus each person is an embedded part of a group, 'one in which kin and clan members are considered as much a part of the self as one's own arms and legs' (Lambert 1993). We have noted the 'skin' and moiety structure of traditional First Nations Australians in discussion of marriage patterns in Chapter 2. A good place to learn how this system of patterning works in detail, is by viewing the University of Sydney, 'Kinship Learning Module', particularly 'skin names'.

The concept of relationships goes further, including with animals (totems mentioned above) and indeed, all things. Yunkaporta talks about 'kinship-mind', whereby in 'Aboriginal worldviews, nothing exists outside of a relationship to something else'.

In order to ensure this pattern of inter-relationships continues in the right way, traditionally a baby girl is 'promised' to a future husband, sometimes already a full-grown man. According to Hiatt, among the Gidjingali (Arnhem Land, Northern Territory), the mother had the right to decide where her daughter would be promised, usually in consultation with her brothers (a relationship that is usually very strong in matrilineal societies). Among the Warlpiri people (Tanami Desert, Northern Territory) at least, it should be noted that the mother also had the right to select the 'mother-in-law' for a son, that is, the woman who would be suitable to give birth to the girl who will become his wife. The mother announces this by the order of the women dancers at the initiation of the boy (D Bell 1983). These rights are in line with women's responsibility in matrifocal cultures for ensuring strong relationships. Once a baby girl becomes the man's 'promise wife' he is obliged to contribute to the welfare of her family – 'he marries her land and people as well and must serve them as a husband serves a wife' (HR Bell 1998).

Upon marriage then, a husband inherits responsibility for his wife's country and must learn how to participate in the ritual life of her tribe. The woman does not relinquish responsibility for her country but must now learn all she can of 'women's business' in her new clan. Unlike most matrifocal cultures the wife moves to live with her husband's clan – this occurs too in Polynesian culture (Chapter 10).

The Oldest Continuous Living and Thriving Culture

As Hannah Bell details clearly in her work about the traditions of the Ngarinyin people, for a First Nations Australian young woman living the traditional lifestyle, marriage and moving to the new clan is done in a very careful way, whereby her clan travels to the camp of the betrothed, where other clans also meet up with them. Prior to travelling, the young woman has been instructed in what to expect and prepared by her female relatives for the sexual act (HR Bell 1998; Flood 2019; Lawlor 1991). The betrothed husband has received instruction from the older men and spent time with an older law/lore woman who teaches him how to behave in intimacy with a woman. This information is not entirely new; Lawlor contends that watching adults engaged in intercourse was a major pastime of children as they approached adolescence.

When the clan arrives, the couple go off for a week with an Elder, to live together, learn each other's ways and preferences and get to know each other, without intercourse, under the watchful eye of the Elder. After this week, the marriage ritual is performed. The couple retire and consummate the marriage, again under the eye of the Elders who are available to consult, should any issues arise. This is an amazing extent of care for their wellbeing and safety, especially for the young woman, expressed through these traditions. It hints at a matrifocal past, the values of which respect sexuality as healthful, it ensures balance and the wellbeing of the woman. Other tribes have other similarly careful processes – in the 1880s Parker collected stories of the Euahlayi tribe (north-central New South Wales through to south-central Queensland) whose marriage preparation occurred through various stages over several months for the young woman (Lambert 1993).

Relationship that includes rebirth

In First Nations' myth there is a constant reference to birth, death and rebirth, which is a key component of the matrifocal belief system. These tales state quite clearly that Ancestors return as 'spirit-children' who, sometimes with the encouragement of human ritual in song and dance, move into the body of a woman, who then becomes pregnant (Andrews 2019; HR Bell 1998). A similar conception belief sometimes occurs in matrifocal cultures, whereby either the role of the sexual act in procreation is not known, or if it is known, it is not identified as the cause of conception alone (not all intercourse leads to pregnancy, for example). In Ngarinyin culture, in the ideal situation, the spirit child identifies itself to the husband who sees the child when the husband is in the state between wakefulness and sleep. Lawlor claims this tradition is typical in Australian First Nations beliefs. The same night the wife dreams of a child in a dream-like vision. 'Her body jolts. The spirit child has been planted.' (HR Bell 1998).

The Dreaming

A commonly used term for the mythic world of First Nations Australians is the 'Dreamtime' or the 'Dreaming' ('which existed prior to the appearance of the manifest world' [Lambert 1993]). Westerners tend to think of this as a time in history, in a linear sense. But traditionally, First Nations people do not (D Bell 1983; Andrews 2019), instead they experience time in a cyclical fashion (Stanner in Flood 2019; Andrews 2019) where the Dreaming both holds stories of ancient happenings and is also alive now, surrounding people and available to dip into (Pike 2013; Griffiths 2018) – as the parents above would have in seeing their unborn baby, in this case as a child already. Lawlor characterises this as moving through space, rather than time, and in a circle of life, death, rebirth.

Some deeply spiritual men and women have the skills to slip into the Dreaming and return (HR Bell 1998), with new songs, rituals or to see patterns emerge in a rock face that are new information from the Ancestors, to be painted. This Australian expression of spirituality has a parallel in the ancient shamanic practices seen in Europe in the cave-paintings of the Palaeolithic era. The Australian development of rock painting may have occurred at about the same time as that in Europe, or somewhat earlier – Flood suggests 50,000–45,000 BCE.

As Hannah Bell reports:

> For the Ngarinyin, the world is received and transmitted through direct communication with nature, understood in ritual through performing and visual arts, and consolidated into laws of being and doing through the medium of dream in readily accessible altered states of consciousness.

Creator women, as in many parts of the world, are known also in Australian First Nations' myth, as is usual in matrifocal culture. (It is to be noted that some First Nation people, particularly in south-eastern Australia, recognise a male ancestor as the creator being.) An example is Gulaga, ancestral creator for the Yuin people of the south coast of NSW. Now embodied as a sacred mountain, she is the mother of the Yuin, and the source of all cultural and spiritual connection.

The being called Gadjeri, or in other places Mingari (Pike 2013) is known over a wide area of northern Australia. Her name means 'old woman', in terms of sacredness more than age. She is the 'sacred mother', or 'mother of us all'. She symbolises the productive qualities of all natural things, including people (Encyclopedia.com). She is the Earth Mother (Pike 2013). In other cultures she would be called a Mother Goddess.

Kunapipi is another name for this mythic female being, and she gave birth to men, women and other species as she travelled (oxfordreference.com) and placed spirit children in the landscape (who would then enter and fertilise passing suitable women). With other female beings, she performed rituals using sacred objects. In the story the mythic man observes that the women have sacred objects and steals these from them. Thus, women lost the ability to carry out this form of sacred ritual and men obtained ritual power (Encyclopedia.com).

This is not the only First Nations Australian story of the sacred objects and/or abilities of women being taken from them by a man or men. For example, Foster recounts a tale from northern Australia of Python Woman, a creator being, who also distributed spirit children. She was accosted by some men who took some of her law/lore. This law/lore became an extremely important men's ceremony and is now controlled by men.

In a Ngarinyin story, a man created some sacred items, but kept them for himself. Knowing this, two men came to his camp when he was away hunting. His wife, who was blind, was there alone and the men stole some of the items (HR Bell 1998). In effect the items were stolen from a woman's care, who was blind to the possibility of their theft and the danger the men presented. From these stories it would seem then, that in the earliest times, women were the protectors of sacred knowledge, they were the shamans, priestesses or law/lore women (as occur in matrifocal culture). Then, at some point men took some of the ritual for themselves.

The Oldest Continuous Living and Thriving Culture

The last story is traditionally seen as a tale in favour of sharing. It may be so, but it is also a tale reflecting a forcible shift to a more male-oriented power system. In earlier chapters of this book we saw that this was a change that also happened for cultures in other parts of the world.

Changes into elements of patriarchy

One wonders why the women accepted this shift – another of these theft stories provides an insight. Lambert recounts the Djan'kawu story of the Dhuwa moiety of the Yolŋu people of northeast Arnhem Land. The Djan'kawu were sisters 'who created our world' (Gay'wu Group of Women 2019) who arrived from an island across the sea and travelled from east to west, naming the creatures they saw, giving birth to many moieties, providing the people with language, ritual and myth, and allowing their possessions to turn into features of the landscape (e.g. rocks offshore are the upturned boats they used). They carried with them many 'emblems of power and sacred ritual' (Lambert 1993).

At one point, they left their dilly bags full of sacred objects hanging in a tree while they went to the mangroves to collect crabs and shellfish. The men then crept out from a secret ceremony ground, stole the dilly bags and took them back to the men's ceremony ground where women may not follow, because they are women.

According to Lambert's recounting of this, when the theft was discovered by the sisters, 'the older sister considers that it may be time for them to relinquish their power and allow men, for a period, to take control by possessing the sacred bag. The sisters understand that as women the knowledge is innate within them and that, besides, they have their uteruses, which hold not the symbolic but the actual power of creation'. This is supported by the Gay'wu Group of Women who write of this story 'They didn't take away giving birth to children and so they didn't take away our power to create'.

Lambert asserts that, 'Traditional Aboriginal Society is founded on the pre-eminence of the characteristics of the Universal Feminine, epitomised by its unwavering respect for the earth, which Aborigines refer to as "the mother"… '. Balanced with this, she refers to the Universal Masculine attributes 'such as limitation, order, structure and definition'.

According to Lawlor, 'Among early contact tribes there was very little evidence of wife-beating, very few illicit marriages, and no evidence of prostitution for pay, … '. Yunkaporta (2019) refers to homosexual males being regarded as having special powers in calming distraught children and mediating disputes. In Tiwi Society he states that transgender people have been known to carry important cultural knowledge and conduct their own ceremonies.

In contrast to this overall peaceful telling, infractions of traditional law/lore could generate severe violence, including spearing, into the legs or to cause death. By the time of the arrival of Europeans, the culture that had originated in matrifocal values like 'receptivity, mutability, interrelatedness, and diffusion' (Lambert 1993) had moved heavily toward masculine values, to retribution and punishment. Yunkaporta (2019) comments that 'Punishment is harsh and swift, but afterwards there is no criminal record, no grudge against the transgressor'.

A woman accused of seeing men's ritual objects (which, it would seem, had once belonged to women) could be offered a choice of punishment between death, or rape by every man of the tribe until the men were satisfied (Flood 2019). There is no way of knowing how ancient or recent this practice is, but it would have to indicate how far the culture had moved from its matrifocal origins, where the cruel and brutal punishment of group-rape would never be a sentence brought down on a woman. Colonial settlers in Tasmania noted the scars and brutal treatment meted out to the First Nations women there, by their husbands (Flood 2019). Yunkaporta proposes that such reports already reflect 'fragmented societies whose governance structures had been severely disrupted' by first-contact encounters, rather than truly traditional behaviours. Certainly, in some places there were protections for women, such as being able to appeal to those who had arranged their marriage, for aid with an unsuitable husband (D Bell 1983).

At the end of the last ice age sea levels began to rise as the ice melted. The climate improved and so did the productivity of the land, leading to increased population. However by 10,000 BCE large coastal areas had become drowned, including the valley of Sydney Harbour. With the loss of the lands of coastal people there was no choice but to move inland. As Flood says, 'Displacement and population growth apparently led to increasing warfare and territoriality, changes reflected in rock paintings'. It is probable that the specialised 'death spear' (up to 40 sharp stone flakes set into two grooves on the shaft) was developed at this time (Flood 2019). When hunters become warriors, some fundamentals of matrifocal cultures change. This chapter has indicated the lifestyle areas in which this may have occurred.

Dating for this is highly speculative. Lawlor proposes that the decline of matriarchies, including for First Nations people, began with the ending of the last ice age. In Europe he marks this with the 'Aryan invasions', being the same group for which I have used the term Kurgan/Yamnaya people (Chapter 7), who moved into matrifocal Europe at about 5,000 to 4,000 BCE. Presumably, these people were developing their patriarchal tendencies prior to that, perhaps in the period 10,000 BCE (above, Flood 2019) to 5,000 BCE. As Lawlor indicates, First Nations Australians may, at the same time, have been doing something similar. How this could occur in such a synchronistic way would deserve much further study, although Lawlor proposes a theory to do with changes in the magnetism of the Earth. The important point is that changes did happen.

The story of the Djan'kawu sisters recounted above, gives us a way to further understand this change. At the base of it is men's desire to find a way to share in the deep 'power of creation'. There are aspects of men's ceremony that illustrate that desire to share some of the exceptional sacredness of women's business, based on women's bleeding and ability to give life.

The sacred blood of women

Menstrual blood is seen as extremely powerful and something men should have nothing to do with (D Bell 1998). 'A man may not touch, smell, or see the blood of the womb for fear of his very life. He is in mortal danger if he is careless at this women's time' (HR Bell 1998). The women retreat together during their bleeding time, knowing that menstrual blood is too powerful and dangerous for menfolk, and no man will approach where they are camped (HR Bell 1998). This contrasts with the Western attitude under patriarchy where a menstruating woman is seen as unclean, rather than sacred (Lawlor 1991).

Red ochre represents this blood and is, as we saw in other chapters, considered highly sacred. Trading for it occurred across vast distances in Australia. Only exceptional law/lore men were permitted to paint their bodies with red ochre in the design. Men who were healers, law/lore men and emissaries were designated Australia-wide with red and white lines painted across the nose and cheeks – they could travel anywhere unimpeded (Poulter and Nicholson 2018).

In some tribes women used ochre in deep healing rituals, in others they might use blood but never red ochre (only white or yellow) as red is considered men's business. Where women do use it, it is for sacred use such the initiation rites for girls, rubbing it into lines cut into the body (D Bell 1998, speaking of the Ngarrindjeri people, Lower Murray, South Australia) so that the scar would heal as a raised line ('cicatrisation'). Other tribes used clay or ash (Flood 2019) of particular plants that inhibit bleeding, for this purpose.

Initiation for young men usually involved circumcision (e.g. the Ngarinyin of the Kimberley [HR Bell]; also in Central Australia [D Bell 1983, 1998] and also mentioned by Hiatt 1991; Flood 2019; Lambert 1993) so that, like women, they would actually bleed into the Earth 'their flesh and blood spilling into the Earth as a sacrifice in sacred consecration of the place where they belong, the renewal of the tribe in the land to which they are now biologically joined' (HR Bell 1998). Lambert claims that in this process dependency on a human mother is 'transformed into a mature bond with the Universal Feminine, "the mother earth," who will be his new guide and provider'.

According to Hiatt, initially the women objected to this ritual and it could take days before the mother provided her required consent. Even so, when the boy was taken by the men, the women set up wailing in genuine grief at losing the child to the men, although, of course, they knew what was going to happen and when (Lawlor 1991; D Bell 1998). The initiation would 'mark the novitiates' passage out of women's control' (D Bell 1998). Lambert says that the mothers at this point must relinquish the close bonds of a mother with her child so that he can move on into the roles of manhood. This relinquishment is the basis of the women's grief.

When the boy is taken he is secluded with the older men, who cut themselves and smear the boy with their blood, symbolising that he has begun his second emergence from the womb of life (Lawlor 1991), this time through men. There are other First Nations' male bleeding rituals (Lawlor 1991) that I have chosen not to detail here.

Lawlor believes that ' … underlying the Aboriginal world view is the belief that people only reach fruition by accepting the risk and adventure of continual death and rebirth … ' and each successive ritual of initiation offers this opportunity to men throughout their lives. It provides the opportunity not to suffer pain, but to utilise trance-skills to rise above pain and fear. Women, on the other hand have fewer such rituals because '… during pregnancy, childbirth, and menstruation … women, by their very nature, continually participate in the initatic experience … '.

Women's business and men's business

Within the information above, we see reverence and great respect for the powers of women, which are, similarly, embedded in matrifocal cultures. We also see an effort by men to achieve some extra authority, which may have moved too far, into patriarchal ways. In Australian First Nations' culture, there is a clear allocation of some ritual and knowledge to women and others to men, there are also joint ceremonies. This practice is now usually referred to as 'women's business' and 'men's business'.

The Oldest Continuous Living and Thriving Culture

Anthropologist Dianne Bell states the 'the separation of the sexes does not solve the tensions engendered by male-female relations: it merely orders certain aspects of the sets of relationships within and between the domains of men and women ... the relation between the sexes ... an ever-shifting, negotiable balance'. Women's rituals are a part of this balance. The desire for balance is intrinsic to First Nations' culture (Lawlor 1991) which is a value also held by matrifocal cultures. The Gay'wu group of Women (2019) state that 'men's and women's knowledge balances each other. It is entwined, it is not separate'.

As part of this, stories often have a women's side and a men's side (D Bell 1998). Each group respects the law/lore that the other is responsible for. The men will not go near a women's ceremony, and will 'travel circuitous routes to avoid even sighting the area' (D Bell 1983). Although the men know some of the stories and activities, they will not speak of them, but refer to the women to share this information or not. The women treat men's business in the same way. This balance is seen in other ways – women and men usually seek out food separately, when there are events that need collaboration, such as setting fire to grass to flush out game, or creating an eel race in the river, the collaboration is negotiated by mutual consent (Hiatt 1991), as is typical in a matrifocal culture. Similarly, decision-making is by consensus, without the idea of a chief (Flood 2019), and based on the acceptance by all of the law/lore.

In earlier chapters, we have spoken of the matrifocal principle of two – there are always two that must operate in harmony with each other, neither can have success alone. This principle is explicit in Australian First Nations' culture too. 'In all of Creation there are always two ... Always two – that is the Law.' (HR Bell 1998). Lambert contends that 'the Aboriginal worldview can be seen as founded upon a distinct twoness' originating with the two realms of the Dreaming and 'earthly creations, or physical reality'.

Goettner-Abendroth speaks of the 'twinship' of two equivalent powers in matriarchies, particularly between women and men. Dianne Bell, uses the word 'complementarity' for this relationship in all things, within the Australian First Nations' belief system. Hannah Bell gives a sample list of twos in Ngarinyin law/lore that includes bones and dust; rock and sand; animal blood and vegetable; mother and father; red ochre and white claypipe. The Universe is seen in terms of complementarities and balance, and as part of this, humans reflect this principle too. The Australian First Nations' traditional culture sought a peaceful balanced world, just as matrifocal cultures do.

Avoidance of war is a typically matrifocal behaviour and in First Nations' Australia there were no wars of conquest (Graham 2021). Ability as a warrior or hunter gave you no special privilege, but did gain respect and recognition. Conflicts occurred, surprise attacks occurred, though they were not permitted under traditional law/lore. Twenty-eight days' notice of a conflict was expected to be given and both sides had to have a similar number of men involved (Poulter and Nicholson 2018). Often women were asked to adjudicate between two opposing groups of men as ' ... it was women who were responsible for mitigating the violence of tribal conflicts to ensure that justice took place' (Lambert 1993). Women as peacekeepers is a feature of matrifocal communities.

Power in society could not be earned by force, but by 'the twin test of character and knowledge' (Poulter and Nicholson 2018). The required character traits were of 'humility, patience and inclusion'. A person could not nominate themselves for high office. The number of senior Elders was strictly balanced between the skin groups and each gender, so that 'power could never be concentrated in one group, one gender, one family or one clan' (Poulter and Nicholson 2018). Additionally, 'there are no headmen, chiefs, leaders ... no single man is elevated' so that he could direct or control other people (Lambert 1993; Lawlor 1991). This egalitarian approach is typically matrifocal.

A federated economy

Poulter and Nicholson report that traditional Australia operated a kind of federal system, starting with a few clans who spoke the same language. Each of these language groups in turn formed part of a broader cultural federation of perhaps a half-dozen language groups. Each of these federations then established trade, travel, cultural exchange and diplomatic relations with other federations. 'There was therefore an embedded sense of common identity across the whole of Australia, and this was evidenced by the fact that all the people in the centre of Australia knew it was an island.' (Poulter & Nicholson 2018).

In 1951, the anthropologist, Ronald Berndt noted the practice of 'dzamalag' among the Gunwinggu people of western Arnhem Land, Northern Australia. This was the practice of a gift economy, as we have noted previously occurs in matrifocal cultures to confirm relationships of friendship and kin. Lambert reports that ' ... "free-giving" and generosity are fostered in Aboriginal children at a very young age'.

Given this, and the federation structure, we could expect that a gift economy would have been widespread. This is confirmed by the work of Isabel McBride, a professional archaeologist who was able to trace a complex system of exchange based on stone axes.

An example is greenstone axes from a quarry in Victoria moving through networks, over 1,000 kilometres, across south-eastern Australia (Griffiths 2018). Lawlor states that for First Nations people, 'status relates directly to the capacity to take part in reciprocal exchanges'. Graeber reports on a gift-giving event, indicating that it included dancing, singing, the exchange of sexual activity, and giving of goods such as tobacco, serrated spears and European cloth. According to Graeber, barter, on the other hand, was used where a long-term trust had not been established.

It is known that at times of plenty, clans would gather together for cultural events, marriage and building good relationships. The 'host' people didn't demand payment for their food. Pascoe states that 'one of the central tenets of trading was the sharing of resources', pointing out that events like the bunya nut harvest (south-eastern Queensland) and the Bogong moth season (around much of the Australian coastline and mountains) would have been opportunities for gatherings, as would the eel season in Victoria.

Is this a matrifocal culture?

Dianne Bell contends that First Nations women have been disproportionately affected by the coming of colonial settlers. In particular, by the loss of their traditional lands and food production activities; by the Western patriarchal system including only men in decision-making, removing the continual dialogue that had enabled women to participate actively; and because of the stereotypes of women held by the settler population (as domestic workers and sex objects), that forced First Nations women into a diminished area of action.

The Oldest Continuous Living and Thriving Culture

It is unlikely that Western people today would accept the idea of separation of women's business and men's business in their lives. The experience of the unequal distribution of tasks based on gender under patriarchy has been too damaging to both sexes and women have fought long and hard to remove these constraints. What we can consider perhaps, is the notion of balance, of an equal dialogue and the principle of two-way thinking. In any discussion there may be at least two sides, other than female and male, for example, 'We have considered the effect on the water, what about the land?'.

This chapter has been about exploring whether First Nations' cultures can be considered matrifocal. When we compare them with the matrifocal principles discussed most fully in Chapter 3, I don't think it is possible to say that they are. Nevertheless, I think the roots of the culture were matrifocal and over an extensive period of time (65,000 years) evolved into a way of life that is truly unique and complex, with a highly-developed spirituality. It was so different from the European worldview that there was no way for real mutual understanding and respect to occur, at the outset. It is to be hoped something close can be achieved now, over 230 years later.

Women have their way of looking at the world and men have tended to another way. For too long in Western culture we have had one-way thinking, under the domination of male figures in powerful positions. We now know it doesn't work, and that better outcomes can be achieved by allowing space for both perspectives to be respected and heard, with a consensus outcome that works for everyone.

Ancient Ways for Current Days

Postscript

I recognise that the spirituality of the First Nations peoples is intrinsically connected to this ancient land of Australia and that I am a newcomer. In my search for understanding and meaning I respect and honour that connection and do not in any way wish to cause offense in doing so.

CHAPTER 12

Modern Matrifocal Re-emergence

Without women there is no freedom. Until women educate and empower themselves, there won't be freedom.
Painted large on a wall in the women's village of Jinwar, in Syria.

So, have we been talking about an ancient tradition sadly now passing, to be swallowed up by Western values and the nuclear family? A worn-out format, curious but irrelevant? Some women think not, and are reinventing a new model for themselves. Below we look at three examples, one from Kenya, one type in both Australia and the USA, and the most recent in Syria.

Women's unity – Umoja, Kenya

Is there a future for matrifocal systems? There are women of the Samburi tribe in Kenya, who possibly don't know about the ancient and current matrifocal traditions, but are nevertheless taking action to take control of their lives by walking out on domestic violence, female genital mutilation, forced marriages and rape, in other words, men. They have left their men in the village of their childhood or marriage and gone and built first one village, Umoja, and then more.

Umoja was started in 1990 by 15 women who became stigmatised in their communities after they were raped by British soldiers from a base at nearby Archer's Post, a trading centre bordering Samburu and Isiolo. Some of the rape survivors say their husbands accused them of bringing dishonour to their families and threw them out. They found a piece of land, moved there and named it Umoja – Swahili for 'unity'.

In that first village established 30 years ago, there are no men allowed, though women may have lovers who they meet away from the village. Sons who accept matriarchal rule may stay. In huts protected by thorny brush to keep away intruders, 48 women live with their children. When a man trespasses, the women notify the local police, who either issue a warning or arrest the culprit – depending on the number of offenses.

The women have built everything. They make traditional jewellery and sell it to Westerners for an income. The men say it is not natural, mainly because 'these women cannot be controlled'! In subsequent villages, the women have allowed adult men to live with them if they reject the traditional Samburi values and recognise that women are the decision-makers of the town. You can find videos of these villages (and of Jinwar, below) on YouTube.

Umoja has grown into a refuge, welcoming women escaping abusive marriages, female genital mutilation, rape and other forms of assault. Even some women whose husbands have died have found solace and a home there. They run a school, cultural centre and campsite for tourists visiting the nearby Samburu National Reserve. They create complicated colourful beaded jewellery and other traditional craft for sale.

In the true matrifocal way, all women have equal status with each other and all decisions are made together.

Womyn's Lands – USA and Australia

In the late 1960s and during the 1970s Western women lived under many more strictures than they do now. Access to divorce was poor and seen as shameful, abortion illegal, women could not borrow money without a male guarantor, children born out of wedlock were routinely removed from their mothers, no single parent benefit existed, homosexuality was a sin or a disease to be cured and was generally reviled, and domestic violence was condoned.

In these circumstances, some courageous groups of women began to move out of mainstream society, creating homes and villages for themselves in country isolation, where they could live freely the way they wanted, close to the Earth. Men were absolutely excluded from these communities, although today some do allow men to visit. Generally speaking they are referred to as 'Womyn's Lands'. Such communities included lesbians and some were exclusively safe havens for lesbians. Several of these established themselves in close proximity in northern NSW in Australia, and exist in various degrees still today (Hall 2019).

Womyn's Lands now practise various forms of lesbian separatism, an idea which emerged as a result of the Radical Feminist movement in the late 1960s. Lesbian separatism is based on the concept that women must exist separately from men, socially and politically, in order to achieve the goals of feminism – to gain women's liberation through separation from mainstream patriarchal society. Certainly, the idea of separation from patriarchal societies is one often adopted in matrifocal communities (which included women and men) in the past.

Women-only communities were established in Australia, New Zealand, America and Western Europe. In Australia, the main community of this sort was called Amazon Acres, established in 1974, renamed The Mountain in the 1980s. It was on 1,000 acres of native bushland, about 400 kilometres north of Sydney. The aim was for a self-sustaining utopia where women lived free of men, riding horses, building shelters where needed and living naked if the weather allowed. There was no electricity and huts and homes were quite basic and built entirely with hand-tools. Like matrifocal communities, decisions were made by consensus and childcare and chores were shared. More than a thousand women have come and gone from The Mountain to date (Hall 2019), with 10–100 women and girls living there at any one time. The community is now home to a diminishing group of women who live there full-time or occasionally, and open to further women interested (Sitka 2019).

It is reported that there are one hundred or so remaining women-only communities in America, and these mainly trace their roots to the original 'Pagoda by the Sea', founded in St Augustine, Florida, in 1977. A product of the 1970s gay rights and women's liberation movements, a group of women made their way to Florida to live together on a beach where no men were allowed.

For 15 years, the Pagoda had hundreds of female visitors, and a small core community of 12 cottages. In the 1990s, some of these women relocated to a mountaintop in rural Alabama. They formed a camp called Alapine Village which still exists today. According to their website, the village:

> ... is home to a diverse group of womyn who celebrate many spiritual paths, pursue a variety of outdoor activities, and enjoy vegetarian and gluten-free to omnivorous diets. Residents are full-time, part-time, or seasonal. ... We currently range in age from 50s to 80s but welcome women of all ages.

The women run their own businesses, are employed locally or retired. They live and work the land together in an eco-friendly, community-based and strictly man-free lesbian community.

Today such communities struggle with numbers as the original founders age, the wider world provides conditions more tolerable to women, including lesbians, and a radical feminist analysis wanes.

Women's Land – Jinwar, Syrian Kurdistan

Now, in the autonomous region of north-east Syria/west Kurdistan, Kurdish women have created Jinwar, a village built and inhabited by women of all cultures and beliefs who, having survived Islamic State (ISIS) and civil war, wish to live apart from male violence. They are fleeing a rigid family structure, domestic abuse and the horrors of civil war such as rape, displacement, being sold and treated as slaves, and the potential of death.

Similar to the African example, men may visit Jinwar by daylight but cannot stay overnight. In fact the idea for the village was partly inspired by Umoja. Commenced in November 2016, built in 2018, 'Jinwar' means 'Womens' Land' in the Kurdish language. The women want to experience freedom, democracy and a new form of life, different from the restricted one that has been imposed upon them for thousands of years. One shaped by the women themselves, and their goal is self-sustainability.

The women built 30 houses of adobe (mudbrick) which required only freely available resources, in line with their concern for the environment and to reduce waste. Their buildings line three sides of a common space, creating a triangle. They also have a communal bakery and kitchen, a children's park, a natural medicine clinic, a school, a small museum and the Jinwar Academy where many practical skills are taught. The women have completed beautiful murals, representing the ideals of the community, on the outside of their buildings. The idea is to create more of these eco-villages across the Syrian Kurdistan region.

Kurdish, Yazidi and Arab women all live in harmony there. Each family has some land allotted to them in open fields where they grow their food, which is a source of confidence and pride. A wide range of fruit and vegetables are grown. Renewable energies are used, mainly solar power (Lopez 2020).

The commune is self-governing and an assembly is held every month where women contribute ideas, are heard, and all contributions have the same value. The women take turns each month to act as leader of the village. At the meeting tasks are also distributed, allowing women to learn how to do different jobs (Lopez 2020). One roster is to keep track of comings and goings, including at night when the women on the roster carry a weapon for security.

The women want to challenge conservative, patriarchal ideas and establish the reality of the free, independent woman. They are influenced by the concept of Democratic Confederalism, which is based on the ideas of Abdullah Ocalan, a Kurdish nationalist and political activist, about women's freedom and self-administration of different ethnic and social groups (Vaughan 2019). Democratic Confederalism includes a framework that reflects many of the principles that matrifocal societies have traditionally shown. These include local assemblies, decisions made communally, the custodianship of property rather than ownership, the application of ecologically sound principles, and promotion of women's rights.

At the time of writing the women of Jinwar are in danger from the border war between Syria and Turkey and they are appealing to anyone who can intervene to stop the violence to do so. In November 2019, they had to withdraw from the commune due to the threat of Turkish invasion, but have since returned.

Women turning their backs on patriarchy

All of the models discussed in this chapter have emerged from utter desperation or frustration with the constraints for women under patriarchy, the lack of safety for women it represents, all stemming from the loss of respect for women and their life-bringing and nurturing role.

There are men who are also less than satisfied, and while a growing group, they are vastly overshadowed by those completely committed to male supremacy and the violence they perpetrate. The groups discussed in this chapter all exclude men from the day-to-day life of women. This is not the traditional matrifocal way, but it may be a new way for women until men find ways to abandon the toxic masculinity that has developed under patriarchy.

Ancient Ways for Current Days

It seems that, when women are pushed to their limits they will abandon a society run on patriarchal values. It is to be hoped that we can take the time to look at matrifocal ways of being, for the good of both women and men worldwide, to see what can be learned and adopted, before more of the ruthless behaviour toward women is perpetrated.

Alesali and Zdanowicz on CNN reported the words of Emin, one of the women of Jinwar: 'Jinwar is life's spirit, nature's spirit and free woman's spirit … I wish that we could build more Jinwars in every region so that no woman should be subjected to injustice'.

CHAPTER 13

Creations of Nature – Our Kin

> Farm and land and animals need nurturing. Sometimes the women haven't been allowed to express that nurturing side that I think the land really benefits from. Not by being dominated but by being nurtured and encouraged. It's just nice to have a bit more balance now I think women are allowed to be part of the picture a lot more and I think that's quite important.
>
> **Garlone Moulin, a woman grazier, Mt Pleasant Station, Queensland, Australia, in the video 'River to Reef'.**

In 2019 more than 11,000 scientists around world (153 countries) signed a scientific paper that declared a climate emergency. According to the World Wildlife Fund's (WWF) 'Living Planet Report 2020', over the past 50 years, humans have killed almost 70 per cent of terrestrial biodiversity, and 50 per cent of freshwater biodiversity, on the planet. This particularly impacted species in Latin America and the Caribbean.

Our relationship with Nature is broken

As the WWF says, 'The findings are clear: our relationship with Nature is broken'. They also point out that there is a direct relationship between what we do in nature and the emergence of infectious diseases, which have increased dramatically over the last 80 years. The COVID-19 pandemic that emerged in 2020 is not a freak occurrence: it is part of this escalation. In his book *How Contagion Works* author Paulo Giordano says that the more we become aggressive towards nature, the more we push into rich biodiversity and tropical forests, the more we put ourselves at risk. In the process, bacteria that once lived inside the gut of extinct animals are forced to look elsewhere for somewhere to live. As well, in his view, the growing need for food is forcing millions of people to resort to eating animals that should be left alone.

Due to climate change the world is experiencing unprecedented and devastating weather events, including cyclone, flood and fire. In 2020, Australia experienced megafires, wildfires of never before seen proportions that shocked the world. More than 100,000 farmers had properties or livestock affected by the fires, with an estimated 12 per cent of the national sheep flock and 9 per cent of the cattle herd killed or affected (Flannery 2020). In the same fires, 143 million wild animals including mammals, reptiles, birds and frogs were killed or displaced (WWF). Species extinction from these fires is possible and still being explored. In the 2019 Amazon Rainforest fires, created purely for private profit, 2.3 million animals died. Due to the climate emergency, overheating of the seas is killing coral beds, seen in the coral bleaching events in the Great Barrier Reef of Australia.

The WWF holds humans alone responsible for the situation, pointing to growth of human consumption, population, global trade and urbanisation over the last 50 years. Destruction of forests for agriculture is responsible for 80 per cent of global deforestation. Where and how people produce food is one of the greatest threats – if current habits remain the same even more clearing will have to occur (to create 10–25% larger agricultural space in 2050 than in 2005). Yet, around the world approximately one third of all food produced for humans is wasted.

There are many grassroots initiatives to tackle the climate change issue, such as the actions by the Extinction Rebellion movement, or the school strikes initiated by school student Greta Thunberg in her determination to do something to get recalcitrant decision-makers to take action on the topic. She stared down the United Nation's 2019 Climate Action Summit attendees saying, 'How dare you! How dare you look away … and come here saying that you're doing enough?'

Human destruction requires human intervention

David Attenborough has said that once nature determined which species survive. Now humans determine how nature survives. He offers a plan that he says would enable both humans and animals to thrive:

- a rapid transition to renewable energy
- an end to land clearing
- rewilding on land and marine reserves.

Within this, he emphasises the need to improve the lives of the world's poorest and for strong systems of accountability. He says, 'we often talk of saving the planet … the truth is we must do these things to save ourselves'.

Ancient Ways for Current Days

Tim Flannery has written extensively on the climate emergency and in his book *The Climate Cure* elaborates 'we need to fight three critical battles':

- cutting fossil fuel use decisively and deeply
- minimise damage that the planet will suffer as a result of greenhouse gases already emitted and to come
- development of a new, clean economy with the capacity to draw CO_2 out of the air at scale.

The group of scientists with which I opened this chapter propose the solutions to these human induced problems lie in human actions such as reducing the:

- fertility rate
- amount of air travel
- meat production.

Naomi Klein points to the 'Green New Deal' proposed by Alexandria Ocasio-Cotez and other Democrats in the United States, which she sees as an eminently feasible plan of action. No doubt it is applicable for any country. It proposes that the US government:

- wean the United States from fossil fuels
- curb planet-warming greenhouse gas emissions across the economy over the next 10 years
- guarantee new high-paying jobs in clean energy industries
- ensure that clean air, clean water and healthy food are basic human rights.

Ending any reliance on the use of fossil fuels, is a key part of all of these proposals. Fossil fuel companies are huge and influential. These companies know that they are not part of the solution but want to survive. Thus they have placed themselves in positions to exercise an unwarranted degree of influence on decision-makers, who react to a fear of the loss of jobs if these industries are not propped up, instead of looking to the longer-term future and putting their effort into building up industries that will support human survival, such as renewables and other sustainable technologies.

If we had remained with the matrifocal model we would not have got to this position. The matrifocal model is a social system inculcated with respect for Nature and the need for humanity to reflect and enhance the natural world. While we need to implement all the plans and initiatives recommended above, I would also contend that developing a respect for all species will help us to recognise the noblest nature in ourselves. Patriarchy certainly does not.

Climate change is a gendered issue, first because it is mainly men who run the companies that create it. It affects women disproportionately due to existing gender inequalities and rigid gender roles. For example, 90 per cent of the 150,000 people killed by the 1991 Bangladesh cyclone were women (Bambrick 2015). Women face additional challenges in meeting the rising energy, transport and food costs associated with climate change. In times of stress family violence increases and a range of mental health issues increase for women. Women are more likely to be living in rented or public housing accommodation which is less likely to be climate-proof. They have fewer resources for disaster preparation, mitigation and rehabilitation. A matrifocal system would put the needs of women and children centrally, while ensuring the needs of everyone in the group were addressed. However, under patriarchy there are many groups of people disadvantaged and left behind.

Ancient Ways for Current Days

The disaster of alienation from Nature

As we learnt in earlier chapters, China was one of the places where early matrifocal cultures were originally to be found, inclusive of respect for Nature. Values from that time are repeatedly reflected in the Chinese worldview in many historic texts. Carr-Harris recounts one by Chuang Tzu (written in the third century BCE):

> [The] long-gone Era of Great Purity [was] a time in which people knew their mothers but not their fathers, and lived in a state of innocence. They were genuine, simple, spontaneous and direct in their conduct. They were in harmony with the seasons and with the ways of nature. Animals and humans did no harm to one another. … this paradise was destroyed when people first began controlling fire, mining, felling trees, hunting and fishing. During this period, referred to as The Great Cosmic Struggle, their perfect life was destroyed because they lost touch with the all-important patterns of nature.

The matrifocal Khasi people of north-east India, described in Chapter 10, have an ancient myth that once there was a sacred ladder between heaven and Earth, resting on the sacred Lum Sohpetbneng mountain peak. The people were in 16 clans and could once move freely between both heaven and Earth via the ladder. Then one day they were tricked into cutting down a divine tree, a serious error which prevented them from getting to heaven forever. Seven families were on Earth at the time and nine in heaven, each group trapped and separated from each other, such is the result of lack of respect and honouring of the natural world.

Even in religions of 'The Book', the worst punishment God could inflict on Adam and Eve was that they were cut off from immersion in, and the bounty of what the natural world represented, shown in the Garden of Eden.

All elements of Nature are kin

According to the UN Environment Program, in the culture of the Maori people of New Zealand, the people 'view the life surrounding them as kin … or relatives'. If we take the longest view of course, we are indeed all from the same primordial soup from which single, then multiple cell organisms began, starting the chain of life and growth on Earth.

Traditional First Nations Australians each have a totem animal which they are tasked with caring for, including the myths associated with it. Their sacred, mythic forbearers often turned themselves into land features or birds or animals at the conclusion of their story. The land and its creatures were sacred. Munya Andrews, a Bardi woman from the Kimberley region in Western Australia, affirms 'our connection, our kindredness and our Oneness with all of nature', including 'so-called inanimate objects' and states that the feeling of '*kindredness* that Indigenous people feel towards their fellow creatures and their environment' is their gift to the world.

Salmon continues that, in Indigenous belief, 'Without human recognition of their role in the complexities of life in a place, the life suffers and loses its sustainability'. As his main example of this belief system he provides a tribe, of which he is a part, in Mexico, the Raramuri. We would have to admit that this perspective has been proven true when we look at the devastation patriarchy, and capitalism as an outgrowth of it, have brought to pass, from absolute failure to care for natural life – our kin.

Connection to Nature supports psychological wellbeing

The Australian First Nations elder Mary Graham, a Kombumerri woman from Queensland, offers a reversal of the Western ideas of relationship with land. She speaks (2021) of the land as caring for and ensuring the well-being of its people. It is custodian of people. 'The land invents us, looks after us and keeps us human'. In turn we must be custodians for the well-being of the land.

We find that the health benefits of returning to an awareness of nature are mutual. The Earth may heal, and so do we. Assistant Professor Gregory Bratman and his colleagues say that various research ' ... has found that the psychological wellbeing of a population can be associated, in part, with its proximity to green space, blue space (i.e. aquatic and marine environments), and street trees or private gardens ... nature experience is associated with psychological wellbeing'. The results are experiences of joy, positive mood and alertness; a sense of wellbeing; ability to engage socially and manage your life; a sense of meaning and purpose in life; decreases in mental distress; improved memory and attention, imagination and creativity; and improved performance of children at school. They comment that opportunities for these experiences are reducing across the globe and argue against this.

Through the new therapeutic approach of 'eco therapy' people experiencing mental health challenges are benefiting in the ways identified above from treatment that involves doing things outside in nature. Activities can include adventure therapy, animal-assisted interventions/therapy, doing work to look after animals on a farm (called 'care farming'), conservation, green exercise therapy, doing art in or with nature, social and therapeutic horticulture and wilderness therapy (Mind Inc 2021). Health benefits can result from as little as caring for an indoor plant.

Ancient underground nurturing

The biologist Suzanne Simard is a professor of forest ecology at the University of British Columbia. It was her research that identified the fungal threads that link nearly every tree in a forest. 'Carbon, water, nutrients, alarm signals and hormones can pass from tree to tree through these subterranean circuits' (Jabr 2021). This ancient underground partnership links trees even of different species to benefit from each other. A dying tree may send a substantial share of its carbon to its neighbours. A sapling planted outside this network, in plantation rows, for example, is 25 per cent less likely to survive than one growing inside the diverse forest.

Darwin popularised the concept of the 'survival of the fittest'. It turns out the 'fittest' may be those who are linked to, and supportive of, each other. Matrifocal culture bases its precepts in observation of nature and espouses cooperative, supportive processes. Perhaps there is an ancient wisdom here we should return to, sooner rather than later!

CHAPTER 14

Regaining the Motherworld

> I used to think that top environmental problems were biodiversity loss, ecosystem collapse and climate change. I thought that thirty years of good science could address these problems. I was wrong. The top environmental problems are selfishness, greed and apathy, and to deal with these we need a cultural and spiritual transformation.
> And we scientists don't know how to do that.
> **James Gustave (Gus) Speth, American environmental lawyer and advocate (1942–present)**

An ancient Iroquois prophecy foretold that in a future time the Grandmothers would come together to light the way for the people. In 2004 the first gathering of 13 Grandmothers from different First Nations people around the world came together to fulfil the prophecy. They came because of their belief that we are now at a critical time in human history and that if we do not change our ways of relating to each other and our Mother

Earth, we will face cataclysmic consequences (https://www.grandmotherscouncil.org).

We face those consequences now.

One of the Grandmothers said of women that we are the only ones who can carry more than one spirit at a time. This is a reference to the ancient matrifocal principle that not only are women to be honoured for bearing life, but for providing the means for the rebirth of a spirit once more into the world. I am not going to discuss the nature of spirit and the truth (or not) of rebirth, but it is certain that only women can hold two life energies – their own, and their offspring in the womb – sometimes multiple offspring. Vaughan-Lee, the Sufi Master, expresses a similar view, that it is only a woman who is 'able to be a place where the light of the soul takes on a human form and remains true to its essential nature'.

Rebirth is a concept held to be true by millions of people around the globe. For interest sake, it's worth noting that it was a close thing that Christianity didn't include rebirth. Western, especially Christian, readers are best not to feel too alien and dismissive of the concept, as theologians in early Christianity, such as Origenes, Basilides and St Gregory taught various forms of reincarnation of the soul as a matter of course. This concept was only written out of Christianity at the Fifth Ecumenical Council of Constantinople in 553 CE, under Emperor Justinian, when the Church officially declared the doctrine to be heresy. Avraham Azulai was a fifteenth century 'Kabbalist' studying this esoteric side of Jewish philosophy. He incorporated reincarnation as a key tenet to tackle war, destruction, and man's inhumanity to his fellow man – in other words the excesses of patriarchy. For those interested, he also prophesied that a significant spiritual transformation would begin to take hold beginning with the year 2000, a time we are now in.

Regaining the Motherworld

In this current time, Vaughan-Lee teaches that the Earth absorbs spiritual energy, which ancient people knew and provided it in abundance through their rituals, which kept the entity we call Earth healthy, attuned. Non-Indigenous people no longer have those rituals, although there are an increasing number working together to offer modern interpretations. Throughout the centuries there have been small groups, mainly women, who have maintained the spiritual rituals of connection to Earth. What were those witches in the Middle Ages actually doing, dancing in circle in a grove of trees? Not conjuring up the devil as the Church hierarchy would have it, that's for sure. They were dancing in honour of the Earth, the skies and waters, usually personified into a Goddess and some Gods. The Church captured and burnt the ritualists, leaving the Earth, in that area at least, without such spiritual sustenance.

This concept will be very hard for the rational thinker to manage, because reason alone is a narrow band of knowledge and system of thinking that has come to dominate (rather than participate) to our disadvantage. Were First Nations Australians, for example, wasting their time for 65,000 years when they nurtured the spirit of their country with ritual, song and dance? They were not – those that do it still, are not. Their level of communication without writing and across long distances, is just one form of evidence – for example, knowing ahead of time that people from far away would arrive on a certain day; creating healing magic at a distance that was effective, and also the energy of punishment, when the receiver did not know anyone was targeting them but felt the effects (HR Bell 1998). The traditional First Nations people in Australia certainly could direct energy where it was needed on their country.

Creating a different future

To create a different future, Vaughan-Lee says one of the first steps needed is for women 'to forgive the masculine, or men, for what they have done'. He recognises though, that, understandably, many will not, 'because men have made a real mess. I mean a real, *real* mess – people can see the ecological devastation but most people can't see the spiritual desecration that has been done.' He contends that women's bodies and cycles are sacred in a way that is not true for men. This relates to the 'two spirits in one body' ability mentioned earlier. This means that the spiritual work that is needed can only be done by women, he imagines in circles, all around the globe. This has to do with 'healing and transmuting the Earth so it can once again function as a living spiritual organism'. This is an enormous expectation of women, but as a key matrifocal principle says, there are always two – and men have important and different roles.

I mentioned in Chapter 1 the Gaia Hypothesis, developed by the scientist James Lovelock. This proposes that the Earth operates as one integrated being, which he called Gaia, after the Greek Goddess. The Earth has its own systems and life forms on it that respond, through the natural systems of the Earth, to perpetuate the conditions for life on the planet. As there are always two – Gaia needs the physical *and* the spiritual healing to return to balance.

In Vaughan-Lee's view, the role of men is to protect women in this work – to value it and consciously protect it, not allow it to be interfered with. He points out that there are many forces in the world that will not want 'the world to be activated again' and will oppose women regaining their power. Implicit in this thought is the need for men to undertake critical work on themselves, so that they can be in the mind frame that will allow them to feel supportive, and then move to a position where they will defend such work.

Men have lost much of their own self-balance in creating patriarchy. Using the principle of two, we all have masculine and feminine energy. Men in large part have left behind their own internal feminine. A woman can also do this, to her detriment, under patriarchy. We see women in high office who believe they can only succeed 'in a man's world' by being as ruthless as the men. We see others, who are informed by a feminist analysis, who do place the needs of women in a central position. We all need to reinforce our feminine aspects to be truly balanced humans. Men in matrifocal societies enjoyed the benefit of this balance in themselves and in their world.

Taylor, who holds a doctorate in psychology, talks of his travel experience of coming in contact with the world of Minoan Crete (a matrifocal culture discussed in Chapter 9) and a yearning it brought him for something similar. He feels that if that came to pass 'it won't necessarily be because women are in power, but because the drive for power and the structures that support it are absent, replaced by empathic connection with nature, other human beings and other living beings, and the whole cosmos'. In other words, a matrifocal society. He feels that in Minoan Crete neither women nor men were afflicted with what he calls an 'over-developed ego'. In contrast, people living under Western values have a strong sense of individuality, which can make us feel disconnected from people and nature and even our own bodies. Like most people of the Western world I prize my individuality and its expression. Yet it is in community, in connection to other people, working together with shared values towards a positive goal that brings the greatest feelings of satisfaction. We will all need to be less self-centred if you like, to solve the current conundrum.

We have two responsibilities: one is to take action in the outer world and the other is to undertake the necessary and critical inner work. Woodman said the 'great work of our time' is to bring the feminine into this culture and that it's not an easy path. 'How does each one of us contribute? Believe it or not, it's done in the most personal ways. Take time to listen to your dreams, to write them down. Take time to recognise that there are things going on within you that need to be felt, or said, or lived, or grieved. Pay attention to these things both in yourself and in the people in your life. Pay attention to the authentic self.' Are you wanting to scoff? Look again, how easy would these things really be for you? Possibly harder if you are a man, since it can also challenge a woman. This is personal work.

Much of what needs to happen now requires fundamental change. I have proposed that first, it is important to know that patriarchy is only 4,000 years old at the most and there is another model, the matrifocal way that more than met our needs, and existed in the world possibly for over 200,000 years (Berekhat Ram figurine, Chapter 1). Second, that the matrifocal model offers an approach that may be adapted to function for us again, now that we are at a time of profound dissatisfaction with the place to which our patriarchal system has brought us.

An invitation to discuss and explore

I did not write this book because I have the answers, but to contribute to the information that we need to create them, to raise the questions. I invite you all to discuss and debate the principles with your friends and colleagues. Perhaps the following exploration of the utility of the main aspects of matrifocal culture may prove useful in such discussions.

Regaining the Motherworld

Goettner-Abendroth defines matriarchies as:

- Societies of economic mutuality, based on the circulation of gifts
- Non-hierarchical, horizontal societies of matrilineal kinship
- Egalitarian societies of consensus.

The necessary conditions for this are:

In matrifocal cultures, mothers are at the centre of society (shown by matrilineal descent and the mothers' power of economic distribution). The necessary conditions for this are:

1. Women are respected and valued
2. Equality, consensus and peace
3. Balance between the sexes
4. Matrilineal kinship
5. Economic mutuality
6. Relaxed enjoyment of sexuality
7. Shared politics
8. Spirituality – Goddess, the ancestors and the natural world
9. Principle of two.

Let's look at what these might mean in a little more detail.

1. Women are respected and valued

Matrifocal cultures hold that mothers are at the centre of society. Respect for women means that the woman's needs are put first. The values of mothering: being considerate and nurturing, showing tolerance, being adaptive, caring for those most in need and being cooperative, are paramount. Women are treasured for their ability to give life, which is not a licence to overpopulate – matrifocal

> cultures have always found ways to control the number of offspring produced, for the capacity of the geographical space, and food production system available. Care of children is central and shared.

With regard to the care of children the Deep Ecology practitioner Joanna Macy feels '… all the children for centuries to come are my children'. This has to be the view to emphasise that what we do to the planet now will be either endured or enjoyed by future generations.

With women respected and valued there would be no more social messages as given in Western society that are negative, violent, disrespectful of anyone, and in particular, women and children. In my view, what benefits the marginalised flows through to benefit all. What benefits the privileged benefits the privileged. A culture based on women and children benefits all. Tyson Yunkaporta, writes (2019) 'those two together, mother and child, are the pivotal relationship in any stable society'.

A focus group of women about this principle advocated that pregnancy and birth should be revered and celebrated; women should be supported in women's circles and we should bring back more communal responsibility and support for childrearing because, according to an African proverb, 'It takes a village to raise a child'.

What does your group think?

2. Equality, consensus and peace

> Matrifocal cultures are egalitarian societies of consensus, which are non-hierarchical, horizontal societies of matrilineal kinship which promote dialogue. In this way people work collectively to

ensure peace, with no class system. On a given topic the group would start discussions at the grassroots, for example in the clan home, then to a wider group and so on. At any point the decision thus far can be returned to the grassroots, and if they disagree they can reformulate it and propose it again.

Clark (in Biaggi 2005) states that majority-rules voting is not the way to make significant changes in social institutions. 'In fact, voting inevitably leaves one side – as much as 49 per cent of a society – dissatisfied and feeling coerced.' She provides an example with regard to war: ' ... we now have a dangerously over-armed planet ... trapped in an institutionalised militarism that threatens to become an evolutionary cul-de-sac. ... the world's citizens are overwhelmingly against acts of violence as a solution to human differences, regardless of their particular leader's opinion'. Our current decision-making structures do not allow this strong preference for peace to be reflected in the outcomes.

Carr-Harris expresses that, for the Western world at least, we can create a matricentric future without guns or violent revolution, because we are simply returning to our true human nature 'to create and maintain a matricentric social order compatible with our biology, one in which children hold centre stage, and peaceful, mutual nurturing is universally accepted as the order of the day.'

Equality, (and equity) at a societal level requires evening out the income spread. On this, see the principle on the economy.

One action would be to make clear and act on our commitment to the Charter of the United Nations, developed 75 years ago. 'To work collectively to ensure peace and security. To build relations between nations based on equal rights and self-determination of peoples. To solve global problems through international cooperation. And to promote respect for the human rights of all.' (Smith and Cockayne 2020).

Carr-Harris believed that we should promote equality and consensus communities of resilience by establishing child-centred, agricultural collectives of no more than 500, as that number has been shown to be 'the maximum human optimum for a healthy, viable egalitarian community'.

A focus group of women about this principle were concerned about the challenges of consensus over the 'majority rules' approach that we tend to have now. Would it mean everyone lived in big groups? How could this be achieved? Or perhaps the decisions could be made in citizen groups, or gender groups rather than co-habitation groups?

What does your group think?

3. Balance between the sexes

> In matrifocal cultures women and men receive equal dignity – they are in balance. Women and men respect each other's dignity, value and spheres of responsibility in a true balance between the sexes, rather than the dominance of one over the other. This creates a relationship of working together, with equal dignity and respect.

There may be some concern that this principle leads to sex role stereotyping, something women and some men have been attempting to break free of, at least since the 1970s. In the past it often has proscribed female and male roles, although in this book we looked at a couple of matrifocal cultures where, while the task was gendered, if a person of the other gender wished to undertake the task they could. Today we will want greater fluidity

Regaining the Motherworld

than that. The central principle is that no one gender is valued more highly or given more privilege because of their gender, and that the needs of each is respected (for example the three days of seclusion while menstruating illustrates respect for a sex-based difference. People who did not menstruate would not need or expect this leave).

Both women and men will need to change to rise to the ideal expressed in this principle. Orenstein undertook comprehensive interviews with young men between the ages of 16 and 22, and they shared with her many raw revelations that revealed a deep desire for more expansive ways of being a man. Some were struggling with conflicting social messages about respect and sexual conquest; there were boys who want closeness but lack the social skills to achieve it. Orenstein reports that one sexually active college student said his most intimate act was holding hands. She provides a vision of how boys can move forward as better men.

It is my hope that Goettner-Abendroth is correct in stating that matriarchal understanding 'can support men in their alternative movements, giving them another way of identifying as men by demonstrating that war and violence are not the innate heritage of mankind.'

I have referred to the Kurdish people in this book (Chapter 12), who always seem to be under attack. Without their own recognised state they are at odds with a number of governments. But I wonder how much their vision for how they want to live is really the concern to their opponents. Their philosophy is expressed through Abdullah Ocalan's writing. He was caught (with USA assistance) and convicted by the Turkish Government, for being involved in the creation of an armed organisation (Kurdish Workers' Party). He has been held on an island since 1999 and from that prison has published several books. He has said 'the need to reverse the role of man is of revolutionary importance. ... Woman's success is the success of society and the individual at all levels. The twenty-first century must be the era of awakening; the era of the liberated, emancipated woman. ... [There are] three aspects crucial for the realisation of a democratic modernity-system: a society that is democratic as well as economically and ecologically moral.' Matrifocal culture has delivered this in the past, can it assist today?

A focus group of women about this principle confirmed that they felt that women were not supported by the current practice of moving away from their family of origin upon marriage. Healing between women and men is needed before real trust can be regained. Will the underlying wariness of women towards men ever disappear? Women who have benefited from colonial thinking have a great challenge in truly knowing how to move from that mind frame to remove the assumptions of the colonialist from their language. How will men ever manage to do this with regard to women?

What does your group think?

4. Matrilineal kinship

> In matrifocal cultures, biological descent is traced through the mother's line, and the mother's brother (not the biological father) is the male role model/parent for children. Brothers, not the husband ensure the material needs of the sisters. This principle may include being matrilocal where, in a sexual partnership, the woman stays with her biological family and the man moves to her household/compound, or travels there for the evening.

We can now manipulate conception from outside the human body and some look towards the creation of a technological womb.

But when it comes down to it, we still need genetic material and should technology fail, where shall we turn? To women of course.

It makes sense that our primary descent should be traced through our mothers who gestate and care for us at our most vulnerable – in the womb and after birth. While parthenogenesis does occur in the animal and plant worlds it is yet to be found viable in humans. We require both sperm and egg to reproduce. Women and men in this regard need each other.

If women are to have free choice of sexual partner in the future with no ongoing ties unless the woman decides to, it is logical that her children trace their lineage through her, their mother. As things stand of course, the last or 'surname' is the link between generations, and currently everyone has this name from a man – their father or for women sometimes their husband. Perhaps women need to create new last names to commence their 'line'.

It is unlikely that we will move to brothers providing for their sisters – in a time when we need to control population the chance of having a brother may diminish, or women without a brother would need to adopt one! Will women ever again allow themselves to be financially dependent on a man?

A focus group of women about this principle felt it is important not to forget the women in our line – 'our Motherline'- and to honour their hard work and care. Just recognising the male line seems unbalanced and unfair, interesting as their stories may be. Using the father's name for children is a clear statement of 'ownership' that we could do without in thinking about children. What about the practice of girl children having the mother's name and boy children the father's?

What does your group think?

5. Economic mutuality

> Matrifocal cultures are societies of economic mutuality, based on women's power of economic distribution, including the circulation of gifts. Traditionally, matrifocal cultures were agricultural, but today they can be engaged in all spheres of life. A sharing economy is intrinsic to economic mutuality and the concept of accumulation is condemned. The main woman of the clan, or matriarch, is the custodian of the clan land and property. Money or other acquisitions are given to the women to manage. In this culture one undertakes sharing and giving away out of an abundance, a gift-giving economy, calculated to ensure the wellbeing of all ages and stages of life for the group.

This topic seems to raise the greatest debate, some of which is explored here.

If we continue at the current rate 'all modern economic analysis agree that we will probably reach the most blatant split between the haves and the have-nots in world history' (Risch 2016). This is a major threat to democracy, let alone a consensus society, and it calls for a new system, to allow more equitable distribution of the achieved surplus gains. Does the matrifocal system offer a way to do that?

Author Genevieve Vaughan argues that the previous matrifocal gift economy has been commandeered over time by the capitalist system in ways such as privatisation of water, patenting of life forms, the commodification of traditional knowledge, creating scarcity, assuming the gift of women's labour in the home and one could add, not recognising the free services that the ecosystem provides, such as bees to fertilise crops. Neither does capitalism 'make good' when it has finished with the natural world, such as rewilding after mines are no longer deemed productive or cleaning up toxic waste.

The attributes regarded as male, for Vaughan, are those lauded by capitalism, such as independence, aggression, competition and domination. It may be that a return to an economy of mutuality can best be achieved when we stop valuing a masculinity that denies its feminine side. Vaughan believes that restoring the gift way threatens the capitalist way and the more it can be instituted the more 'we can create a gift economy, make peace, and accumulate the abundance for all that is necessary to make it work.'

Researcher, author and publisher Susan Hawthorne advocates the creation of a system based on biodiversity, recognising the contribution of the natural world. 'Human work could … [be] to leave the world a richer place, a world with the possibility of sustaining itself for many tens of thousands of years.' (Hawthorne 2002). Trade would be about sustaining life, 'developing creativity and innovative systems for survival of communities, cities and geographic regions'. Consumption, which is currently at an unsustainable level, would be reduced, the sense of need replaced by a meaningful life experience.

In the view of Carr-Harris the economy would need to be in two parts – the local economy and a surplus sector to free the first from the demands of the second. In her child-centred communities, title to the land would be inalienable from residents legally recognised as child guardians. 'With necessary food production and distribution in their own hands, people would no longer be vulnerable to the demands of an all-powerful, male dominated corporate elite.' The ultimate goal would be to create communities of peace in which to properly socialise our children.

Ancient Ways for Current Days

A focus group of women about this principle was of the view that there is a rise of the 'sharing economy' these days. There are food swap events where people bring their excess produce and swap for the excess that others have of something else. There are local websites where give-away goods (not just food) can be displayed and a person who needs that item can arrange to come and get it. During the COVID-19 lockdowns food sharing opportunities sprang up for people unable to get to supermarkets in neighbourhoods. There were already shelves of books to take away that some people had placed in their front yards. This focus group observed that women naturally are in charge of markets and they keep the family together – women are nurturers by nature and want everyone to be fed and safe, so are still to this day building connections. We need to overcome the 'scarcity' mentality in current capitalist society. Some do that by 'dumpster diving', others by creating food banks. We need new perspectives on gender. How might we build more respect for women and empower women as custodians of the land?

What does your group think?

6. Relaxed enjoyment of sexuality

> Sexuality is valued highly in a matrifocal culture and being satisfied sexually is regarded as leading to health, peace and a positive, creative culture. Romantic sexual liaisons occur. Choice of sexual partners and gender is respected.

In a world which honours this principle we would abandon the adulation of the idea of one partner for life, certainly as the main source of self-definition. One monogamous sexual partnership would be just one of the options. This principle would not condone any non-consensual arrangement between partners, such as wife-swapping, a practice where a woman will not know who she will be having sex with until the evening ends. Women will cease to be sexual property.

You will recall the open sensuality of the Minoan people of Crete (Chapter 9), which was a world where women felt free and safe to have their breasts exposed to public view. Historian Elinor Gaddon contends that the Minoan women and men were both frankly sexual, celebrating life. For her 'taming of the Goddess under patriarchy led to the gradual erosion of sexuality'.

A focus group of women about this principle stated that relaxed enjoyment of sexuality does happen in some relationships. These women agreed that there is considerable discussion and action about this in these times, so that it is gradually becoming a more balanced situation with women enjoying their part in the sexual/sensual experience. Women are seeing that they have the right to expect this and are taking back power in sexual matters in their lives. In the view of the women in this focus group, men do not change until they have something to move on to. Women can define this. However, they were also concerned that women do still get labelled as 'sluts' if they openly enjoy their sensuality and it is not easy for women to be sexually liberated. They also thought that if there were lower rates of marriage and if it were more acceptable not to get married, it would allow for an easier 'parting of the ways' as things alter in the lives of the people involved in any relationship.

What does your group think?

7. Shared politics, a relationship society

> In matrifocal societies men represent their community on federal matters, balanced with women in charge locally and at home. No man is elected to represent the clan at the local council unless the women approve and their approval can be withdrawn. Alliances in the wider world are based on good relationships, creating confederates of equals. All of this facilitates peace – a key matrifocal value.

This principle does not deny democracy, however it is a different approach from the way we view democracy and would require some new understandings and a substantial reset within it. How could decisions come to grassroots groups for discussion and comment under this form of democracy? How would issues be initiated locally and taken up, as well as coming down from the decision-makers? What government would accept such oversight of their policy platform? Perhaps government would be formed by representatives from neighbourhood groups. Perhaps forums of consultation attached to parliament is an option – not unlike that proposed by First Nations people in Australia in the 'Uluru Statement from the Heart' in 2017. This called for a constitutionally enshrined First Nations voice to parliament. It was quickly rejected by the Australian government but is still on the table as far as First Nations people and supporters are concerned.

Is it any longer an option to contain women to the home and local domain? And don't we want men to be more engaged as fathers and identify with the home front? Certainly, if national decisions cannot be vetted by women, then women must be in the places where these decisions are made. According to cultural historian and systems scientist Riane Eisler (in Biaggi 2005) '[there is] considerable empirical evidence across diverse cultures and income groups that women have a higher propensity than men to spend on goods that benefit children and enhance their capacities'. Early attention to the needs of children and their learning is a major contribution to them becoming positive community members in adult life. This is but one example of how priorities could change.

In the past, marriage between clans was a way to create understanding and good relations. In the modern world this approach is an unlikely one, but the skills of women in building friendships and accord remain a resource that is underutilised.

Eisler chooses the word 'partnership' for matrifocal society. She proposes that in an 'integrated partnership political agenda' a new 'partnership' approach is needed to childhood relations, gender relations, economics and finally 'cultural beliefs, myths, and stories that support partnership'. For the last she states that we humans live by stories and that we cannot solve our problems with the same mindset that caused them. Einstein is reputed to have said something very similar – 'No problem can be solved from the same level of consciousness that created it'. Eisler continues 'If we believe male-dominance, violence, and oppression are inevitable, decreed by God or our genetic evolution, we won't even try to create a more humane way of life. It's time to free our enormous evolutionary gifts – our extraordinary capacities for empathy, creativity, caring and conscious choice … '.

Like Eisler, the mathematical physicist and Deep Ecology practitioner Brian Swimme also believes that we humans need a new story. He points out that other creatures have meaning in their DNA – they know what they are about. We need a new cosmic story. In his view the last 400 years of science have provided the foundation for that story. For the first time we can agree on the basic story of the galaxies, planets, life forms. In his view only in the last few decades has this become coherent, and now we can live in accord with that knowledge and find a fundamental pathway to a vibrant life.

A focus group of women about this principle felt that more women need to take an active role in politics, just as Jacinda Ardern in New Zealand and Kamala Harris in the States have done. They wondered if we could return to the clan of the Grandmothers and the council/counsel of wise, older women. It was felt that currently women are involved in grassroots politics and also have a significant say in who is elected to parliament. Could the parliament adopt egalitarian principles of rule that lead to peace?

What does your group think?

8. Spirituality – Goddess, the ancestors and the natural world

> It is an ancient matrifocal belief that the Earth is female and generates life, and so the Earth is the body of the Goddess. Women too generate life and so embody the Goddess. Ancestors are revered, the most ancient are women leaders who took their people to a new land and who, over time, gained the stature of myth and came to be regarded as a Goddess. Megaliths are a form of ancestor honouring that a few cultures continue to this day. Rebirth is part of the belief system, for which women are required. Women are the priestesses, responsible for ritual and ceremony, accompanied by some men. There is no religious hierarchy. Seasonal festivals occur based on the fertility or dormancy of the earth, with life-stage ceremonies interspersed. The patterns of nature inform human behaviour and we are part of, love and nurture, the natural world.

Much has been said on this topic at the start of this chapter. Art historian Elinor Gadon (1989) has noted:

Regaining the Motherworld

Until women can visualise the sacred female they cannot be whole and society cannot be whole. ... But this is not just a women's culture; men need the Goddess as well. ... In time the new iconography will include images of the male principle but they have yet to evolve. ... it is clear that any attempt to counteract the alienation we experience in this culture must be an attempt to restore the so-called feminine aspect to men's nature – and to stop demeaning the femaleness in ourselves.

The Italian philosopher, Daniele Bolleli feels that ' ... Empathy toward other living things should be one of the very first lessons instilled by all religions' and he feels that we need new rituals 'to awaken us to the fact that we are not separate from the land, water, and sky'.

Writer and Goddess researcher Elizabeth Childs Kelly is of the view that remembering the sacred female does not necessarily require creation of a new religion, 'The Sacred Feminine calls for something different'. Yet both authors agree we need to heed the call for deep respect and reverence for all planetary life. The importance of reconnecting to the natural world on a deeply inner level cannot be underestimated. It is one of the most joyful and meaningful options available to us. With that sense of connection, we will be prompted to once again treat all life as our kin, a reciprocal caring relationship.

In a practical sense, Macy recommends use of the Precautionary Principle in decision-making about the human interface with the environment. Developed by scientists and lawyers in the Science and Environmental Health Network it requires that 'When an activity raises threats of harm to human health or the environment, precautionary measures should be taken even if some cause and effect relationships are not fully established scientifically.' This approach requires us to explore the range of safe alternatives, including no action at all. With a renewed connection to nature this would be a basic assumption in our approach to new endeavours – at the moment it would be largely excluded or minimised in industrial or mining developmental planning.

A focus group of women about this matrifocal principle were of the view that Goddess spirituality, respect for ancestors and elders and alignment with the natural world, are all on the rise. They felt that women rise when things are in chaos and now is such a time. It will take a long time but will be like breathing in, out, in. It will involve very uncertain times: patriarchy, which is chaos, then healing and growth, then chaos again, followed by more healing and growth. This change is inevitable.

What does your group think?

9. Principle of two

> In matrifocal cultures the principle of two supports balanced collaboration between two equivalent powers, whether cosmos and Earth or any other two aspects of the natural world; between two people, two genders, and including two points of view. This is the twin-ship of female and male which promotes parity between different, and at the same time complementary energies. Further, each part must cooperate with the other, rather than being opposed, for anything to be successful. It leads to finding the commonality in debate rather than focusing on the difference.

I might not have emphasised the Principle of Two were it not so strongly expressed in First Nations culture in Australia, particularly illustrated in the work of H.R. Bell, sharing the Ngarinyin culture of the Kimberley (Chapter 11). As a minimum, discussions could be expected to have two sides represented and not the two opposing views of the current parliamentary system. This approach is used at the United Nations where the two different perspectives have a representative each who go with a facilitator to a separate room and work out a compromise or a more effective way forward. It is the principle of consensus which women have used historically and for the last few decades in the development of women's services.

A focus group of women about this principle felt that under this we could embrace diversity and principles of cooperation and collaboration. One way to express this might be intercultural women's events such as sharing different culturally specific foods at a 'Harmony Day' event. It was suggested that we could explore ways for Yin and Yang energies to be shared within each person.

What does your group think?

You too can do something

We have come to an end in considering the suitability of applying matrifocal principles today. We have established that contrary to popular understanding there has been a long history of peaceful mother and child centred cultures, unfortunately interrupted by the wrecking ball of the pursuit of patriarchy.

Mary MacKillop (1842–1909), now known as Saint Mary of the Cross, is Australia's only saint. She started her own order of nuns where everyone was of the same status and elected their leader from their ranks. Mary spent her life dedicated to bringing education to disadvantaged children and assisting others who were marginalised and in trouble, particularly women. She had a founding effect on education in Australia. A determined woman, she found ways to operate to the good of women and children in a patriarchal religious system. At one point she was excommunicated because she discovered that children were being abused by a priest and went public with the information. She nevertheless remained firm in her convictions, and kind. She encouraged everyone to be a change agent:

You can't do everything
You can't do nothing
But you can do something.

Far from the patriarchal teachings of the Catholic Church, I have written here about the peaceful matrifocal past that lasted possibly 200,000 years. I think we should consider what worked so well in those communities of peace, in this time when we know that patriarchy, an aberration of 4,000 years, is failing us so badly. It may be said that I am a dreamer. But think about it and you will know from deep within that I am a truth-teller, because the message appeals and resonates. For those who also wish something like the matrifocal way were the case today – one by one and together, we can make it so.

Bibliography

Adler RD (2001) 'Women in the Executive Suite Correlate to High Profits', *Working Paper European Project on Equal Pay*, Pepperdine University, California.

Allam L (19 Jan 2020) 'Right fire for right future: how cultural burning can protect Australia from catastrophic blazes' *The Guardian*, Australian Edition, accessed 4 August 2021.

Alesali L and Zdanowicz C (4 May 2019) 'After surviving ISIS and a civil war, these Syrian women built a female-only village', *CNN*, accessed 4 August 2021.

Andrews M (2019) *Journey into Dreamtime*, Ultimate World Publishing, Victoria.

Ates M (2002) *Mythology and Symbols*, Mehmet Ates, Turkey.

Attenborough, D (2020) *A Life on Our Planet: My Witness Statement and a Vision for the Future*, Ebury Press, UK.

Australian Institute of Health and Welfare (2020) *Sexual assault in Australia*, Canberra.

Bachofen JJ (1973) *Myth, Religion and Mother Right*, Princeton University Press, New Jersey.

Bambrick H (26 Oct 2015) 'Worldwide, climate change is worse for women' *The Conversation*, accessed 4 August 2021.

Basham AL (1969) *The Wonder that was India – A Survey of the History and Culture of the Indian Sub-continent before the Coming of the Muslims*, Sidgwick & Jackson, London.

Bell, D (1983) *Daughters of the Dreaming*, Melbourne, Allen & Unwin, Sydney.

Bell, D (1998) *Ngarrindjeri Wurruwarrin: A World that Is, Was, and Will Be*, Spinifex Press, Melbourne.

Bell, HR (1998) *Men's Business/Women's Business. The Spiritual Role of Gender in the World's Oldest Culture*, Inner Traditions International, Rochester.

Benhaiem A (10 Oct 2019) 'What This Researcher Discovered After Years of Studying Matriarchal Societies', interview with Heide Goettner-Abendroth, *HuffPost* France, accessed 4 August 2021.

Berndt RM and Berndt CH (1952) *The First Australians; Aboriginal Traditional Life – Past and Present*, Ure Smith publisher, Sydney.

Ancient Ways for Current Days

Bevis S (23 Apr 2016) 'Enduring Legacy of Wandjina', *The West Australian*, accessed 4 August 2021.

Biaggi C (Ed) (2005) *The Rule of Mars – Readings on the Origins, History and Impact of Patriarchy*, Knowledge, Ideas & Trends, Manchester.

Blakemore E (15 March 2019) 'Surprising DNA found in ancient people from southern Europe', *National Geographic*, accessed 4 August 2021.

Blumenfield T (2009) 'The Na of Southwest China: Debunking the Myths'(PDF) University of Washington.

Bocquet-Appel JP, Demars PY, Noiret L and Dobrowsky D (2005) 'Estimates of Upper Palaeolithic meta-population size in Europe from archaeological data', *Journal of Archaeological Science*.

Bolelli D (2013) *Create Your Own Religion – A How-to Book Without Instructions*, The Disinformation Company, New York.

Boyce J (July 2021) 'Transforming the national imagination – Bruce Pascoe and the *Dark Emu* debate', *The Monthly*, Schwartz Media, Melbourne.

Boyd B (2018) 'An Archaeological Telling of Multispecies Co-Inhabitation – Comments on the origins of agriculture and domestication narrative in Southwest Asia', *Multispecies Archaeology*, Pilaar B and Suzanne E (Ed) Routledge, New York.

Braafladt K (2003) 'Mysteries of Çatalhöyük', *Science Museum of Minnesota*, accessed 4 August 2021.

Bradley, J (7 Nov 2020) 'Warriors in a call to arms on climate', *The Age*, Melbourne.

Bratman, G et al. (24 Jul 2019) 'Nature and mental health: An ecosystem service perspective', *ScienceAdvances*, accessed 4 August 2021.

Breines I, Connell R and Eide I (2000) *Male Roles, Masculinities and Violence – a culture of peace perspective*, UNESCO.

Briffault R (1996) *The Mothers. A Study of the Origins of Sentiments and Institutions*, 3 vol, Johnson Reprint Corporation, New York.

Bryant W and Bricknall S (2017) *Homicide in Australia 2012 – 2014 National Homicide Monitoring Program report*, Australian Institute of Criminology, Canberra.

Cameron, D (1981) *Symbols of Birth and of Death in the Neolithic Era*, Kenyon-Deane, London.

Cameron, D (1981) *The Ghassulian Wall Paintings*, Kenyon-Deane, London.

Bibliography

Cameron J, Moseley K and Ray V (1985) *New Insights into Pre-History*, unpublished manuscript, Melbourne.

Carr-Harris L (2011) *The Descent of Religion: Its Evolution from Nurturing to Bullying and Back!*, Grey Fox Publishing, USA.

Carter NM and Wagner HM (2011) 'The Bottom Line: Corporate Performance and Women's Representation on Boards (2004–2008)', *Catalyst*, Common Good Press, USA.

Chaloupka G (1993) *Journey in Time: The World's Longest Continuing Art Tradition*, Reed Books, Sydney.

Chapman B (17 Oct 2018) 'Majority of the world's richest entities are corporations, not governments, figures show', *Independent*, UK, accessed 4 August 2021.

Kelly EC (16 Nov 2019) 'When God was a Woman – An introduction to the wisdom of the sacred feminine', *Human Parts*, accessed 4 August 2021.

Christ CP (22 Feb 2021) 'What If We Begin from the Hypothesis that Ancient Crete Was Matriarchal, Matrifocal, and Matrilineal?' *Feminism and Religion*, accessed 4 August 2021.

Coimbra FA (2015) 'Neolithic Art, Archaeoacoustics and Neuroscience', *Archaeoacoustics 11: The Archaeology of Sound*, Publication of the 2015 Conference in Istanbul, Eneix, L (Ed), OTS Foundation.

Mark JJ (13 Nov 2012) 'The History of Ancient India', *World History Encyclopedia*, accessed 4 August 2021.

Corbett, R (19 Nov 2014) 'A journey deep inside Spain's temple of cave art', *BBC Travel*, accessed 4 August 2021.

Crittenden AN and Schnorr SL (20 Jan 2017) 'Current views on hunter-gatherer nutrition and the evolution of the human diet', *American Journal of Physical Anthropology*, accessed 4 August 2021.

Cummings V and Richards C (2016) 'The essence of the dolmen –The architecture of megalithic construction' in Robin G, D'Anna A, Schmitt A and Bailly M (2016) *Functions, uses and representations of space in the monumental graves of Neolithic Europe*, Presses Universitaires de Provence, France.

Daly M (1978) *Gyn/Ecology: The Metaethics of Radical Feminism*, Beacon Press, Boston.

Dames M (1976) *The Silbury Treasure: The Great Goddess Rediscovered*, Thames and Hudson, London.

Dames M (1996) *The Avebury Cycle*, Thames and Hudson, London.

Debertolis P, Coimbra F and Eneix L (2015) 'Archaeoacoustic Analysis of the Hal Saflieni Hypogeum in Malta', *Journal of Anthropology and Archaeology*, 3(1), American Research Institute for Policy Development.

Debertolis P, Earl N and Zivic M (2016) 'Archaeoacoustic Analysis of Tarxien Temples in Malta' *Journal of Anthropology and Archaeology*, Vol.4, No. 1, American Research Institute for Policy Development.

Devereux P (2000) *The Sacred Place – The Ancient Origin of Holy and Mystical Sites*, Cassell & Co, United Kingdom.

Douka K, Efstratiou N, Hald MM, Henriksen PS and Karetsou A (April 2017) 'Dating Knossos and the arrival of the earliest Neolithic in the southern Aegean', *Antiquity*, 91(356):304–321.

United Nations Environment Program (26 Apr 2017) 'Indigenous people and nature: a tradition of conservation', UNEP, accessed 4 August 2021.

Edwards EL (n.d.) 'Human Sacrifice in Anemospilia Reexamined' research paper in Acedemia.edu.

Evely D (1999) *Fresco: A Passport into the Past – Minoan Crete through the eyes of Mark Cameron*, British School at Athens, Athens.

Farrell PB, (2 Sept 2014) '7 Reasons women will lead the new world order', *MarketWatch*, accessed 4 August 2021.

Feldman R, Gordon I, Zagoory-Sharona O and Leckman, JF (1 Apr 2010) 'Oxytocin and the Development of Parenting in Humans', *Biological Psychiatry*, 15 August 2010, 68(4):377–382.

Flannery T (2020) *The Climate Cure: Solving the Climate Emergency in the Era of COVID-19*, Text Publishing, Melbourne.

Flood J (28 May 2019) 'Explosion from the Steppe? The distribution and origins of the Y-Haplogroup R1a' draft, accessed 4 August 2021.

Flood J (2019) *The Original Australians – The Story of the Aboriginal People*, 2nd Ed, Allen and Unwin, Sydney.

Foster J with Derlet M (2013) *Invisible Women of Prehistory – Three million years of peace, six thousand years of war*, Spinifex Press, Melbourne.

Fran J (19 Jan 2020) 'Feeling anxious and powerless? Australia's only saint had advice', *The Sydney Morning Herald*, accessed 4 August 2021.

French M (2008) *From Eve to Dawn: A History of Women in the World, Volume 1: Origins*, The Feminist Press, New York.

Bibliography

Fuller D reporting on Narasimhan VM and Patterson, Nick (2019) 'The Formation of Human Populations in South and Central Asia', *Science*.

Gadon EW (1989) *The Once and Future Goddess – A Sweeping Visual Chronicle of the Sacred Female and Her Re-emergence in the Cultural Mythology of Our Time*, Harper & Rowe, San Francisco.

Garrison LT (3 Mar 2017) '6 Modern Societies Where Women Rule', *Mental Floss*, accessed 4 August 2021.

Gay'wu Group of Women (2019) *Song Spirals – Sharing women's wisdom of Country through songlines*, Allen & Unwin, Sydney

Gerlich R (Dec 2018) 'The Creation of Patriarchy: How did it happen?', reneejg.net, accessed 4 August 2021.

Gimbutas M (1974) *Gods and Goddesses of Old Europe*, Thames and Hudson, London.

Gimbutas M and Dexter MR (Ed) (1999) *The Living Goddesses*, University of California Press, USA.

Gleeson-White J (1 Aug 2021) 'What really counts? How the patriarchy of economics finally tore me apart', *The Guardian Australia*, accessed 4 August 2021.

Goettner-Abendroth H (2012) *Matriarchal Societies: studies on Indigenous Cultures across the Globe*, translated from German by Karen Smith, Peter Lang Publishing, New York.

Goldberg A, Günther T, Rosenberg NA and Jakobsson M (2017) 'Ancient X chromosomes reveal contrasting sex bias in Neolithic and Bronze Age Eurasian migrations', *Proceedings of the National Academy of Sciences*.

Gould-Davis E (1973) *The First Sex*, Penguin Books, London.

Graeber D (2011) *Debt: The First 5,000 Years*, Melville House Publishing, Brooklyn.

Graham, Mary (2021) Online seminar 'Regenerative Songlines', Australian Earth Laws Alliance, Queensland.

Gray M (n.d.) 'Neolithic Temples of Malta', *World Pilgrimage Guide*, accessed 4 August 2021.

Greenlee C (10 Dec 2000) 'Goddesses 25,000 BC', *Then Again Info*, accessed 4 August 2021.

Griffiths B (2018) *Deep Time Dreaming – Uncovering Ancient Australia*, Black Ink, Carlton.

Hall S (2016) *Amazon Acres, You Beauty; Stories of Women's Lands, Australia*, Shall Publishing, Wollongong.

Hall S (2019) *Shelters and Buildings; Stories of Women's Land Australia Volume 2*, Shall Publishing, Wollongong.

Handwerk B (11 Feb 2019) 'Europe's Megalithic Monuments Originated in France and Spread by Sea Routes, New Study Suggests', *SmithsonianMag.com,* accessed 4 August 2021.

Hawkes J (1977) *The Atlas of Early Man*, MacMillan, London.

Hawthorne S (2002) *Wild Politics*, Spinifex Press, Melbourne.

Haque U (6 May 2021) 'What it Means to Live in an Abusive Society, and Why We Do', *Eudaimonia and Co*, accessed 4 August 2021.

Haque U (24 April 2020) 'America's (Still) Committing Economic Suicide – Why America is Facing Unprecedented Economic Disaster' *Eudaimonia and Co*, accessed 4 August 2021.

Hardy SB (1999) *Mother Nature: A history of Mothers, Infants, and Natural Selection*, Pantheon books, New York.

Hiatt LR (1991) *Kinship and Conflict. A Study of an Aboriginal Community in Northern Arnhem Land*, Various editions 1965–1991, The Australian National University, Canberra.

Hodder I (Jan 2003) 'Men and Women at Çatalhöyük', *Scientific American Inc.*, 290.

Hodder I (Mar 2016) 'Understanding Çatalhöyük and the Origins of Settled Life'. Melbourne University, March 2016, Public Lecture.

Hodder I (2014) *Research Interests*, Ian Hodder website, accessed 4 August 2021.

Hoffman DL, Standish CD, Garcia-Diez M, Pettitt PB, Milton JA, Zilhão J, Alcolea-González JJ, Cantalejo-Duarte P, Collado H, de Balbín R, Lorblanchet M, Ramos-Muñoz J, Weniger GC and Pike AWG (23 Feb 2018) 'U-Th dating of carbonate crusts reveals Neandertal origin of Iberian cave art', *Science*, 359(6378):912–915.

Humphreys C (4 Mar 2020) 'We've lost the wisdom of Solomon', *Pursuit*, University of Melbourne, accessed 4 August 2021.

International Labour Organisation (2015) 'Women on Boards: Building the female talent pipeline', ILO, Switzerland.

Jabr F (30 Jan 2021) 'The Social Network', *The Age*, Melbourne.

Bibliography

Jusseret S and Sintubin M (eds) (2017) *Minoan Earthquakes – Breaking the Myth through Interdisciplinarity. Studies in Archaeological Sciences 5.* Leuven University Press, Belgium.

Kabbalah Centre (7 Feb 2012) 'Rav Avraham Azulai', *KC*, accessed 4 August 2021.

Keller ML (1998) 'Crete of the Mother Goddess: Communal Rituals and Sacred Art', Revision, 20(3):12–16.

Kelly EC (16 Nov 2019) 'When God was a Woman – An introduction to the wisdom of the sacred feminine', *Human Parts*, accessed 4 August 2021.

Kerns CJ (2016) 'Monuments from the doorstep: exploring the temporal, spatial and social relationship between chambered cairns and settlements during the Orcadian Neolithic', in *Decoding Neolithic Atlantic and Mediterranean Island Ritual* (2016) Nash G and Townsend A (Eds), Oxbow Books, Oxford.

Klein N (2019) *On Fire: The Burning Case for a Green New Deal*, Allen Lane, UK.

Klein N (2014) *This Changes Everything*, Simon and Schuster, USA.

Kralik M, Novotny V and Oliva M (2007) 'Fingerprint on the Venus of Dolni Vestonice 1', *Anthropologie*, Brno, Czech Republic, Masaryk University and The Moravian Museum.

Kreisberg G (4 Aug 2014) 'Mission: Malta – Exploring the Sound and Energy Properties of Ancient Architecture', Graham Hancock, 2014, accessed 4 August 2021.

Kurup, RG (2014) *Rising Daughter Silent Mother and Fading Grandmothers – A study of Female Sexuality within a North Malabar Nayar Family Structure*, CinnamonTeal Publishing, India.

Lal BB (2007) *Demolishing the Steppe Sons Hoax, recollecting BB Lal's plea to abandon 19th century Aryan Invasion paradigms*, Lecture conference paper, 2–6 July 2007, Italy.

Lambert J (ed) and Parker, KL (1993) *Wise Women of the Dreamtime – Aboriginal Tales of the Ancestral Powers*, Inner Traditions International, Rochester, Vermont.

Larsen CS, Knüsel CJ, Haddow SD, Pilloud MA, Milella M, Sadvari JW, Pearson J, Ruff CB, Garofalo EM, Bocaege E, Betz BJ, Dori I and Glencross B (25 Jun 2019) 'Bioarchaeology of Neolithic Çatalhöyük reveals fundamental transitions in health, mobility, and lifestyle in early farmers', *Proceedings of the National Academy of Sciences*, 116(26):12615–12623.

Law S (5 Oct 2010) 'Dads, Too, Get Hormone Boost while Caring for Baby', *Live Science*, accessed 4 August 2021.

Lawlor R (1991) *Voices of the First Day – Awakening in the Aboriginal Dreamtime*, Inner Traditions International Ltd, Vermont USA.

Levine R, Rodrigues A and Zelezny L (2008) *Journeys in Social Psychology – Looking Back to Inspire the Future*, Psychology Press, East Sussex.

Lewis-Williams D and Pearce D (2009) *Inside the Neolithic Mind – Consciousness, Cosmos and the Realm of the Gods*, Thames & Hudson, London.

Lim L (19 Mar 2007) 'Painful Memories for China's Footbinding Surviviors', *NPR*, accessed 4 August 2021.

Llamas J (Apr 2017) 'Female Circumcision: The History, the Current Prevalence and the Approach to a Patient', *University of Virginia School of Medicine*.

Lobell JA (May/Jun 2015) 'The Minoans of Crete', *Archaeology*, accessed 4 August 2021.

Loose R (2010) 'Archaeoacoustics: Adding a Soundtrack to Site Descriptions', *Papers of the Archaeological Society of New Mexico*, 36, Albuquerque, New Mexico.

Lopez JM (15 Mar 2020) 'Jinwar, the Middle East's first feminist commune for Arab, Kurdish, and Yazidi victims of Islamic State', ABC News, accessed 4 August 2021.

Mackey, Mary (1993 - 1998) *The EarthSong Trilogy: The Year the Horses Came; The Horses at the Gate; The Fires of Spring*. Onyx Publications, Nashville, Tennessee, USA.

Macy J (2007) *World as Lover, World as Self – Courage for Global Justice and Ecological Renewal*, Paralax Press, California.

Malmstrom H, Linderholm A, Skoglund P, Storå J, Sjödin P, Thomas M, Gilbert P, Holmlund G, Willerslev E, Jakobsson M, Lidén K and Götherström A (19 Jan 2015) 'Ancient mitochondrial DNA from the northern fringe of the Neolithic farming expansion in Europe sheds light on the dispersion process', *Philosophical Transactions of the Royal Society B*, 370(1660).

Marak Q (2014) 'Megaliths and Living Cultural Traditions' in Sengupta S (ed.) *Explorations in Anthropology of North East India*, Gyan Publishing House, New Delhi.

Marinatos N (1984) *Art and Religion in Thera – Reconstructing a Bronze Age Society*, I. Mathioulakis & Co, Athens.

Marsden, H (8 Mar 2018) 'What are matriarchies, and where are they now?', The Independent, accessed 4 August 2021.

Bibliography

Marshack A (1972) *The Roots of Civilization: the Cognitive Beginning of Man's First Art, Symbol and Notation*, McGraw-Hill, New York.

Mattison SM, Scelza B and Blumenfield T (2014) 'Paternal Investment and the Positive Effects of Fathers among the Mosuo of Southwest China', *American Anthropologist*, 116,(3):591–610.

McCoid, CH and McDermott LD (Jun 1996) 'Toward Decolonizing Gender: Female Vision in the Upper Palaeolithic', *American Anthropologist*, 98(2):319–326.

McDonald P (Aug 2020) 'A Great Awakening with Many Dangers: What has the #MeToo Movement Achieved?', *Centre for Justice Briefing Paper*.

Meadow R and Kenoyer JM (n.d.) Harappa Archaeology Research Project, Various papers, full publication awaited, Harappa.com, accessed 4 August 2021.

Mellaart J (1965) *Earliest Civilisations of the Near East*, Thames and Hudson, London.

Mellaart J (1975) *The Neolithic of the Near East*, Thames and Hudson, London.

Metcalfe T (Mar 2021) 'Ancient woman may have been powerful European leader, 4,000 year old treasure suggests', *National Geographic*, accessed 4 August 2021.

Mind.org (May 2018) 'How can nature benefit my mental health?', accessed 4 August 2021.

Morgan E (1982) *The Aquatic Ape*, Souvenir Press, London.

Mor B and Sjoo M (1991) *The Great Cosmic Mother – Rediscovering the Religion of the Earth*, American Edition, Harper One (a Harper Collins imprint), USA.

Muller MN, Thompson ME and Wrangham RW (2006) 'Male Chimpanzees Prefer Mating with Old Females', *Current Biology*, 16(22).

Narang A (2015) 'Archaeocoustics: Necessity for the study of Acoustics of selected Ancient Architecture', MSc Audio Production, University of Salford.

Narasimhan VM et al. (6 Sept 2019) 'The formation of human populations in South and Central Asia', *Science*, 365(6457).

Nash J (1978) 'Women and Power in Nagovisi Society', *Journal de la Societe des Oceanistes*, 60(34):119–126.

National Museum, Copenhagen, Denmark (n.d.) 'How did the burials take place?', NMD, accessed 4 August 2021.

Ncube J (2015) *African Queens and Empresses: Uncovering a forgotten history to pave the way to a bold future*, Action Support Centre for conflict transformation.

O'Neil D (2012) 'Primate Behavior: A Survey of Non-Human Primate Behavior Patterns' Behavioral Sciences Department, Palomar College, accessed 4 August 2021.

Orenstein P (2020) *Boys and Sex: Young men on Hook-ups, Love, Porn, Consent and Navigating the new Masculinity*, Souvenir Press, London.

Parker C (Feb 2014) 'Costa Rica in Focus – Bribri, un matriarcado modern: Costa Rica's living Matriarchy', *Intercontinental Cry*, accessed 4 August 2021.

Pascoe B (2018) *Dark Emu*, Magabala Books Aboriginal Corporation, Broome, Western Australia.

Pearson MP and Willis CC (2011) 'Burials and builders of Stonehenge: social identities in Late Neolithic and Chalcolithic Britain' in Furholt M, Luth F and Muller J (eds) *Megaliths and Identities – Early Monuments and Neolithic Societies from the Atlantic to the Baltic*, Dr. Rudolf Habelt GmbH, Bonn.

Petrie CA, Bates J, Higham T and Singh RN (2016) *Feeding ancient cities in South Asia: dating the adoption of rice, millet and tropical pulses in the Indus civilisation*, Antiquity Publications Ltd, UK.

Pike AN (2013) *Karani Bunpi: Living Women's Sacred Ceremonies. First Australian women's daily spiritual life in the Channel Country from the research and life's work of A.M. Duncan-Kemp*, A.N. Pike publisher, Cudgera Creek, New South Wales.

Ponting G (2007) *Callanish And Other Megalithic Sites Of The Outer Hebrides*, Wooden Books Ltd, Glastonbury, Somerset, U.K.

Poulter J and Nicholson UB (2018) *Australian Sovereignty – Past and Present*, Submission to Australian Parliament 2018 – Joint Select Committee on Constitutional Recognition Relating to Aboriginal and Torres Strait Islander Peoples.

Primeau KE and Witt DE (25 Oct 2017) *Soundscapes in the Past: A GIS Approach to Landscape Scale Archaeoacoustics*, A paper presented at the Frontiers in Archaeological Sciences symposium, Rutgers University.

Ramirez PB, Behrmann RdB and Bermejo RB (2015) 'Graphic Programmes as Ideological Construction of the Megaliths: The South of the Iberian Peninsula as Case Study' in Rocha L, Bueno-Ramirez P and Branco G (eds) *Death as Archaeology of Transition: Thoughts and Materials*, British Archaeological Reports, International Series 2708, Oxford.

Ratnagar Shereen (2018) *The Magic in the Image: Women in Clay at Mohenjo-Daro*, Manahar Press, New Delhi.

Refrew C and Bahn P (1991) *Archaeology: Theory, Methods and Practice*, Thames & Hudson, New York.

Bibliography

Rigby S (2021) 'Neanderthals could talk like humans, study suggests: Our cousins' ears were tuned to the frequencies used in human communication', *Science Focus*, accessed 4 August 2021.

Reich D (18 Jun 2020) 'The Truth About Us, and Where We Come From', online lecture for New Scientist Live, YouTube.

Rintoul S (12 June 2021) 'For the Record', *The Age Good Weekend*, Melbourne.

Risch R (2016) 'How did wealth turn into surplus profit? From affluence to 'scarcity' in prehistoric economies', in *Rich and Poor – Competing for resources in prehistoric societies*, Meller H and Jung R, Halle (Saale), Germany.

Risch R, Meller H and Gronenborn D (2018) Preface to *Surplus without the State – Political Forms in Prehistory*, Halle (Saale), Germany.

Shugg GR (6 Nov 2020) 'Ritual, Urbanism, and the Everyday: Mortuary Behavior in the Indus Civilization', in Betsinger TK and DeWitte SN (eds) *The Bioarchaeology of Urbanization*, Springer, Switzerland.

Rodenborg E (1991) 'Defence of Marija Gimbutas' Thesis about Old Europe', translation-summary from Swedish by Kvilhaug M, *MMS Scholars*, accessed 4 August 2021.

Romey K (12 Nov 2019) 'Exclusive: This 7,000-year-old woman was among Sweden's last hunter-gatherers', *National Geographic*, accessed 4 August 2021.

Rutter JB (4 Mar 2017) 'Ancient Minoan Religion', *Brewminate*, accessed 4 August 2021.

Sahlins M, Lee RB and DeVore I (1968) *Notes on the Original Affluent Society*, Man the Hunter conference, Aldine Publishing Company, New York.

Sajo J (n.d.) 'A winter-solstice visit to the ancient marvel of Newgrange', *International Travel News*, accessed 4 August 2021.

Salmon E (Oct 2000) 'Kincentric Ecology: Indigenous Perceptions of the Human-Nature Relationship', *Ecological Applications*, 10(5):1327–1332.

Sample I (7 Dec 2018) 'Earliest plague strain found in Sweden holds clue to stone age migration from east: Pandemic could explain the crash in European population 5,500 years ago and influx of people from the Eurasian steppe', *The Guardian*, accessed 4 August 2021.

Sanchez-Quinto F, Malmström H, Fraser M, Girdland-Flink L, Svensson EM, Simões LG, George R, Hollfelder N, Burenhult G, Noble G, Britton K, Talamo S, Curtis N, Brzobohata H, Sumberova R, Götherström A, Storå J and Jakobsson M (7 May 2019) 'Megalithic tombs in western and northern Neolithic Europe were linked to a kindred society', *Proceedings of the National Academy of Sciences of the United States of America*, 116(19):9469–9474.

Schauer P, Bevan A, Shennan S, Edinborough K, Kerig T and Pearson MP (20 Dec 2019) 'British Neolithic Axehead Distributions and Their Implications', *Journal of Archaeological Method and Theory*, 27:836–859.

Schwartzberg L (director) (2019) *Fantastic Fungi* [motion picture], Moving Art, USA.

Sever, OB (14 Oct 2011) 'Göbekli Tepe's Oldest Temple in the World – an Archaeological Stone Age Site in Anatolia', *Electrum Magazine*, accessed 4 August 2021.

Shannon L (2019) 'Dancing Our Way Home: Indigenous European Wisdom in Balkan Circle Dance', *2019 Conference Proceedings: Cultural, Intercultural and Transnational Dialogues in Dance and Spirituality: The Journal of Dance, Movement & Spiritualities and Intellect Publishing*, Moving Soma cultures, Cheltenham, England.

Shinde V (1 Feb 2016) 'Harappan Civilisation: Current Perspective and its Contribution', *American Institute of Sindhology*, accessed 4 August 2021.

Shinde VS, Kim YJ, Woo EJ, Jadhav N, Waghmare P, Yadav Y, Munshi A, Chatterjee M, Panyam A, Hong JH, Oh CS and Shin DH (21 Feb 2018) 'Archaeological and anthropological studies on the Harappan cemetery of Rakhigarhi, India', PLOS ONE, 13(2).

Silva M, Oliveira M, Vieira D and Brandão A (Dec 2017) 'A genetic chronology for the Indian Subcontinent points to heavily sex-biased dispersals', *BMC Evolutionary Biology*, 17(1).

Singh, RN and Dailey JD (3 Aug 2016) 'Honor killing', *Encyclopedia Britannica*, accessed 4 August 2021.

Sitka C (independent scholar) (July/August 2019) 'The Origins of Patriarchy: Parts 1 & 2' [radio interview], Radio 3CR, Melbourne.

Sjogren KG (2011) 'Megaliths, landscapes and identities: the case of Falbygen, Sweden' in Furholt M, Luth F and Muller J (eds) *Megaliths and Identities – Early Monuments and Neolithic Societies from the Atlantic to the Baltic*, Dr. Rudolf Habelt GmbH, Bonn.

Smith L and Cockayne J (Nov 2020) 'Why we need a feminist foreign policy', *The Saturday Paper* No 329, Melbourne.

Snow DR, Wang JZ, Weina G, Mitra P and Giles CL (Oct 2010) 'Determining the Sexual Identities of Prehistoric Cave Artists using Digitized Handprints— A Machine Learning Approach', *Proceedings of the ACM Multimedia Conference*, Florence, Italy.

Soetens K (2008) 'The Source Goddess of the Chauvet Caves', *Goddess Alive!*, 14 Autumn/Winter, UK.

Steimer-Herbet T (2018) *Indonesian Megaliths – A forgotten cultural heritage*, Archaeopress Publishing Ltd, University of Geneva.

Bibliography

Steinem G (Jul 2020) 'Gloria Steinem and Ronan Farrow in Conversation' [video], Pioneer Works, July 2020, on You Tube.

Stone M (1976) *When God Was a Woman*, Marboro Books, New York.

Streffon C (Feb 2010) 'Windfarm Threat to Callanish Sleeping Beauty', The Megalithic Portal, accessed 4 August 2021.

Tait C (2017) The Heart of Neolithic Orkney, Charles Tait Photographic, Orkney.

Tano S (2021) 'Inside the last matriarchal society in Europe: Tiny Estonian islands where women make the rules and till the land – and men take a back seat', Daily Mail online, accessed 4 August 2021.

Taylor, SE (2003) *The Tending Instinct: Women, Men, and the Biology of Relationships*, Holt Paperbacks, New York.

Taylor SM (Jan 2015) 'If Women Ruled the World – Is a Matriarchal Society the Solution?' *Wake Up World – it's time to rise and shine*, accessed 4 August 2021.

Thompson JE, Parkinson EW, McLaughlin TR, Barratt RP, Power RK, Mercieca-Spiteri B, Stoddart S and Malone C (28 Apr 2020) 'Placing and remembering the dead in late Neolithic Malta: bioarchaeological and spatial analysis of the Xagħra Circle Hypogeum, Gozo' World Archaeology, 52(1):71–89.

Towers R, Card N and Edmonds M (2015) *The Ness of Brodgar*, Orkney Media Group, Great Britain.

Trump DH (2002) *Malta – Prehistory and Temples (Malta's Living Heritage)*, Midsea Books, Malta.

Turkic World (n.d.) 'Kurgan Culture – A critique of Ch. 10 *The Civilisation of the Goddess* by Marija Gimbutas', Turkic, accessed 4 August 2021.

Uesugi A (ed) (2018) *Current Research on Indus Archaeology: South Asian Archaeology Series 4*, Kansai University, Osaka.

Underwood G (1977) *The Pattern of the Past*, Abacus, London.

United Nations Environment Programme (26 Apr 2017) 'Indigenous people and nature: a tradition of conservation', UNEP, accessed 4 August 2021.

University of London, UCL Social Research Institute (2001–2008) *Millennium Cohort Study* Centre for Longitudinal Studies.

Uribe-Bohorque MV, Martinez-Ferraro J and Garcia-Sanchez IM (2019) 'Women on boards and efficiency in a business-orientated environment' in *Corporate Social Responsibility and Environmental Management*, 26(1).

Vaughan G (2019) *The Maternal Economy and Patriarchal Capitalism*, conference speech posted on Magoism.net.

Vaughan-Lee L (2017) *The Return of the Feminine and the World Soul*, The Golden Sufi Centre, Point Reyes, California.

Ventura F and Hoskin M (Jul 2014) 'Temples of Malta', in Ruggles C, *Handbook of Archaeoastronomy and Ethnoastronomy*, Springer, New York.

Violatti C (6 Apr 2018) 'Aryan' *Ancient History Encyclopedia*, accessed 4 August 2021.

Volk, AA and Atkinson JA (May 2013) 'Infant and child death in the human environment of evolutionary adaptation', *Evolution and Human Behavior*, 34(3).

Von Petzinger G (2017) *The First Signs: Unlocking the Mysteries of the World's Oldest Symbols*, Atria Books, New York.

Walden C (21 Sept 2019) 'The happiness load is on women', *The Age*, Melbourne.

Walker ML and Herndon JG (2008) 'Menopause in nonhuman primates?' *Biology of reproduction*, 79(3):398-406.

Ward NN (2018) *Ninu – Grandmother's Law. Autobiography of Nura Nungalka Ward*, Magabala Books Aboriginal Corporation, Broome, Western Australia.

Workplace Gender Equality Agency (2012) *Workplace Gender Equality Act 2012*, WGEA, accessed January 2021.

Wragg Sykes R (2020) *Kindred: Neanderthal Life, Love, Death and Art*, Bloomsbury Sigma, London.

Whiting K, Konstantakos L, Sadler G and Gill C (2018) 'Were Neanderthals Rational? A Stoic Approach' *Humanities*, 7(2):39.

Whitely DS (2008) *Cave Paintings and the Human Spirit – the origins of creativity and belief*, Prometheus Books, New York.

Wiley-Blackwell (2 Aug 2008) 'Biological Fathers Not Necessarily The Best, Social Dads Parent Well Too', *ScienceDaily*.

O, The Oprah Magazine (Sept 2009) '8 Ways of Looking at Power', *O*, New York City, accessed 4 August 2021.

World Wide Fund for Nature (2020) *Living Planet Report 2020*, WWF, accessed 4 August 2021.

Wright S (23 Mar 2018) 'Adjusting to Parenthood', *EPIC Assist*, accessed 4 August 2021.

Yunkaporta T (2019) *Sand Talk – How Indigenous Thinking Can Save the World*, Text Publishing, Melbourne, Australia.

Index

Note: images are identified with bold page numbers

A

abortion, 212, 269
Adat law, 230–233, 249
Afghanistan, 67, 195
Africa
    Akan people, 85
    Ashanti people, 84–85
    Berber people, 80
    Homo sapiens, 143
    matrifocal societies, 84
    migration, 152
    Queen Yaa Asantewa, 85
    Tuareg people, 80
    women and self-defence, 83
Agia Triada, **179**
agriculture
    agrarian festivals, 77
    Americas, 81–82
    animals, 36, 44, 45, 50, 55–56, 116, 163, 195
    arable land, 83
    arid environment, 151
    Australian First Nations people, 164, 211, 242, 243
    Aztecs, 213–214

    crop developments, 36, 44, 45, 55–56, 195, 211
    environmental degradation, 131, 277
    future generations, 294
    gender roles and responsibilities, 83–84, 173, 191, 217, 227
    Goddess role, 123–124
    impact of colonisation, 244
    Indus Valley region, 210–211
    irrigation, 195, 243
    matrifocal societies, 61–62, 75, 80, 278
    Minangkabau people, 230
    mono-crops, 213–214
    nomadic people, 153
    organic, 237
    respect for the environment, 165
    ritual practices, 108–109
    tools, 109–111, 195
    traditions, 243
    Yamnaya culture, 114
'Ain Ghazl, 41–42, **42**
altars
    See megaliths; sacred places
altered state of consciousness
    See shamanism; trances

American First Nations People
　Apache people, 95
　custodians of nature, 68
　Hopi pueblo people, 80
　Iroquoi, 68, 69–70, 285
Anatolia, 43, 148–149, 178
ancestors
　connection with, 36, 47, 50–51,
　　53, 54–55, 56, 96, 97, 246, 247,
　　253
　honouring, 76–77, 80–81, 98, 102,
　　126–127, 223, 225, 304
animals
　agriculture, 36, 44, 45, 50, 55–56,
　　116, 163, 195
　Australian native, 155
　in the Bible, 27
　boars, 51, 171, 194
　bulls, 50, 51, 182, **183**, 185, **186**,
　　192
　castrated, 195
　cave paintings, 21, 24, 32, 41, 67,
　　247
　control of, 24, 48, **49**
　domesticated, 36, 44, 45, 50, 116,
　　124, 151, 152, 195
　extinction, 28, 148, 276, 277
　in healing processes, 282
　horned and horns, 19, 20, 24, 50,
　　51, 185
　horses, 51, 148, 151, 152, 153, 154,
　　156, 208, 270
　Indus Valley region, 208
　megaliths, 105
　as offerings, 188
　procreation, 141, 296
　represented in art, **23**, **29**, 38, 39,
　　47, 48, **49**, 51, 52, 124, 126, 172,
　　179, **181**, **183**, **186**, 187, **188**,
　　199, **200**

respect for, 27, 29, 56, 232,
　242–243, 248, 250, 280, 281
sacrificed, 78, 124, 127, 154, 188,
　222, 225
skins as clothing, 24
skulls, 24, 50
slaughter of, 222
spiritual propagation, 242–243
under stress, 137
survival, 277
as symbols, 30, 50, 78, 105, 126,
　248, 281
teeth as jewellery, 24, 126
See also agriculture; goddess-
　animal connections; human-
　animal connections; human-
　plant-animal relationships
archaeoacoustics
　See archaeological findings;
　megalithic structures, sound
　resonance; megaliths, sound
　resonance; stones, acoustic
　properties; temples, sound
　resonance
archaeological findings
　astronomical events, 32–33
　Avebury earthen henge, 106
　burial sites, 201, 206
　calendars, 32, 121
　Çatalhöyük, 44–56
　cave art hands, 30–31
　drainage system, 94
　evidence of fire, 152
　female figurines, 10, 16, 43
　fingerprint, 16
　Göbekli Tepe, **38**
　Hypogeum, **126**, **128**
　Israel, 8
　Knossos, 189–190, **191**
　male figurines, 24

Index

Mnajdra temple, **118**
Mohenjo-Daro, **203**
Newgrange burial chamber, **93**
sound resonance, 98, 100–101
tools, 46–47, **110**, 111, 113, 178, 263–264
Venus of Laussel, 19
See also cave paintings; figurines; megaliths; statues
artefacts
double axe, 178, **179**, 190
Indus Valley region, 199, 211
jewellery, 11, **12**, 24, 111, 126, **179**, 190, 191, **196**, 201, **202**
seals, 190, 199, **200**, 205, 209
skulls, 42, 43, 50, 52, 54
tools, 11, 109, 111
See also burials; sacred artefacts
Aryan people, 206, 208, 209, 219, 225, 257
Ashanti people, 84–85
Asia
genital mutilation, 167
human sacrifice, 169
Indus culture, 210
matrifocal societies, 81, 220
megaliths, 89
migrations, 148, 220
Neanderthals, 142
women, 169–170
See also China
Assyria, 211–212
astronomy
knowledge of, 93, 172, 206
links with, 94–96
megaliths, 96, 103, 105
menstruation cycle, 33
and temples, 120
Australia
animals, 155
colonisation, 211, 240
domestic violence, 166, 169–170
gender employment prospects, 172
matriarchal future, 267
population movements, 81
sexual harassment, 165
'terra nullius,' 211
violence against women, 166, 169–170
violent crimes, 173
'Womyn's Lands,' 269–270
Australian First Nations people
agriculture, 242
beliefs and understandings, 242–243, 252
birth control, 155
cave paintings, 247, 253
culture, 54
Dravidian people, 246
Dreamtime, 247, 252–253
egalitarian, 155
gender roles, 243, 261
'gift economy,' 263–264
and healing processes, 95
housing, 243–244
impact of colonisation, 240–241, 264–265
initiations, 95, 259–260
and matriarchal societies, 246, 248
migration, 155
moieties, 54, 249–250, 255, 262
mythologies, 281
oral traditions, 245, 287
palaeolithic art, 23
patrilineal, 248
and peace, 262
procreation, 252
relationship credence, 262

relationship with the land, 155, 165, 244, 282
sexual mores, 169
shifts to patriarchy, 255, 257–258
songlines, 79
totem animals, 248, 281
trade, 263
Austria, 12–13
authority shared, 210
See also mothers, authority; symbols, of authority; weapons, symbols of authority; women, and authority
Avebury, 106–107, **107**, **108**, 113
Aztecs, 213–214

B

Babylon, 210, 211
belly
in constructions, 91, 93, 107, 108
sculptures, 20, 30, 118, 129
Berekhat Ram, 8, **9**
Bible, the, 27, 161, 180
biodiversity, 275–276, 299
biological
family relationships, 53, 58, 144, 296
fathers, 63, 222, 228, 231, 296
links with nature, 259
birds
Bible, the, 27
carvings, 37, 39
in mythology, 281
paintings, 51
sculptures, 126
as symbols, 186–187
totems, 22
zoomorphic features, **22**

birthing
animals, 101
and felines, 39, **49**
places of, 26
represented in art, 39, **40**, **49**, 50, 107–108
represented in constructions, 94, 106–107, 108
symbols, 13, 33
boars, 51, 171, 194
bonding
See relationships
bones, human, 47, 48, 55, 87, 90–93, 126, 127, 166
Britain
colonised Australia, 240
cultural misconceptions, 62
in India, 216, 222
Khasi people, 222
megaliths, 38–39
See also England
Brodgar, Ness or Ring, 102–103
Buddhism, 229
bulls
celebrations and festivals, 182, 185
represented in art, 50, 51, **183**, **186**, 199
burials
artefacts, 48, 111–112, 126, 190, 191
communal, 113
Crete, 190
egalitarian, 113, 126–127
Harappa, 201
Homo sapiens, 143
in houses, 47–48, 53
Indus Valley region, 206
megaliths, 92, 152
Minoan, 182

Index

Mohenjo-Daro, 201
Nagovisi people, 235
Neanderthal, 143
placement of bodies, 24, 33–34, 91–92
Rakhigarhi, 201
shell adornments, 33, 126
stone chambers, 89–96, **90**, 100, 113
underground temples, 126
Wales, **90**
See also ritual practices

C

Callanish Stones, 79, 103–105, **103**
capitalism
    economy, 298–299
    and food distribution, 163
    societies, 61, 298–299
Carnac megaliths, **101**
carvings
    art, 39
    birds, 37, 39
Çatalhöyük
    a commonwealth, 210
    constructions, **45**
    gender equality, 210
    house interior, **47**
    matrifocal cultures, 54
    movements of people, 178
    settlement, 43–46
    See also archaeological findings; figurines; homes and housing; sculptures and reliefs; trade
cats
    See felines
cave paintings
    Altamira, 10, 28–29, 31–32
    animals, 21, 24, 32, 67, 172, 247
    astronomy, 32, 33
    Australian, 246–247
    Australian First Nations people, 253
    charcoal, **29**
    dating, 32
    hand and foot prints, 30–31
    Homo sapiens, 10
    males, 24
    materials and colours, 30
    Neanderthal, 143
    Palaeolithic, 21–23
    ritual practices, 25
    Trois Freres, 28–29
    warfare, 257
    See also rock shelters
celebrations and festivals
    agrarian, 77, 108–109
    artefacts, 185, 187
    bull-leaping, 184
    coming of age, 228
    food, 264, 307
    harvests, 185
    honouring the dead, 77, 225
    Kerala, 217
    Khasi people, **224**
    Mosuo people, 228, 229
    seafaring, 184
    summer solstice, 229
ceremonies
    artefacts, 112
    honouring the dead, 223–224
    initiation, 74, 228
    pagan, 107–108
Chalcolithic, 43–44
Chauvet, 28–29, **29**, 31
chief, 61, 62, 68, 92, 112, 154, 236, 261, 263
children
    adoption, 228

Australian First Nations people, 263
awareness of sexual intercourse, 251
clothing, 216
death rates, 15
fingerprint, 17
fingerprints, 21, 31
footprints, 31
illegitimate, 269
Minangkabau people, 233
Mosuo people, 229
and parent relationships, 53
protection of, 75, 137, 138, 144–145, 150, 227
treatment and standing, 216
See also relationships

China
foot-binding, 166
marriage customs, 67
matrifocal cultures, 280
Mosuo people, 226–229
population movements, 81
Qing dynasty, 166
roles of daughters, 76
Yeoh culture, 24
See also Asia

Christianity
Church of Rome, 163
Emperor Theodosian, 159
influence of, 26–27
Khasi people, 225
monasteries, 161
Mother Mary, 75
Nagovisi people, 234
and paganism, 95
and rebirth, 286
Sophia, 26
and witchcraft, 286

circles
chambers, 89
dancing, 86, 186, 287
gift-giving, 71, 72
in hairstyles, 14
of life, 252–253
sound resonance, 127–129
of stones, 37–39, 80, 89, **90**, 96, 98, 99–101, 102–106, **103**, 115, 127, 247
women's, 292
Xaghra Circle, 126
circumcision, 259
See also genital mutilation
civilisation
matrifocal societies, 211
oecumene, 210
patriarchal, 7, 158, 211–212
climate
change, 208–209, 277–278, 279
emergency, 275–277
liveable, 36
clothing
animal skins, 24
on figurines, 16–17, **196**
Mosuo initiation, 228
colonisation
Australian First Nations people, 240–241
impact on agriculture, 244
impact on women, 264
communal living
agriculture, 185
burials, 113, 182
children's areas, 272
dancing, 186
decision making, 273
food distribution, 182
future generations, 292
gatherings, 121

Index

housing, 228, 231
kitchens, 183, 272
Mosuo people, 228
shared propety, 195
waste management, 204
communism, 62
companies
See economy
conception, 25, 252, 296
conflicts
absence of, 41, 66
Australian First Nations law, 262
interpersonal, 56
resolution, 232
consensus
Australian First Nations law, 261
future generations, 265, 294, 298, 307
Khasi, 222
matriarchies, 61, 291
matrifocal, 133, 292
Minangkabau, 232
The Mountain, 270
Neolithic, 37
and power of two, 67–70
when not reached, 82
See also decision making; politics
constructions
bridges, **223**
burial chambers, 90–91
crystals, 95
earthquake resistance, 182
Hopi pueblo people, 80
Khasi people, **223**
megaliths, 80, 89, 91
mudbrick, 45–46, 80, 117, 182, 272
protection of, 203
See also homes and housing

control
See power
cowrie shell
See shells
Crete
art, 182–183, **183**, **184**, 185, **187**, **188**, 192, 194
earthquakes, 193–194
egalitarian society, 190
Goddess, 178, 180–181, 184–185, 187, 189
Horns of Consecration, 185, **186**
infrastructure, 180–182
lifestyles, 190
migration, 194
Mount Juktas, 185
Neolithic era, 178
religion, 180, 189
women, 191
See also burials; hierarchies; Minoan culture; sacred places; violent eras
cycles
life, 68, 77, 154
lunar, 105
represented in megaliths, 105
seasons, 68
Czech Republic, 16

D

dance, 53, 76, 86, 108, 186, 191, 229, 250, 252, 287
Danube society, 210
death rates
children, 15
by gender, 165
decision making
Australian First Nations people, 261
Democratic Confederalism, 273

future generations, 294, 302–304
Minangkabau people, 232
See also communal living; consensus; politics
destruction
culture, 206, 240
dealing with, 277, 286
environment, 229, 277
diet, 15, 16, 41, 45, 55, 209, 243, 276
See also food supply; health
diseases and infections
See health
divorce
attitudes to, 269
Khasi people, 221
Mosuo people, 226
See also marriage
DNA identifying population movements, 113–114, 149, 201
dolmens
See megaliths
domestic violence, 166, 169–170, 212, 269, 279
domination
among primates, 139
of animals, 154–155
in capitalist societies, 299
Christianity, 27
of environment, 28
by fathers, 63
future generations, 294
Kurgan people, 152–153
male, 7, 148, 165, 174, 265, 299
under one-god religions, 7
patriarchal societies, 63, 178
in storytelling, 153–154
by the victor, 158
and violence, 152–153, 158
See also patriarchal societies; power

Dravidian people
See India
dreams
Dreaming Goddess, **128**, 129
and kinship, 155, 248
See also mythologies; trances

E

Earth
and astronomy, 113
Australian First Nations people, 259
Bible, the, 27
burials, 219
connection with, 153, 154, 165, 269
energies, 78, 189
female, 14, 68, 304
and food supply, 124
Gaia hypothesis, 26
geological features, 79, 113
a Goddess, 26
healing, 282, 288
and moon, 105
mother links, 16, 41, 92
powers of, 77, 127
respect for, 256
seasonal knowledge, 15–16, 77
spiritual connection, 280, 287
Earth Mother
See Mother Earth
earthquakes, 193–194
ecology, 9, 28, 283
economy
accumulation, 61, 298
capitalist societies, 298–299
economic mutuality, 70–71, 74, 291, 298, 299
'gift economy,' 71, 72–73, 111, 116, 221, 234, 263–264, 298

Index

shell valuables, 234–235
surplus, 195, 221, 243, 298, 299
women, 172
egalitarian societies
    Çatalhöyük, 52
    hierarchies, 37
    Indus culture, 210
    Nagovisi culture, 235–236
    Neolithic era, 35
    symbols of, 92
Egypt, 167, 210
El Castillo
    cave paintings, 28–29
    caves, 31, 32
    hand and foot prints, 31
elders
    care of, 61, 217
    and food distribution, 54
    knowledge and wisdom, 216, 251, 262, 282, 306
    and migration, 82
    oral histories, 82
    respect for, 28, 306
England
    genital mutilation, 167
    megalithic tombs, 92
    Stonehenge, 99
    Yamnaya culture, 114
    See also Britain
engravings
    of animals, 24
    of men, 24
environment
    custodians of, 241–244
    deforestation, 131–132, 229
    degradation, 131, 229, 276–277
    ecology, 283
    The Flood, 148
    future generations, 278, 305–306
    impact of changes, 148
    matrifocal societies, 278
    regard for, 28, 222–223
exchanging and sharing
    See economy
extinction
    See animals

F

families
    biological, 53, 58, 144, 296
    Çatalhöyük, 47, 52
    extended, 163
    future generations, 297
    nuclear, 163
    See also ancestors
fathers
    biological, 63, 222, 228, 231, 296
    dominant, 63
    future generations, 302
    Kerala, 217
feasts
    honouring the dead, 77, 98, 102, 224
    hosting, 116, 236
    ritual practices, 218
felines
    and birthing women, 39, **40**, 48, **49**
    cats, **181**, 206
    with the Goddess, 48
    tigers, **199, 200**
    See also cats
female body image
    cosmetic treatments and surgery, 168
    fashion, 167–168
females
    See women
fertility and life
    control of, 212

    and diet, 55
    Goddess, 56
    Hohle Fels Goddess, 11
    and infertility, 78
    links, 28–29
    links with nature, 28–29
    Mother Earth, 77
    represented in art, **198**
    ritual practices, 25, 26
    and sacrafice, 78
festivals
    See celebrations and festivals
figurines
    Berekhat Ram, **9**
    breasts of, **12**, **13**, **17**, **18**, **19**, 43, 48, **49**, **60**, 118, **128**, 129, **181**, 197, **198**
    clothing, 16–17, **181**
    Dolni Vestonice, 16, **17**
    history of, 10
    Hohle Fels, 10, 11–12, **11**, 14
    Homo erectus, 8–9
    Indus Valley region, **196**, **197**, 198, **202**
    Kostenky, 12
    males, 208
    Minoan, 186
    Mother Goddess of Çatalhöyük, 48, **49**
    symbols of abundance, 11, 14, 48, 124, 167, 187, 198
    Tell Ramad, 43
    Venus of Lespugue, 16–18, **18**
    Willendorf, 12–13, **13**
    See also Goddesses; statues
First Nations people
    See American First Nations People; Australian First Nations people
food supply
    abundance, 15, 45, 55, 100, 177, 243
    for the afterlife, 199
    Australian First Nations people, 165
    and capitalism, 163
    celebrations and festivals, 264
    control of, 164
    current practices, 277
    diminished, 77, 84, 209
    distribution, 54, 84, 164, 212, 214, 227, 264, 300, 307
    future generations, 278–279, 292, 299
    gender equality, 164
    Goddess role, 52, 77
    hunter gatherer societies, 139
    impact of colonisation, 264
    inequality, 214
    insufficient, 276
    men's roles, 84
    nomadic lifestyles, 243
    storage, 189
    women's roles, 70, 72, 75, 212, 235, 243
    See also diet
foot-binding, 166
France
    Carnac, 101
    caves, 16–17, 21, 28
    Dordogne, 32–33
    megaliths, 88, **101**
    rock shelters, 32–33
    Venus of Laussel, 19–20
frescoes
    Crete, 182
    gender representations, 192
    in homes, 190
    Minoan, **184**

Index

Minoan Bull-leapers, **183**
natural world, **188**
friezes
    animals, 124, 187
    natural world, 186
    Tarxien temple, **123**, 124
future generations
    agriculture, 294
    child rearing, 292, 303
    decision making, 294, 302–304
    environmental protections, 305–306
    eradicating violence, 293
    family relationships, 297
    gender roles, 294–295
    leadership, 294
    links with nature, 293, 305
    marriage, 301
    matrilineal kinship, 296–297
    peace, 293–294
    sexual mores, 300–301
    sharing economy, 298–300
    spiritual guidance, 303–305
    trade, 299

G

Gaia hypothesis, 26, 28
    gender roles
    adoption for, 228
    alternate, 75
    future proposed, 294–295
    in tasks, 66
    transgender, 256
    See also Australian First Nations people; food supply; homosexuals; lesbians
genital mutilation, 167
genocide and massacres, 162, 169–170, 240, 241
Ggantija temple, 119

gift-giving
    and connectedness, 54, 72–73, 102, 263–264
    Mother Earth, 20, 41, 71
    Neolithic Malta, 116–117, 121
    property distribution, 221
    shells, 73, 234
    sign of respect, 111
    social alliances, 72–73, 111
    Tobriand islanders, 71–73
    See also economy
Göbekli Tepe, 37, **38**, 39, **40**
goddess-animal connections, 19, 50, 51–52, 56, 200
goddesses
    anatomical developments, 74
    and animals, 199
    architectural representations, 117–118
    of death, 225
    death and regeneration, 178, 225
    as deities, 8, 56
    Gaia hypothesis, 26
    and harvests, 107–108
    healers, 185
    Khasi people, 225
    life giving, 14, 101–102
    in patriarchal myths, 158
    represented in art, **200**
    snakes, **181**
    Tarxien temple, 122–124, **123**
    terminology, 10
    See also figurines
Goddesses
    Aegean, 67
    Dolni Vestonice, 16, **17**, 31
    Harappa, **196**, **199**, **200**
    Laussel, **19**, 20
    Mehrgarh, 197, **198**

Minoan, **184**
Minoan-Mycenaean, **197**
Mohenjo-Daro, **197, 200**
North African, **60**
Poppy, **193**
gods
    Khasi, 225
    in Minoan Crete, 180
    patriarchal, 154
    power of, 154
    represented in art, 7
    time of appearance, 7–8, 157
Golan Heights
    See Berekhat Ram
graves
    See burials
Great Goddess
    See Mother Goddess
Greece
    Herodotus, 155–156
    temple sleep 'enkoimesis,' 129
    women, 158, 191
greenhouse gases, 278

H

Hagar Qim temple, **120, 121**, 122, 123–124
hairstyles
    Indus, 197
    with circles, 14
Hal Saflien Hypogeum, 125–127, **126, 128**, 130
Halaf, 210
Han people, 226
Harappa
    city design, 203–204
    decline, 206–209, **207**
    goddesses represented in art, **199, 200**
    lifestyles, 203–206

matrifocal societies, 201
seals for commerce, **200**
health
    COVID-19, 276
    and diet, 55
    diphtheria, 240
    and environment, 55, 237, 305
    future generations, 278, 294
    influenza, 240
    leprosy, 209, 240
    links with nature, 282–283
    living conditions, 55
    malaria, 240
    measles, 240
    plague, 152
    and sexuality, 64, 86, 251, 300
    smallpox, 240
    symbols of, 129
    tuberculosis, 209, 240
    typhoid, 240
    typhus, 240
    venereal disease, 240
    and women, 172
    See also mental health
hierarchies
    Crete, 190
    Minoan, 190
High God
    See Sky God
Hinduism
    Aryans, 208
    Kali, 74
mythology, 78
Hohle Fels, 10, 11–12, **11**, 14
homes and housing
    altars, 179
    ancestral links, 47, 51, 76–77
    Australian First Nations people, 235, 243–244
    burials in, 47–48, 53

Index

burnt, 152
Çatalhöyük, 45–46
children, 217
clans, 61, 63, 67, 70, 83, 221–222, 228, 232, 293
cohabitation, 36, 47, 58, 228, 296
communal, 48–49, 228, 231
construction, 45–48, 81, 120, 182, 190, 203–204, 272
egalitarian societies, 52
grain storage, 48, 195, 204
hearth, 36, 46, 77, 228
homelessness, 172
interiors, 46–47, **47**, 51, 52, 190, 199, 204, 205–206
men, 62, 71–72, 226
men's roles, 227
Minoan, 190
Mohenjo-Daro, **203**
Mosuo people, 228
Neolithic Malta, 117
ritual practices, 112, 183
sanitation, 55, 172, 204
for security, 138
for survival, 15
temporary, 37
vacinity, 91
violence in, 169
women, 58, 66, 71–72, 158, 226, 268–271, 279, 302
women's roles, 70, 139, 227, 235, 298
Homo sapiens
   Africa, 143
   burial practises, 143
   cave paintings, 10
homosexuals
   public opinion, 269
   same-sex love, 75
   in Tiwi Society, 256
   See also gender roles; lesbians

Hopi pueblo people, 80
horns
   Goddess symbols, 20, 50, 185
   represented in art, 19, 20, 50, 51, 185
horses, 51, 148, 151, 152, 153, 154, 156, 208, 270
human-animal connections, 24, 29, 51–52, 280, 282
human-plant connections, 27–28, 43
human-plant-animal relationships, 27–28, 29–30
   See also relationships
humans
   brain development, 142
   development, 136–137, 140
   gender equality, 164–165
   language development, 143
   speech development, 142–143
   zoomorphic features, 49–50
   See also fathers; men; mothers; parenting; relationships; women
hunter gatherer societies
   Çatalhöyük, 43–44
   diet, 55
   and farming societies, 39, 52, 88
   gender roles, 139
   lifestyle, 15–16
   shamanism, 24–25
   skills and knowledge required, 242
hypogeum
   See Temples, underground

I

India
   caste system, 208–209, 219–220
   clan councils, 196
   Dravidian people, 209, 246

Kerala, 216–218
Khasi people, 61, 80, 220–226, 280
matrifocal societies, 209, 216–218
migrations, 152, 209
Indonesia, 21, 80, 89, 181, 230–233, **231**, 240, 249
See also Adat law
Indus Valley region
agriculture, 195, 210–211
animals, 208
Aryan people, 206
burials, 206
commerce, 201
a commonwealth, 210
constructions, 210
decline of culture, 208–209
gender equality, 210
goddesses, **196, 197, 198, 199, 200**
industry, 201, 210
lifestyles, 201–203
matrifocal societies, 205, 210
megaliths, 204
migrations, 206, 219
population, 202, 204
Sanauli, 206
settlements, 201–203
statues, **207**
trade, 205, 209
water supply, 208–209
yoga, 199
Industrial Revolution, 163
infanticide, 212
initiation
females, 74, 85, 259
Hal Saflien, 127
males, 85, 250, 259–260
Mosuo people, 228
See also ceremonies

Iran, 195, 206
Iraq, 195, 211
Ireland
burials, 93–97
megaliths, 88, 97
Islam, 26–27
Israel, 8, 38, 43
Italy, 110–111, 116

J

jewellery
See artefacts
Jordan, 41–42
Judaism
matrilineal, 157
reincarnation, 286
and women, 26–27

K

Kenya, 267–269
Kerala
See India
Khasi people
See India
kinship
Australian First Nations people, 45, 54, 211, 248, 249–250, 262–263
future generations, 291–292, 296
genetic studies, 92
human-plant-animal relationships, 28, 281
intermarrying, 53, 69
loss of, 214
matrifocal alliances through, 68
matrilineal, 69, 291–292, 296
See also ancestors; families; relationships
Knossos
Horns of Consecration, **186**

Index

Labyrinth of, 190, **191**, 194
temples, 178, 188–190
Kurgan people, 148–149, 152–153, 257
See also Yamnaya

L

Lammas Eve, 107–108
language, 33
Lascaux caves, 10, **23**, 24, 28–29
Laussel, 19–20
leadership
    balanced, 294
    female participation, 164–165, 170–171
    future generations, 294
    shared, 272
lesbians
    communities, 271
    same-sex love, 75
    'Womyn's Lands,' 269–270
    See also gender roles; homosexuals
Lespugue, Venus, 16–18, **18**, 67
Levant region, 111
lifespan, 15
literacy rates, 165

M

Maesmor Mace, **110**
Malta, 32
Malta
    Dreaming Goddess, **128**
    goddesses, 132
    Hal Saflien Hypogeum, 125–128, **126**, 130
    megaliths, 38, 76, 79, 89, 91, 97
    Mnajdra, 118, 120, 121, 122
    priestesses, 131
    Santa Lucija, 126
    temples, 101, 115, 116, 117, 118–119, **118**, 120–124, **120**
    Xaghra Circle, 126–127
    See also Ggantija temple; Hagar Qim temple; megalithic structures; Tarxien temple
Maori people, 28
marriage
    age at, 158
    arranged, 169, 250
    Australian First Nations people, 250–251
    future generations, 301
    inter-clan, 68–69
    intermarrying, 53
    in matrifocal societies, 66
    Minangkabau people, 231
    monogamy, 155–156, 221, 226
    Mosuo people, 229
    Nagovisi people, 235
    politics, 82
    polyandry, 66–67
    rites and expectations, 153
    virginity, 158
    'visiting' or 'walking,' 221, 226, 231
    See also divorce; also relationships
masculinity
    See men
massacres and genocide, 162, 169–170, 240, 241
matriarchal societies
    Australian First Nations people, 246
    defined, 59, 61
    gender roles, 75
matrifocal cultures
    abolished by law, 216
    China, 280
    and Christianity, 158–159

matrifocal religions, 74, 76, 77, 78,
 143–145, 154, 229
matrifocal societies
 agriculture, 278
 American First Nations People,
  69–70
 Asia, 81
 Australian First Nations people,
  248
 birth and rebirth, 24, 33, 77, 286,
  304
 and communism, 62
 Council of Mothers, 133
 cycle of life, 94–95
 decline, 150–151, 194
 economic management, 71, 74,
  298
 egalitarian, 66, 67, 75
 environmental regard, 28
 features of, 61, 65–66, 291–307
 female earth deity, 14
 female initiation, 74
 future generations, 267–269
 gender roles, 72, 139, 262
 human sacrifice, 78
 India, 209, 219
 Indus Valley region, 201
 Jewish people, 156
 Kerala, India, 218–219
 kinship groups, 54
 land ownership, 225–226
 leadership, 84–85
 lifestyles, 36–37, 52–53
 matriarchs, 76–77
 Mehrgarh, 201
 Melanesian people, 71–73
 Minoan, 192
 and patriarchal aggression, 83
 and peace, 86, 262
 principle of two, 261

religions, 76, 143–144
respect for nature, 279
ritual practices, 77
sexual partners, 64
shift to patrilineal, 148, 149–151,
 153
tolerance within, 82
matrifocal societies today
 Bribri people, 236–238
 Jinwar, 271–273
 Khasi people, 220–226
 Minangkabau people, 230–233
 Mosuo people, 226–229
 Nagovisi people, 233–236
 Tobriand islanders, 71–73
 Umoja people, 267–269
matrilineal
 Australian First Nations people,
  248
 future generations, 296–297
 India, 216–218
 Jewish people, 156
 Khasi people, 221
 Mosuo people, 226
 shift to patrilineal, 112
megalithic structures
 construction, 89, 91, 133
 features of, 96–97
 Ggantija temple, 119
 Malta, 38, 115, 117, 131, 133
 Newgrange, 93
 Orkney Islands, 96, 102, 112
 sound resonance, 99–100
 tombs, 92, 152
megaliths
 altars, 98, **120**, 124, 224, 225,
  247–248
 Asia, 81, 89
 and astronomy, 96, 105, 120
 Atequera Dolmen, 96

Index

Australia, 247
Britain, 38, 90, 95, 107
and burial mounds, 88
dolmens, 97–98, 99
features of, 103–104, 105
France, 88, **101**
Göbekli Tepe, 37, 39
holes, 121, 122, 124
honouring ancestors, 304
India, 80
Ireland, 88
Israel, 38
Khasi, 80, 223–224, **224**
matrifocal societies, 79, 96
Minangkabau people, 232
Moai, 80
Mohenjo-Daro, 204
mother stones, 225
Neolithic era, 89–92
placements, 124
representations of life, 87, 113
sound resonance, 98–100, 122
symbols of men, 96–97
See also stones
Melanesian people, 71–73
men
    archaeologists and scientists, 59
    bachelor bands, 149–151
    change, 288–289
    in Christianity, 27
    gender balance, 261
    guardianship of women, 158
    'men's business,' 259, 261
    myth of uncontrollable sexual urge, 173–174
    parenting roles, 63–64
    postnatal depression, 144–145
    property ownership, 161
    as protectors, 58, 63–64, 96, 150, 151, 222, 227, 249, 288
    represented in art, 192, 208
    roles and responsibilities, 25, 36, 37, 53, 62, 65–66, 72–73, 83–84, 96–97, 192, 217, 222, 227, 230, 232, 234–236, 249, 288
    sacrifice of, 150
    societies of, 85
    symbols of, 96–97
    violence, 175
    See also fathers; patriarchal societies; relationships; women and men
menstruation
    commences, 74, 218
    cycles, 33, 141
    menopause, 141
    and the moon, 121
    Mosuo women, 229
    sacred, 258
    symbols of, 13, 20, 48, 258–259
mental health
    and environment, 128, 282–283
    increased issues, 279
    and relationships, 174
    and stress, 175, 279
    and women, 279
Mesopotamia
    birthing represented in art, 107–108
    'cradle of civilisation,' 211
Mexico, 28, 281
Middle East, women, 169–170
migration
    See population movements
Minangkabau people, 230–231, **231**
mining
    Aryan people, 206
    and the environment, 165, 237, 280, 298–299, 306
    jadeite, 110–111

Minoan culture
    advancements, 180–182
    art, **183**, 187, **188**
    Goddesses, 178, **181**, **184**, 187
    offerings and gifts, **179**, **184**, 189
    sarcophagus, **179**
    See also Crete
Minoan people
    burials, 182
    decline of culture, 194
    egalitarian, 190
    gender roles, 192
    lifestyles, 182–186, 190
    trade, 192
Mohenjo-Daro
    archaeological site, **203**
    artefacts, **197**, **200**, **202**, **207**
    matrifocal societies, 201
    population, 203
    script symbols, **200**
    See also Indus Valley region
Mongolia, 114
monogamy
    See marriage
monuments
    See megaliths
moon cycles
    represented in art, 33
    understanding of, 15–16
    See also cycles
Mosuo women, 213
Mother Earth
    Australian First Nations people, 253–255, 256, 259
    Bribri, 215, 237
    Bryn Celli Ddu passage, **90**
    daughters, 74
    and the dead, 125, 127
    Gaia hypothesis, 28
    guidance, 71
    Hohle Fels, **11**
    Indus Valley region, 199
    knowledge, 180
    life cycle, 78, 92, 113
    links with women, 74
    matriarchal future, 237
    matrifocal economy, 71
    Minoan, 178
    as mother, 20
    partner, 78
    Poppy Goddess, **193**
    powers, 154
    provider, 77
    rebirth, 87
    and religion, 77
    respect for, 28, 285–286
    Silbury Hill, 107–108, **107**
    spiritual connection, 34, 41
    Sumer, 214
    symbols, 20
    underground temples, 125
    vulva stone, 79
Mother Goddess, 26, 48, **49**, 74, 77, 150, 153
mothering
    and employment, 171–172
    powers of, 62
    roles, 142
    shared, 75
motherlines
    See matrilineal
mothers
    authority, 68–69, 221
    clan leader, 61, 221
    'gift economy,' 71
    postnatal depression, 144–145
    as protectors, 137–138, 145
    venerated, 74

Index

See also parenting; relationships; women mountains, as sacred, 25, 180, 184, 229, 253, 280
murals, 51–52
music
 instruments, 10, 51, 183, 185, **187**, 201
 singing, 100, 108, 121, 130, **187**, 206, 218, 264
 use of, 11, 51, 76, 84, 100, 104, 183, 201
mutilation, genital
 See genital mutilation
mutuality
 See women and men
Mycenaean people, 194
mythologies
 Amazon women, 156–157
 Australian First Nations people, 79, 155, 211, 246, 252, 253–255, 281
 birds in, 281
 Bribri, 237
 Celtic, 78
 embedded in landscape, 79
 Greek, 190
 Hindu, 78
 honouring ancestors, 98, 304
 Iroquoi, 285
 Khasi people, 280
 patriarchal, 158
 representing gender roles, 158
 Sirens, 132
 and tribal lands, 155
 Ulysses, 132
 See also Australian First Nations people, Dreamtime

N

natural world
 Australian First Nations people, 249
 future generations, 293, 305
 Garden of Eden, 280–281
 links with, 15–16
 Maori people, 28, 281
 matrifocal societies, 278
 relationship with, 229
 respect for, 276, 280
Nayar people, 216–218
Neanderthal
 burial practises, 143
 figurines, 8–9
Nepal, 79
New Guinea
 See Papua New Guinea
New Zealand
 See Maori people
Newgrange, 93–97, **93**
nuclear families
 See families

O

Oracular Chambers, 118, 122, 128–130
oral traditions, 98
Orkney Islands, 38, 92, 96, 102, 112

P

paganism
 ceremonies, 107–108
 goddesses, 74
Papua New Guinea
 matrifocal customs, 71–73
 Nagovisi people, 233–236
Parayan people, 219
parenting
 foster, 53
 future, proposed, 303

future generations, 292
male roles, 63
and patriarchy, 166
positive, 174
and religion, 145
roles, 174
patriarchal religions, 82
patriarchal societies
aggression, 83, 114, 299
attitudes to Goddess, 8
Australian First Nations people, 155, 255
benefits, 172
and capitalism, 169, 281
controlled food supply, 164
defined, 154–155
differs from matriarchy, 52, 59, 65
dissatisfaction with, 273, 308
duration, 290
female compliance, 162–163
and female self-image, 168, 171, 289
Han people, 226
influence on matriarchy, 82, 153, 192, 220
male dominance, 149, 156, 174, 265
and motherhood, 75
and nuclear family, 63
role distribution, 265
and sex, 167, 301
values, 155, 165, 171, 258
worst expressions of, 27, 28, 211, 286
patrilineal societies
Australian First Nations people, 248
and rulers, 161
payment
See economy

peaceful eras, 113, 117, 201
Penang, 230
penis
penis stones, 20, 224
represented in art, 22, **23**, 105
perpetuation of life
See procreation
politics
consensus, 67, 222
Democratic Confederalism, 273
equality, 66, 75
future generations, 291, 296, 302, 304
Iroquois influence, 69
matrifocal, 82
and men, 83, 227, 235
patriarchal, 165
representative, 62, 65, 68, 84, 172, 222, 227, 232, 302, 307
and women, 68, 158, 165, 170, 172–173, 230, 232, 270, 304
See also decision making
Polynesia, 76, 81, 89, 116
population
Europe, 14–15
increase, 36
over-populate, 82
population movements
Americas, 81
Australia, 81
due to climate change, 151–152
due to conflicts, 83
Fiji, 81
Hawai'i, 81
Indonesia, 81
Japan, 81
Jericho, 177
Lebanon, 177
Melanesia, 81
Micronesia, 81

Index

Neolithic era, 88, 116
Palestine, 177
Papua New Guinea, 81
Polynesian people, 81
Russia, 148–149
South America, 81
Taiwan, 81
Ukraine, 148
Vietnam, 81
possessions
    See property ownership
power
    complementary, 235
    control as, 164, 171
    control of animals, 24, 48, **49**
    of creation, 256, 258
    of crystals, 95, 100
    egalitarian, 262–263
    female, 68
    healing, 101
    male, 68
    men over women, 174–175, 211–212
    of menstrual blood, 258–259
    shifts to males, 88–89, 194, 211–212, 255, 257–258
    state control over women, 213
    of two, 67–68, 261–262
    of voices, 132
priestesses and priests
    Agia Triada, **179**
    clan mothers, 62
    healing, 127–128
    hierarchy, 76
    in matrifocal societies, 62, 76, 235
    Minoan, 184, 187
    oracles, 122, 127, 130
    partnership, 131, **179**, 183, 192
    priestesses, 52, 53, 56, 128–129, 131, 153, 180
    priests, 154
    processions, 104, **179**, **184**
    and prostitutes, 212
    ritual practices, 108, 180, 184–185, 187, 222
    shamanism, 76
    trances, 127
primates
    ape families, 138–139
    Danakil region, 139–140
    mating, 141
    Swamp Ape, 136
procreation
    See reproduction
property ownership
    Bribri people, 237
    Khasi people, 222
    matrifocal societies, 225–226
    Minangkabau people, 231
    Mosuo people, 227
    women, 214
prostitution
    absence of, 64
    as trade, 212
pubic triangle, 13, 29–30, 116, 195
    See also vulva
Pulayan people, 219
punishment, Australian First Nations people, 256

Q

quality of life, 164–165
queen, 59, 83–85, 92, 157, 194

R

racism, 158, 226
rape
    absence of, 64
    evidence of, 154
    statistics, 168–169

stigmatism, 268
See also sexual assault; slaves and slavery
Raramuri peoples, 28, 281
rebirth
    Australian First Nations people, 252, 260
    from burials, 33, 87, 91, 182
    and Goddess, 56, 74, 90
    Mosuo people, 228
    as procreation, 74
    reflected in nature, 14, 145
    and religions, 77, 286
    sacrifice and, 78, 225
    shamanism, 24, 76
    women's importance, 24, 33, 77, 286, 304
red
    ochre, 19–20
    temple walls, 126–127
red colours
    on figurines, 197
    and 'men's business,' 259
    Minangkabau ceremonial dress, 231
    pottery, 201
    on statues, 207
    symbol of menstrual blood, 91
    temple interiors, 188
    used on artwork, 30
red ochre
    Australian First Nations people, 258–259, 262
    body paint, 259
    burials, 33, 47, 48, 91
    on figurines, 13, 19–20, **128**, 129
    Neolithic era, 116
    in sacred places, 91, 113, 124–126, 129
    symbol of healthy life, 129
    symbol of menstrual blood, 13, 258
    temple interiors, 124–126, 129
    on Venus of Laussel, 20
relationships
    Australian First Nations people, 249–250
    collaborative, 35, 68, 69, 105, 138, 261, 306
    communities, 102
    families, 138, 217
    father and child, 16
    hierarchies, 149–150
    Khasi families, 222
    matrifocal societies, 53, 82
    men's, 150
    mother and child, 16, 135, 145, 166, 174, 260
    with nature, 281
    nurturing, 248
    sisters and brothers, 71–72, 227–228, 232, 250
    See also human-animal connections; human-plant-animal relationships
reliefs
    See sculptures and reliefs
religions
    Adam and Eve, 280–281
    of the book, 26–27, 280–281
    Buddhism, 229
    Crete, 180, 189
    developing, 36
    future generations, 305
    of the Goddess, 154, 195
    Hinduism, 208
    influence of, 26–27, 165
    Judaism, 26–27
    Mosuo, 229
    one-god, 7

Index

'organic,' 143–145
patriarchal, 7–8, 76, 82, 165, 208
symbols of, 129
women's roles, 52–53, 170, 192
religious books
Apocrypha, 161
Bible, the, 27, 161–162, 180
Deuteronomy, 157
religious traditions, 38–39, 49
renewable energy, 272, 277, 279
reproduction
animals and humans, 296
perceptions, 25, 74, 242–243, 252
roles, 36
ritual practices
and agriculture, 108–109
and crystals, 96
death, 127, 235
fertility, 25, 124
food, 222
healing, 124, 127, 259
initiations, 259–260
men's societies, 256–257
and menstruation, 218
Nagovisi people, 234–235
Oracular Chambers, 122
priesthood, 180
regeneration, 188–189
sacrifice, 127
trances, 24
See also celebrations and festivals; trances
rock shelters
Abri-sous-Roche Blanchard, 32–33
footprints, 247
Rome, 10, 158–159, 167
Rumania, 67

S

sacred artefacts
Australian First Nations people, 255
Labyris, **179**
matrifocal societies, 80–81
Minoan, 178
red ochre, 13
representing bulls, **186**
sacred places
altars, 124, 154, 247–248
artefacts, 111–112
Crete, 188
food storage, 189
France, 20–21
the hearth, 76–77, 124, 228
Hypogeum, 127
matrifocal religions, 76–77
palaeolithic, 21
red ochre, 113
trances, 99, 122, 127, 130
trees, 178, 222, 224, 243, 280, 282, 283
Turkey, 37
See also spiritual environments
sacrifice
animals, 78, 124, 127, 154, 188, 222, 225
humans, 78, 92, 150, 225
same sex
See Kurgan people
same-sex love
See homosexuals; lesbians
Sanauli, 206
Santa Lucija, 126
Scotland
burials, 92, 96
Callanish Stones, 103–105, **103**
'The Clearances,' 163

landscaped representation of birthing, 107–108
megaliths, 102–103
'Sleeping beauty,' 104–105, **104**
script, **199**, **200**, 204–205
See also written language
sculptures and reliefs
birds, 126
Çatalhöyük, 49–50
flint knapping, 11
Goddess of Laussel, **19**
horns, **19**, 20, 50
'Old Married Couple of Sumer,' **213**
sexual attributes, 129
skulls, 42–43
Venus of Laussel, 19–20
zoomorphic features, 49
See also figurines
settlements
burned house horizon, 152
Çatalhöyük, 43–45
expansion, 56
Indus Valley region, 201–203
Knossos, 190
Minoan, 182–185
permanent, 36, 39
'Womyn's Lands,' 269–270
sexism, 168
sexual assault, 168–169, 175
See also rape
sexual harassment, 165–166
sexual instructions, 74, 218, 251
sexual organs represented in art, **13**, 20, **23**, 41–42, 49, **108**, 123, 129
sexual partners
choice, 54, 64, 66, 86, 212, 229, 297
cohabitation, 36, 58
control of, 63

egalitarian, 35
future generations, 297
sexuality
activities, 140
controlled, 169, 173, 174, 212, 226
development, 138, 140–141, 228
enjoyment, 64, 74, 167, 291, 300–301
freedom, 219
future generations, 291, 300–301
and health, 64, 86
male pleasure, 150, 166, 295
respectful, 174, 234
safety, 217
same-sex, 75, 256
valued, 86
Shamanism
altered state of consciousness, 22, 31, 76, 253
art, 31
Australian First Nations people, 253, 254
environments, 21
intelligence, 25
memory, 25
Numic, 95
oral traditions, 25
priesthood, 76
spiritual world, 25
trances, 23, 76
shells
burial adornments, 33, 126, 234–235
gift-giving, 73, 234
inlaid in furniture, 201
jewellery, 73
marriage customs, 235–236
on statues, **207**, **213**
Siberia, 32

Index

Skin groups
   See Australian First Nations people, moieties
skulls
   See artefacts
sky, male power, 68
Sky God, 153–154
slaves and slavery
   Kurdistan, 271
   under patriarchy, 59, 158, 166, 167, 211, 212
   statistics, 169
   of women, 158, 166, 167, 169, 271
sound resonance
   See archaeological findings; megalithic structures, sound resonance; megaliths, sound resonance; stones, acoustic properties; temples, sound resonance
South America, 83
Spain
   Atequera Dolmen, 96
   burial practises, 92
   cave paintings, 21, 28, 31–32
spirals
   Malta, 123, 124, 126, 129
   megaliths, 93, 94, 101, 110
   Palaeolithic, 22, 32
   songspirals, 244
spiritual environments
   artefacts, 112
   Stonehenge, 99–101
   underground temples, 125
   See also sacred places
statues
   'Ain Ghazl, 41–42
   females, 49
   with horns, 24
   Horns of Consecration, **186**
   males, 49
   North Africa, 60
   'Old Married Couple of Sumer,' **213**
   Priest King, **207**
   See also figurines
status
   among nuns, 307
   of ancestors, 98
   Australian First Nations people, 54, 264
   equal, 54, 268
   Khasi society, 221–222
   in matrifocal societies, 52, 268, 269
   of military men, 214
   symbols, 112
   of women, 164, 201, 214
   Stonehenge, 99, 119
stones
   acoustic properties, 93, 98, 99, 100
   birthing stone, **40**
   blocking stones, 90, 94, 96
   Calendar Stones, 121
   Callanish Stones, 79, 102–105, **103**
   capstone, 97
   circles of stones, 38, 39, 80, 90, 96, 99, 100, 101, 102, 103–105, **103**, 106, 115, 127, 247
   female stones, 97, 224
   foundation stone, 61
   male stone, 224
   mother stones, 97, 224–225
   penis stone, 20
   shrines, 79, 80
   stone pillow, 129
   stone rows, 80, 101
   vulva sculptures, 20, 33, 79, 105
   See also megaliths

Sumer, 41, 204, 210, 211, **213**, 214
sun light, 15–16
survival
    animals, 277
    Ashanti culture, 85
    Australian First Nations people, 248
    Darwinism, 283
    future generations, 279, 299
    and Hohle Fels, 11
    of humans, 15, 124, 137, 142, 144, 152, 246
    role of men, 235
    role of religion, 143–144
    role of women, 137, 151, 235
Sweden, 24, 92, 152
symbols
    of agriculture, 108–109
    of ancestors, 281
    animals as, 30, 50, 78, 105, 126, 248, 281
    of authority, 112, 113
    birds as, 186–187
    of birthing, 13, 33
    of breasts, 20, 50
    bulls as, 185
    butterflies as, 178
    cowrie shell as, 33
    of days in a year, 32
    of dualism, 67–68
    eggs as, 18, 67, 125–127
    of fertility, 193
    of goddesses, 185, 195
    graphic codes, 33
    of health, 129
    horns as, 50, 185, **186**
    of hunting success, 31
    labyris, 190
    of luck, 13
    of menstruation, 13, 48, 258–259
    moon as, 108–109
    of Mother Earth, 20
    of nourishment, 20
    number seven, 13
    poppy seeds as, 193
    of powers, 67
    of protection, **224**
    of pubic triangle, 195
    red ochre as, 13, 258–259
    of regeneration, 180
    religious, 129
    shells as, 180
    skulls as, 50
    snakes as, 32, 41, 90, 124, 180, **181**
    of vaginas, 20, 41, **90**, 91
    of vulvas, 33, 79, 108, 110
    of wombs, 33, 91, 93–94, 126
    See also megaliths; pubic triangle; red ochre

T

Tantric traditions, 13
Tarxien temple, 122–124
taxes, 71, 82, 121, 211
    See also economy
technological developments
    bronze, 172, 190, 201
    copper, 201
    frescoes, 182
    gold, 201
    jewellery, 201
    metallurgy, 172, 182, 190, 211
    navigation, 172
    pottery, 172, 182, 201, 211
    sustainable energies, 279
    textiles, 172, 182
    weaving, 172, 182, 201
    written language, 201
Tell Ramad, 43

Index

temples
    access for women, 218
    altars, 124, 154
    astronomical alignments, 120–121
    interiors, 124–125, 129, 182
    Malta, 101
    sound resonance, 101, 122, 127–131
    underground, 125–127
    See also archaeological findings; megalithic structures
textiles
    See technological developments
Tibet, 67, 81, 83, 221, 226
tombs
    See burials
tools
    agricultural, 109–111, 195
    antler picks, 90
    axes, 120, 263
    bamboo, 219
    flint, 90
    hammers, 120
    hand-tools, 270
    hunting, 52, 152, 201
    knives, 120
    levers, 120
    mace, 110
    ritual, 46, 48, 76, 222
    sickles, 195
    wooden, 120
tourism
    Bribri people, 237
    impact on Mosuo people, 229
    Kenya, 269
trade
    animal products, 84
    Çatalhöyük, 46
    cultural exchanges, 263
    future, proposed, 299
    gender roles, 84
    Indus Valley region, 201, 205, 209
    influence on art, 192
    long journeys, 84
    markets, 70–71
    and shared philosophy, 102–103
    shared resources as, 264
    spread of disease, 240
    Turkey, 41
    women's roles, 70–71
trances
    and crystals, 96
    enkoimesis, 129
    fear management, 250
    pain management, 128, 130, 260
    religious traditions, 22
    represented in art, 23–24
    ritual practices, 24
    in sacred places, 99, 122, 127
    shamanism, 23, 76
    and sound, 98
    spiritual connection, 31
Turkey
    agriculture, 195
    birthing represented in art, 107–108
    goddesses, 67
    settlements, 43–45
two, principle of
    Australian First Nations people, 261–262
    balance of collaboration and power, 306
    balanced gender roles, 235, 288
    contemporary responsibilities, 290
    in economy, 299
    feminine and masculine energy, 289

Gaia hypothesis, 288
life energies of women, 286
and nature, 148, 265
partnership, 78
power of two, 68, 69, 222
symbolised, 67
two views, 68, 306–307

U

UN Environment Program, 28
underground streams, 100–101, 122
UNESCO World Heritage sites, 116
urban societies, 79–80
urbanisation, 43–44

V

vaginas
    represented at Long Barrow, 90–91, **90**
    symbols, 20, 41, 91
values
    masculine, 163, 165, 170, 171, 256, 274
    matrifocal, 61–62, 68, 71, 86, 114, 135, 150, 158–159, 173, 192, 218, 251, 280, 291
Venus
    Chauvet, 29–30, **29**
    defined, 10
    Hohle Fels, 10, **11**, 14
    Laussel, **19**, 20
    Lespugue, Venus of, 16–18, **18**
    Willendorf, **13**, 14
    See also figurines
violence
    evidence of, 15, 52
    against women, 256–257
    See also domestic violence
violent eras
    attitudes to, 173
    Australia, 241
    Crete, 194
    migrations, 153
    represented in literature, 162
    warrior skill development, 153
    weapons, 152–153
    witch-hunts, 162
    women's suffrage, 163
    See also peaceful eras
vulva
    cave entrances, 30
    object of worship, 79
    represented in art, 20, 33
    and shells, 33
    symbols, 33, 79, **108**, 110
    Venus of Laussel, 20
    vulva stones, 20, 33, 79, 105
    See also pubic triangle

W

Wa people, 220
Wales
    burial chambers, **90**
    Maesmor Mace, **110**
walking marriage
    See marriage
warfare
    Africa, 83, 84
    Australian First Nations people, 257
    imagery, 194
    Iraq, 211
    Khasi people, 225
    Kurdistan, 271
    women's roles, 70
    See also violent eras
water divining, 100–101
weapons
    arrowheads, 131
    axes, 131

Index

bronze, 152–153
daggers, 131
lack of, 51, 70, 92, 112, 113, 117, 150, 195, 201
represented in art, 154
stone axes, 112
symbols of authority, 112, 113
of war, 59, 131, 152, 154, 219
weaving
   See technological developments
Western cultures, 15, 289
widows, 214
Willendorf, 12–14, **13**
winter solstice, 94–95
witches, 286
witches and heretics
   See violent eras
wombs, 33, 91, 93–94, 126
women
   abortion, 212
   adultery, 212
   architectural representations, 119
   and authority, 61, 66, 68–69, 76, 221, 243
   beautification, 220
   body image, 167–168
   clothing, 192, 216
   control of, 166
   Council of Mothers, 133
   custodians of traditions, 156
   dedications to, 132
   deities, 7–8
   esteemed, 14, 16, 33–34, 64, 154, 192, 201, 261
   financial security, 172
   foot-binding, 166
   genital mutilation, 167
   healers, 162–163
   homelessness, 172
   impact of colonisation, 264–265
   infertility, 212
   inventions, 172
   Khasi people, 225–226
   male guardianship of, 158
   midwives, 162–163
   mutual support, 225–226
   ownership of property, 214
   as peacemakers, 262
   as property, 150–151, 211, 264–265, 271
   protection of, 58, 63–64, 145, 150, 170, 214, 222, 257, 268, 288
   as protectors, 83, 137, 254
   protests for rights, 218
   and religion, 52–53, 74
   represented in architecture, 119
   represented in art, 191–192, 199, **200**
   roles and responsibilities, 24, 37, 52–53, 67, 80, 82, 83–84, 100, 191, 192, 212, 217, 222, 227, 249
   self-defence, 83–85
   self-perception, 167–168
   statues, 49
   and superannuation, 171–172
   symbols of, 96–98
   treatment and standing, 211–212
   violence against, 165–166, 169, 256–257
   voting, 163
   as warriors, 83, 85, 155–156
   witch-hunts, 162
   See also mothers; power; sexuality
women and men
   balance between, 66–69, 75, 86, 155, 235, 261, 275, 291, 294, 302
   dignity and respect, 66, 75, 86, 294

hierarchies, 37
mutuality, 61, 66, 86, 192, 227, 261
oxytocin, 137, 144, 174
relationships, 267
women's business and men's business, 250, 258, 260–261, 266
women's communities
   Jinwar, Syria, 271–273
   Kurdistan, 271–273
   North America, 270–271
   Umoja, Kenya, 267–269
   'Womyn's Lands,' 269–270
'Womyn's Lands,' 269–270
work, hours, 15, 110, 227, 229
written language, 33, 204–205, 211

X

Xaghra Circle, 126–127

Y

Yaa Asantewa, Queen, 85
Yamnaya
   culture, 114
   people, 149, 151–152
   See also Kurgan people
Yeoh culture, 24

Z

Zealand, 92
zoomorphic features, **22**

About the Author

Jennifer Cameron holds a Bachelor of Arts (History, Literature), Diploma of Education, Master of Enterprise Innovation and Graduate Certificate in Sustainability.

Coming from a working class, church-going background, Jenny found herself, contrary to family expectations, at University. It was the 1970s, a time of social foment – anti-Vietnam War and conscription demonstrations and emergence of the Women's Liberation movement. Jenny felt strongly about the rights of those experiencing any injustice and participated in these exciting times, where we came to understand the effects of patriarchy, especially for women.

For over twenty years now, her concerns have extended to the natural world. She felt Nature could not speak out against the desecration governments and companies were causing, so responsible humans had to. Climate change was emerging as a concept – clearly humans were not only causative but would suffer, with the rest of the natural world, if climate change was left unchecked. Jenny characterises the innate energy for life in all things as the Goddess, affirming the crucial role women play in creation and nurturance. Today, Jenny feels, the natural world herself is very strongly speaking with many 'natural' disasters occurring.

As part of a colonising culture in Australia, even as a child Jenny knew something terrible was being perpetrated upon the First Nations people, then called 'a dying race'. She has tried to be respectful of First Nations people's experience and culture.

Ancient Ways for Current Days

Now in her late 60s, Jenny decided that while her brain was still capable of it, it was time to speak up, through a book, written for ordinary folk. *Ancient Ways for Current Days* is the result. Though it includes the terrible effects of patriarchy and unchecked male violence, it is actually an uplifting uncovering of what women and men have been, and in some places still are able to do from a position of mutual respect, in what Jenny calls matrifocal societies. She is very happy to talk to groups about the material she shares in *Ancient Ways for Current Days*.

Contact Jenny Cameron at ancientwaysbook@gmail.com

Acknowledgements

I acknowledge and thank several women in my life who have supported me on this journey.

Firstly, Vera Ray, who went on the original journey of discovery across Europe and Turkey with me, looking for evidence of past matriarchal/matrifocal cultures. I thank her for sharing in a great adventure, and for all the practical support ever since.

Dr Tricia Szirom who urged me to write this book and understood its importance from the start. I thank her for her supportive intelligence over decades to forge together an understanding of Goddess spirituality and the energetic female creative presence in all things.

My daughter Pia Gaia who gives me joy and challenges me, and endeavours to express Goddess values in her life every day.

My partner Margaret de Kam, who believed in me and inconvenienced herself in many ways to support me to complete the book. Her loving constancy and good humour is a wonderful blessing.

Two other women must be acknowledged for their willingness to step forward, volunteering to assist me with their particular skills. Dr Jan Webb is a friend from my first year of school and is a treasure trove of understanding about the construction of the English language. As my first reader, she helped me to hone my wordsmithing and generously assured me it was interesting reading. She made many corrections and prudent qualifications – any faults are my own.

I would also like to thank all the staff and consultants of Ultimate World Publishing, especially Vivienne Mason and Julie Fisher, whose friendliness and professionalism made the publishing process seamless and enjoyable.

Finally, Kaye Moseley, a skilled artist and drawer who has brought the celebration of art to many young people in her time as a teacher. Together with Vera we created an unpublished manuscript about ancient matriarchy in the 1980s, so our journey on this topic is almost as long as our friendship. Kaye created every line drawing in the book, with careful accuracy and skill and I am deeply indebted to her for the hours of work involved. I also thank Kaalii Cargill for her photos, and for sharing the enthusiasm for the subject.

I would also like to acknowledge the men in my life who remind me I can be optimistic about male potential, to live the matrifocal approach, in times ahead.

To all these and many others who have been steadily encouraging in my friendship and family circle: I thank you.

Notes

Ancient Ways for Current Days

Notes

www.ingramcontent.com/pod-product-compliance
Lightning Source LLC
Chambersburg PA
CBHW071725080526
44588CB00013B/1898